POPE PIUS XII LIBRARY, ST. JOSEPH COL

3 2528 07057 9265

SO-DMR-045

Aging in the United States and Japan

A National Bureau
of Economic Research
Conference Report

Aging in the United States and Japan

Economic Trends

Edited by Yukio Noguchi and
David A. Wise

 The University of Chicago Press

Chicago and London

YUKIO NOGUCHI is professor of economics at Hitotsubashi University.
DAVID A. WISE is the John F. Stambaugh Professor of Political Economy
at the John F. Kennedy School of Government, Harvard University, and
area director for Health and Retirement Programs at the National Bureau
of Economic Research.

The University of Chicago Press, Chicago 60637
The University of Chicago Press, Ltd., London
© 1994 by the National Bureau of Economic Research
All rights reserved. Published 1994
Printed in the United States of America
03 02 01 00 99 98 97 96 95 94   1 2 3 4 5
ISBN: 0-226-59018-6 (cloth)

Library of Congress Cataloging-in-Publication Data

Aging in the United States and Japan : economic trends / edited by Yukio
Noguchi and David A. Wise.
        p.   cm.—(A National Bureau of Economic Research conference
report)
    Papers presented at a conference in Tokyo sponsored jointly by the Na-
tional Bureau of Economic Research and the Japan Center for Economic
Research.
    Includes bibliographical references and index.
    1. Aged—United States—Economic conditions—Congresses.
2. Aged—Japan—Economic conditions—Congresses.   3. Aged—
United States—Social conditions—Congresses.   4. Aged—Japan—So-
cial conditions—Congresses.   5. Aged—Housing—United States—
Congresses. 6. Aged—Housing—Japan—Congresses.   I. Noguchi,
Yukio, 1940–.   II. Wise, David A.   III. National Bureau of Economic Re-
search.   IV. Nihon Keizai Kenkyu Sentā.   V. Series: Conference report
(National Bureau of Economic Research)
HQ1064.U5A63474   1994
305.26′0952—dc20   94-14101
                                                                          CIP

⊗ The paper used in this publication meets the minimum requirements of
the American National Standard for Information Sciences—Permanence
of Paper for Printed Library Materials, ANSI Z39.48-1984.

National Bureau of Economic Research

Officers

Paul W. McCracken, *chairman*
John H. Biggs, *vice chairman*
Martin Feldstein, *president and chief executive officer*

Geoffrey Carliner, *executive director*
Charles A. Walworth, *treasurer*
Sam Parker, *director of finance and administration*

Directors at Large

Elizabeth E. Bailey
John H. Biggs
Andrew Brimmer
Carl F. Christ
Don R. Conlan
Kathleen B. Cooper
Jean A. Crockett

George C. Eads
Martin Feldstein
George Hatsopoulos
Lawrence R. Klein
Leo Melamed
Merton H. Miller
Michael H. Moskow

Robert T. Parry
Peter G. Peterson
Richard N. Rosett
Bert Seidman
Donald S. Wasserman
Marina v. N. Whitman

Directors by University Appointment

Jagdish Bhagwati, *Columbia*
William C. Brainard, *Yale*
Glen G. Cain, *Wisconsin*
Franklin Fisher, *Massachusetts Institute of Technology*
Saul H. Hymans, *Michigan*
Marjorie B. McElroy, *Duke*
Joel Mokyr, *Northwestern*

James L. Pierce, *California, Berkeley*
Andrew Postlewaite, *Pennsylvania*
Nathan Rosenberg, *Stanford*
Harold T. Shapiro, *Princeton*
Craig Swan, *Minnesota*
Michael Yoshino, *Harvard*
Arnold Zellner, *Chicago*

Directors by Appointment of Other Organizations

Marcel Boyer, *Canadian Economics Association*
Mark Drabenstott, *American Agricultural Economics Association*
Richard A. Easterlin, *Economic History Association*
Gail D. Fosler, *The Conference Board*
A. Ronald Gallant, *American Statistical Association*
Robert S. Hamada, *American Finance Association*

Charles Lave, *American Economic Association*
Rudolph A. Oswald, *American Federation of Labor and Congress of Industrial Organizations*
James F. Smith, *National Association of Business Economists*
Charles A. Walworth, *American Institute of Certified Public Accountants*
Josh S. Weston, *Committee for Economic Development*

Directors Emeriti

Moses Ambramovitz
Emilio G. Collado
George T. Conklin, Jr.
Thomas D. Flynn
Gottfried Haberler

Franklin A. Lindsay
Paul W. McCracken
Geoffrey H. Moore
James J. O'Leary
George B. Roberts

Robert V. Roosa
Eli Shapiro
William S. Vickrey

Since this volume is a record of conference proceedings, it has been exempted from the rules governing critical review of manuscripts by the Board of Directors of the National Bureau (resolution adopted 8 June 1948, as revised 21 November 1949 and 20 April 1968).

Contents

Preface

This volume consists of papers presented at a joint Japan Center for Economic Research–National Bureau of Economic Research conference held in Tokyo. Financial support from the Department of Health and Human Services, National Institute on Aging (grants P01-AG05842, R37-AG08146, and T32-AG00186), and the Mitsubishi Trust and Banking Corporation is gratefully acknowledged.

Any opinions expressed in this volume are those of the respective authors and do not necessarily reflect the views of the National Bureau of Economic Research, the Japan Center for Economic Research, or the sponsoring organizations.

Introduction

Yukio Noguchi and David A. Wise

The papers in this volume were presented at the first of a series of conferences sponsored jointly by the National Bureau of Economic Research and the Japan Center for Economic Research. Subsequent conferences were held on housing markets in the United States and Japan and on the economics of the family, and the related conference volumes are in preparation. The purpose of the continuing series of conferences is to explore issues that are of concern both in the United States and in Japan. Because population aging poses issues that are of paramount concern in both countries, that topic was chosen to begin the conference series. It is hoped that, as the series progresses, the interaction will promote increased mutual understanding of economic issues and economic behavior in the two countries and in addition will further economic research in the two countries. The goal of this conference was to present discussion papers by Japanese and American authors on comparable topics. The volume contains papers on labor force participation and retirement, the economic status and housing of the elderly, the budget implications of population aging, and the utilization of health care. The discussion of health care in this volume is limited to the United States, but that issue will be the subject of a separate joint conference to be held in December 1994.

Two general concerns are addressed in the papers: one is the economics of the aged, and the other is the economics of aging. The first directs attention toward the present economic status of the elderly, and the second directs attention toward changes that result from and issues that arise because of population aging. The two issues are of course closely related, and some aspects of both are considered in several of the papers. Indeed, studies of the economic status

Yukio Noguchi is professor of economics at Hitotsubashi University. David A. Wise is the John F. Stambaugh Professor of Political Economy at the John F. Kennedy School of Government, Harvard University, and area director for Health and Retirement Programs at the National Bureau of Economic Research.

of the current elderly are in many cases motivated by the recognition that future population aging is likely to bring with it increased concern for the economic well-being of the aged.

The Japanese population will age very rapidly in the coming decades. According to the most recent prediction by the Institute of Population Problems of the Ministry of Welfare (September 1992), the proportion of people age 65 and older is expected to rise from 12.1 percent in 1990 to 25.5 percent in 2020 and 26.0 percent in 2030. These figures are higher than the corresponding figures (23.6 percent in 2020) in the previous prediction (December 1986), on which most of the discussions in the papers by Japanese authors are based. This raises a number of important public policy concerns. Labor force participation, financing Social Security, housing the older population, and health care are of particular importance.

Population aging will also proceed rapidly in the United States in the coming decades, although not as rapidly as in Japan, and the same issues are of major concern. According to the UN publication "World Population Prospects 1990," the ratio of people age 65 and older in the United States is expected to reach 17.3 percent in 2020 and 19.6 percent in 2025. It is our hope that studies of the current situation of the elderly and major trends will help us understand what the future holds and will help inform public policies meant to address these issues.

Current policy discussions are also affected by future considerations. For example, the introduction of the consumption tax, which had long been an important policy issue in Japan, was closely related to the aging problem because its expected role was to finance increasing Social Security expenditures. Therefore, this issue cannot be judged without analyzing population aging. There are other examples in which present economic policies are related to the future aging process. Japan is now asked to adopt policies aimed at expanding domestic demand. Whether to adopt saving-reducing programs or investment-increasing programs depends on the future trend in macroeconomic balance, which is related to population aging.

One of the benefits of the joint research conferences including both American and Japanese participants is that comparisons between the two countries have become possible. We found that there are both similarities and differences in the nature of problems, behavioral patterns, institutional settings, and public policies.

Trends in the labor force participation of older Americans and the primary explanations for these trends are summarized by Robin L. Lumsdaine and David A. Wise. They show that, while the labor force participation rates of men age 60 and older remained essentially constant from 1870 through 1937, those rates then began to decline in the late 1930s and that the fall is still continuing. They attribute the decline to the introduction of Social Security and private pension plans. They emphasize that, for the majority of retirees, support after retirement is provided primarily by Social Security and private pension plans. Most older Americans have very little personal saving. Personal wealth is primarily in the form of housing equity, and housing equity tends not to be converted to liquid assets, as the elderly age. They argue not only that the income from Social Security and firm pension plans allows elderly employees to retire at younger and younger ages but also that the provisions of both Social Security and firm pension plans tend to encourage early retirement. In short, they conclude, although persons are living longer and longer, they are leaving the labor force at younger and younger ages. The trend is unrelated to personal saving; it is associated instead with government promises of Social Security benefits after retirement and the saving by employers for their employees through firm pension plans.

The effect of government pensions on the labor supply of older Japanese is analyzed by Atsushi Seike and Haruo Shimada. As in the United States, the labor force participation of older Japanese is also declining. Still, Japanese labor force participation rates are about twice as high as comparable rates in the United States. For men over 65, for example, the participation rate is 37 percent in Japan, compared with 17 percent in the United States. Seike and Shimada's analysis, however, concludes that the government pension plan for employees contributes significantly to the withdrawal of older employees from the labor force. Seike and Shimada conclude that the Japanese plan earnings test, similar to the U.S. Social Security earnings test, reduces substantially the labor supply of those who are receiving retirement benefits. They tend to reduce their labor supply to avoid the lump-sum tax associated with the earnings test in Japan.

Michael D. Hurd surveys research on the economic status of the elderly in the United States. He concludes that the elderly are at least as well off as the nonelderly and possibly substantially better off. In addition, because much of the income of the elderly, like Social Security, is indexed to inflation, they are well protected from inflation. In the relatively near future, the economic status of the currently retired elderly seems well assured, according to Hurd. In the more distant future, however, when the baby boom generation retires and there are many more retirees per employed person, the financial position of the elderly is much less bright. He suggests that the consumption of the elderly relative to the consumption of employed persons will then be lower than it is today.

Noriyuki Takayama considers household asset- and wealthholdings in Japan. He concludes that, in terms of wealthholding, the elderly are better off than the working-age population. Owing to the rapid rise in the value of Japanese land prices, the difference between the wealth of the old and the wealth of the young has widened. As in the United States, housing equity is the major asset of most elderly households. Takayama emphasizes that, under the current circumstances, a young person who works all his life will still be unable to buy a home in a Tokyo suburb if he has to depend on his own earnings. Takayama also points to the need of older Japanese to liquidate home assets by using equity conversion schemes such as reverse annuity mortgages.

Daniel L. McFadden considers the economic issues of housing the elderly in the United States. He finds that the share of income spent on shelter rises with age, primarily because income falls more rapidly than payments for housing, but also because real housing prices increased substantially at the end of the 1970s. This supports the common perception that the elderly are being squeezed by housing costs. On the other hand, McFadden argues that the pattern of mobility among the elderly and the housing transactions when the elderly move do not suggest a significant "bottled-up" demand for converting housing equity to income. There appear to be no major market barriers that prevent the elderly from making desired transactions between nonliquid and liquid assets. McFadden also suggests that the demographics of the elderly population in the United States and the age distribution of capital gains from housing price increases suggest that the baby boom generation will face more difficult economic circumstances at the end of its life cycle than the previous generation.

Seiritsu Ogura discusses the budget implications of population aging in Japan, with an emphasis on health care and the cost of public retirement benefits. As in the United States, public health insurance in Japan provides health care to the elderly at little or no cost. Apparently as a consequence, the per capita cost of health care for the elderly has risen very precipitously in recent years. Nonetheless, health care cost in Japan is only about 6 percent of GNP, approximately half the cost in the United States.

In 1973, benefits under the Japanese public pension plans were increased substantially, and subsequent costs increased very rapidly. According to Ogura's analysis, the cost of both health insurance and pension plans will continue to increase sharply in the next several decades and will peak around the year 2021, when the cost of government medical programs will be about 50 percent higher than it is today and the cost of public pension plans will double. Together, the two plans will absorb about one-quarter of national income, about 10 percentage points more than the current cost. Ogura questions whether future generations of workers will be willing to continue to support the elderly at the levels at which they have been supported in the recent past.

Alan M. Garber surveys demographic trends that influence the utilization of health care in the United States and examines the key financial issues surrounding hospital and physicians' services for the elderly. He also discusses the obstacles to improved financing and delivery of long-term care. He urges a cautious approach to expanded government financing of long-term care, emphasizing the difficulty of controlling costs for such care. Garber argues that marketing long-term care insurance to younger persons should help prevent the adverse selection that mitigates against selling long-term care insurance to elderly persons. Nonetheless, owing to the open-ended nature of potential long-term care services, he argues that moral hazard will remain an obstacle to the efficient functioning of a long-term care insurance market. As larger numbers of people purchase long-term care insurance, nursing homes are likely to change their character, providing high-quality housing and related services, Garber emphasizes. Many individuals who would not consider entering a nursing home today would be willing to do so if quality improved in this sense. Garber concludes that the development of private financing mechanisms is likely to be the major response to the need for long-term care.

In summary, taken together, the papers in this volume reveal a striking number of similarities between the two countries. The populations in both countries are aging rapidly, although the rate is faster in Japan than in the United States. Thus, true "aging problems" are future problems in both countries. Workers are leaving the labor force at younger and younger ages in both countries, although the trend is much more pronounced in the United States than in Japan. In both countries, the trend may be attributed in large part to public and private pension benefits. Public health insurance that provides health care at little or no cost in both countries contributed to rapid increases in the cost of health care in both Japan and the United States, although the per capita cost in Japan is still only about half that in the United States. Housing equity is the primary asset of both elderly Americans and elderly Japanese. In both countries, the elderly are at least as well off as younger members of the population. Although Japan's national saving rate is much higher than that in the United States, both Japanese and American authors predict that population aging will reduce future saving rates in both countries, largely because of Social Security programs that have become more generous in recent years. Indeed, the Social Security programs in the two countries are rather similar. The cost of health care and, more generally, the prospect of a smaller number of employed persons supporting a growing number of retired persons are important concerns in both countries.

There are of course some differences. For example, the ratio of elderly living together with their children is high in Japan and low in the United States, although the pattern in Japan is rapidly changing in the direction of the U.S. pattern. A special feature of the Japanese economy is the extremely high real estate values, especially in urban areas. Although much of the increase during the late 1980s was due to "bubbles" and real estate prices are falling dramatically in recent years, the values are still considerably higher than in other countries, and homes are the major form of household assets. Since a large fraction of homes are owned by the elderly, this has had an extremely important effect on the wealth of the older population in Japan. The medical care systems are very different in the two countries, although those differences are not emphasized in this volume.

1   Aging and Labor Force Participation: A Review of Trends and Explanations

Robin L. Lumsdaine and David A. Wise

The American population is aging rapidly. Persons 65 years of age and older, who now constitute about one-fifth of the population, will constitute about two-fifths of the population by 2040. In addition, individuals are living longer. Yet the labor force participation rate of older Americans has fallen dramatically in recent years. This paper discusses this trend and the principal explanations put forth to explain it. The paper is in two parts. The first part reviews trends in labor force participation and associated trends in Social Security (SS) coverage, firm pension plan coverage, and other factors that are likely to be associated with the labor force participation trends. The second part of the paper discusses the incentive effects of SS and retirement plans, with emphasis on firm pension plans. The intent is to summarize the facts and the research that has attempted to explain them. The presentation is primarily graphic. We begin with a simple conceptual framework.

1.1   A Conceptual Framework

To help organize the discussion that follows and to put the ideas in context, a conceptual framework of the retirement decision is outlined in figure 1.1,

Robin L. Lumsdaine is assistant professor of economics at Princeton University and a faculty research fellow of the National Bureau of Economic Research. David A. Wise is the John F. Stambaugh Professor of Political Economy at the John F. Kennedy School of Government, Harvard University, and area director for Health and Retirement Programs at the National Bureau of Economic Research.

The authors have paraphrased and borrowed freely from papers by Kotlikoff and Wise (1985, 1987, 1989) and Stock and Wise (1990a, 1990b). Data gathered by several other authors have also been used, often in a format different from the original presentation. In all cases, the original sources are cited. Financial support was provided by the National Institute on Aging (grants P01 AG05842 and T32 AG00186) and by the Hoover Institution.

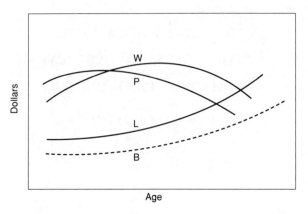

Fig. 1.1   Summary of factors that influence retirement

which summarizes several stylized facts.[1] Several factors have important influences on the retirement decision as workers age. As health and functional ability deteriorate, the disutility of work increases, and the relative desire for leisure increases, indicated by the line labeled L in the figure. Real wage earnings typically rise over some portion of the working life but later decline with age, as indicated by W. Lower wage earnings and greater hardship associated with working tend to increase the incentive to retire. As employees age, they may also accumulate more personal saving, and their entitlement to SS and firm pension benefits increases. Thus, if the retirement age is postponed, employees are able to support a higher level of consumption after retirement. In addition, any given level of personal saving or SS and pension entitlement can support a higher annual consumption level if retirement is postponed; there are fewer remaining years of life over which support must be provided. This is summarized as B in the figure. The larger these benefits, the greater the incentive to retire.

The central theme of the discussion below is the upward shift over time in the relation between benefits and age; given age, SS and pension entitlements have increased. Thus, the incentive to retire has increased. With respect to most of the discussion below, it may be assumed that the relation between real wage earnings and age and the relation between the disutility of work (desire for leisure) and age have not changed over time.

Worker productivity also declines with age. It is often argued that productivity is greater than the wage early in the working life and less than the wage later in the working life. This is the assumption reflected in the relation between worker productivity, P, and the wage shown in the figure. This relation is often put forth as an explanation for the structure of private pension plans, which typically encourage early retirement, as discussed below.

1. Our fig. 1.1 is patterned after fig. 10.1 in Nalebuff and Zeckhauser (1985).

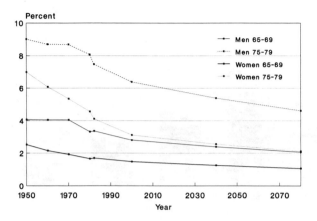

Fig. 1.2   Death rates for men and women, selected ages, by year

1.2   Life Expectancy, Labor Force Participation, and Associated Trends

1.2.1   Life Expectancy and the Age Composition of the U.S. Population

Americans are living longer, and the proportion of the population that is old is increasing rapidly. In 1950, for example, the annual death rate of white men age 75–79 was 90.1 per 1,000; by 1980, it had fallen to 80.7, a 10 percent reduction. Assuming current trends, the projected death rate for the year 2000 is 63.9, a further 21 percent reduction. The reductions for white women are even larger, as shown in figure 1.2.[2]

An implication of the lower death rates is a marked increase in life expectancy, especially for women. Men who were 65 in 1950 could expect to live 12.8 more years; in 1980 they could expect to live 14.2 more years, an 11 percent increase (see fig. 1.3A). Over the same thirty-year period, the life expectancy of women who were 65 increased by over 23 percent, from 15 to 18.5 more years (see fig. 1.3B).

The overall aging of the population probably has more important policy implications than increasing individual life expectancy.[3] The proportion of the population 55 and older has increased from about 15 percent in 1940 to about 21 percent in 1980. By 2020, almost 31 percent of the population will be in this age group (see fig. 1.4A). The elderly (those over 54), who now constitute

2. These data were taken from Poterba and Summers (1987), who obtained their data from the U.S. Department of Health, Education, and Welfare/U.S. Department of Health and Human Services, National Center for Health Statistics, *Vital Statistics of the United States,* vol. 2, *Mortality* (Washington, D.C., 1950, 1960, 1970, 1980).

3. Data for figs. 1.4A and 1.4B are taken from Sandefur and Tuma (1987, table 1) and U.S. Bureau of the Census (1984, table 6).

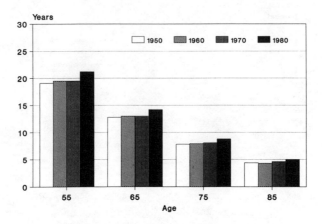

Fig. 1.3A   Life expectancy of men at selected ages, by year

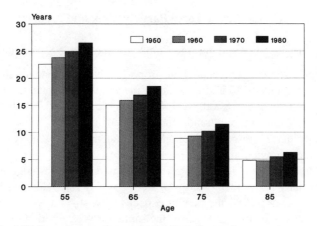

Fig. 1.3B   Life Expectancy of women at selected ages, by year

about one-fifth of all adults, will constitute about two-fifths of all adults by 2040.

The oldest age groups are growing the fastest. Only 0.3 percent of the population was over 85 in 1940; the proportion had increased to 1.0 percent by 1980, mostly since 1960 (see fig. 1.4B). The projected proportion is 2.4 in 2020. The proportion between 65 and 74 increased from about 5 percent of the population in 1940 to close to 7 percent in 1980; the 2020 projection is 10 percent. Thus, an increasingly large fraction of the population is older than typical retirement ages. As emphasized below, the dramatic reduction in retirement ages magnifies this effect.

From the point of view of the individual, increasing life expectancy induces later retirement. If other factors remain the same, longer life expectancy means

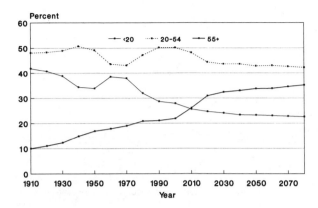

Fig. 1.4A   **Age composition of the U.S. population (1910–80) and projections (1990–2080), selected age groups**

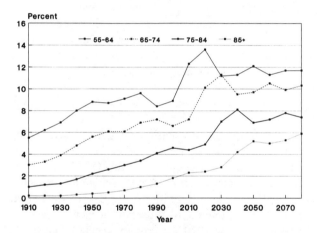

Fig. 1.4B   **Age composition of the U.S. population over 55 (1910–80) and projections (1990–2080), selected age groups**

that any given level of pension and SS entitlement, or of personal saving, must be used to support consumption over more retirement years. From the point of view of society, a larger older population means that a smaller labor force must support a larger number of retirees.

1.2.2   Labor Force Participation

Although a larger and larger fraction of the population is old and individual life expectancy is increasing, workers are leaving the labor force at younger and younger ages. Thus, there are more older people, living longer, working less.

A recent study by Ransom and Sutch (1988) shows that the labor force par-

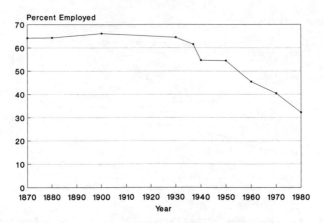

Fig. 1.5A   Labor force participation of men over 60, 1870–1980

ticipation rates of men over 60 were essentially constant between 1870 and 1930. Indeed, according to their study, for most older age groups the rates in 1937 were essentially the same as in 1930. Since that time, the labor force participation rates of older men have fallen continuously. Adjusted for the shift away from agricultural employment, the rate increased from a little over 50 percent in 1870 to almost 65 percent in 1930 and then fell to about 30 percent by 1980. Social Security was introduced under the Social Security Act of 1935. Company pensions were spurred by the Revenue Act of 1942, which granted tax incentives to firms to establish pension plans. The Ransom and Sutch data, based on the decennial censuses, are reproduced in figure 1.5A.

These data, as reported in Sandefur and Tuma (1987), have also been used to construct labor force participation rates by age group for men and women at ten-year intervals, beginning in 1940 (figs. 1.5B–D).[4] The rates for men fell in each age group. For example, 61.4 percent of men 55 and older were in the labor force in 1940, by 1970 the proportion had fallen to 52.7, and by 1985 only 39.6 percent of men in this age group were in the labor force. The participation rates of women 55 and older increased until 1970. But, since

---

4. Labor force participation by gender and age group can be computed from Sandefur and Tuma's (1987) tables 1, 2, 3, and 10. For example, the labor force participation of men in a given age category is equal to the percentage of men in that age group who are employed divided by the percentage of men in that age group (which is given in table 3, panel a). Since the tables are divided by gender and race simultaneously, the percentage of employed men in a given age group is the percentage of white employed men in that age group plus the percentage of nonwhite employed men in that age group. For each race, the percentage of employed men in an age group is the product of the following: the percentage of men of a given race and age that is employed, the percentage of the population of a given race and age that is male, and the percentage of a given age that is a specific race. This information is obtained from tables 10, 3, and 2, respectively. To aggregate age groups, additional information regarding the percentage of the population that is a given age group is required; these data are found in table 1.

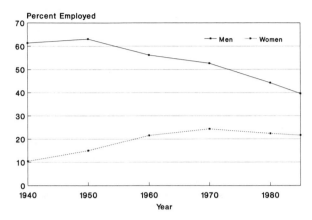

Fig. 1.5B   Labor force participation of men and women 55 and older, 1940–85

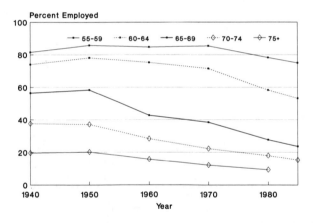

Fig. 1.5C   Labor force participation of men 55 and older, by age group, 1940–85

1970, even the rates for women have fallen (see fig. 1.5B). Indeed, for both men and women there was an abrupt change in labor force participation rates in the early 1970s: for men the reduction was accelerated in most age groups, and for women the rates that had been increasing began to decline.

1.2.3   Associated Trends

What has enabled people to leave the labor force at younger and younger ages and still maintain consumption after retirement? It seems evident that this has been made possible by Social Security benefits and by firm pension plans. Before discussing trends in SS and pension coverage, it is useful to establish first that support in old age is typically not financed by personal saving.

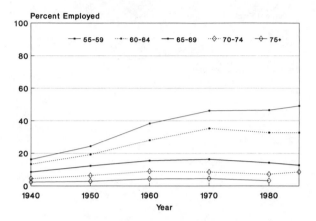

Fig. 1.5D Labor force participation of women 55 and older, by age group, 1940–85

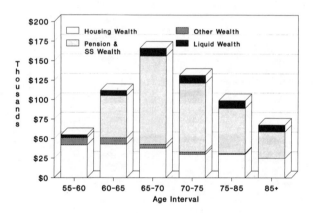

Fig. 1.6A Median wealth by age and asset category, all households

The Composition of Total Wealth

Based on the recent Survey of Income and Program Participation (SIPP), Venti and Wise (1991) have computed the composition of total wealth for all households, for homeowners, and for renters in 1984. The results are summarized in figures 1.6A–C. The amounts reflect median wealth by asset category. It is clear from figure 1.6A that most families approach retirement age with very little personal saving other than housing equity. For example, among households with heads 60–65, the median of liquid wealth is only $6,600; the median of housing equity is $43,000.[5] The majority of families rely heavily on

5. Liquid wealth is broadly defined to include interest-earning assets held in banks and other institutions, mortgages held, money owed from the sale of businesses, U.S. savings bonds, checking accounts, and equity in stocks and mutual fund shares, less unsecured debt.

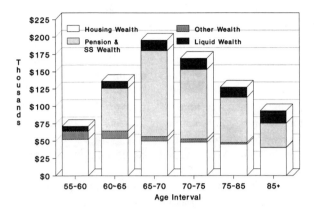

Fig. 1.6B   Median wealth by age and asset category, homeowners

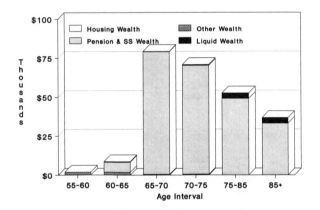

Fig. 1.6C   Median wealth by age and asset category, renters

Social Security benefits for support after retirement and, to a more limited extent, on the saving that is done for them by employers, through defined-benefit pension plans. The SIPP data, from which these figures were computed, allow estimation of the value of SS and pension plan benefits only after the payments are received.[6] Thus, wealth in the form of SS and pensions is re-corded only for persons who have begun to receive the payments. Most persons have retired by 65 and thereafter are receiving the benefits to which they are entitled. About 59 percent of households with reference persons between 65 and 70 receive pension benefits; 89 percent receive SS benefits. The present value of pension and SS wealth is based on life tables together with the amount of the annual payments. Social Security benefits are indexed to inflation; pri-

6. The SIPP data do not contain SS earnings histories (which determine SS benefits), nor do they contain detailed pension plan provisions.

vate pension benefits typically are not.[7] As can be seen from figure 1.6A, SS and pension wealth is by far the most important component of the wealth of most elderly. Among households with heads age 65–70, for example, the median of SS and pension wealth *combined* is $113,400; the median of housing wealth is $38,000, and the median of liquid financial assets is only $10,000. The decline in SS and pension wealth with age is largely an artifact of declining life expectancy. The lower housing equity of older households is a cohort effect and does not reflect a reduction of housing equity as individual households age; in fact, housing equity increases on average as the elderly age; there is little change in housing equity even among families that move from one home to another.

Comparison of figures 1.6B and 1.6C shows that households who rent have substantially less wealth than homeowners in all asset categories. The median total wealth of homeowners is $170,400; the median for renters is $59,300. Renters, who constitute about 20 percent of all households, have virtually no liquid assets.

In summary, the majority of elderly households live on Social Security and pension benefits.

Social Security Coverage

It is clear from figure 1.5A above that the trend toward earlier retirement began between the passage of the Social Security Act in 1935 and the Revenue Act of 1942. The 1942 Revenue Act granted tax incentives to firms to establish pension plans. Indeed, after adjusting for the reduction in agricultural employment, there was a sharp *reversal* in the prior trend toward later retirement, as shown by Ransom and Sutch (1988).

The percentage of persons 65 and older receiving SS benefits increased from about 20 percent in 1940 to 85 percent in 1960; now about 95 percent receive SS benefits (see fig. 1.7). In addition, the level of benefits has increased sharply. The benefits for a retired male worker increased from about 14 percent of median male income in 1950 to 37.5 percent in 1980 (see Tuma and Sandefur 1988). Thus, not only has coverage been extended to virtually the entire labor force, but the standard of living that the benefits can support has also increased sharply.

Firm Pension Plans

The proportion of the *workforce* covered by a firm (or a federal or state or local government) pension plan increased from 23.8 to 48.6 percent between

---

7. The present values of pension and SS benefits are the discounted survival weighted streams of income from each source received by the reference person and the spouse if present. Discounting is at 6 percent, and survival probabilities are calculated from mortality tables by sex. Payments from SS, military pensions, federal employee pensions, and the railroad retirement pension are assumed to be indexed at an annual rate of 4 percent. All other sources of pension income are not indexed in the wealth calculations.

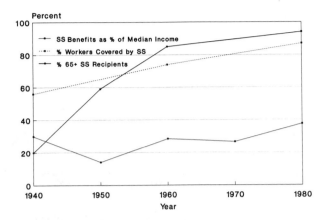

Fig. 1.7   Social Security coverage, recipients, and benefits, 1940–80

1950 and 1979. Now about 50 percent of the workforce is covered by a pension plan. Most of the growth in pension coverage occurred in the 1950s. The proportion of the older *population* (55 and older) collecting pension benefits continues to increase, as shown in figure 1.8.[8] By 1984, 30.8 percent of persons 55 and older and 39.0 percent of persons 65 and older were collecting pension benefits from some sourse, according to the SIPP.

In short, it is evident that the expansion of SS and firm pension plans has allowed and encouraged earlier retirement. In addition to the income incentive created by the entitlement to retirement income, the timing of the accrual of pension entitlements, created by firm pension plan provisions in particular, provides a strong incentive to retire early (as shown in the discussion below). These provisions create large increases and decreases in the *total* compensation from working at particular ages. Thus, the retirement benefit inducement to retire results from both income and price (wage) effects.

The Earnings of Older Employees

Like the earnings of younger employees, the earnings of older workers increased consistently from 1940 to 1970. But, after 1970, the earnings of the oldest employees began to decline, and the earnings of all older workers were declining by 1980 (see fig. 1.9). For example, the average 1985 annual earnings of employees 65–69 were about the same in real terms as they were twenty-five years earlier, in 1960. The earnings of employees 55–59 were lower in 1985 than they were in 1970. These data may be affected by selective retirement of the highest-paid employees and by part-time work, but there is ample evidence of a general decline in real wages across all age groups in the United States since about 1972. Thus, falling real wage earnings may also have contributed to earlier retirement in recent years.

8. Data for fig. 1.8 are taken from Kotlikoff and Smith (1983, tables 3.1.1, 3.1.2, 3.5.1).

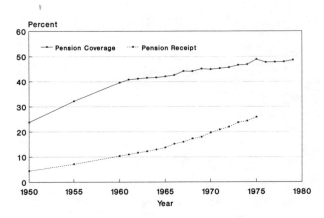

Fig. 1.8   Percentage pension coverage (of all workers 16 and older) and receipt (of population 55 and older), 1950–80

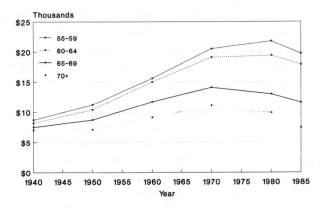

Fig. 1.9   Mean annual earnings of persons 55 and older, with nonzero earnings, by age group (thousands of 1984 dollars)

The Income of the Elderly

Although the labor force participation rates of older Americans have fallen dramatically in recent years, the average income of the elderly has increased sharply. Income data have been tabulated by Hurd and Shoven (1982) for several years between 1963 and 1978 (see figs. 1.10A and B).[9] Between 1960 and 1980, the labor force participation rates of men 65 and older fell by 37.5 percent, from 31.7 to 19.8. Yet the incomes of the elderly increased more than threefold over approximately the same period. The proportion of income from earnings declined, while the proportion from SS, firm pension benefits, and government medical plans increased substantially. The Hurd and Shoven com-

9. The Hurd and Shoven data are based on several U.S. Bureau of the Census, U.S. Department of Health, Education, and Welfare, and Social Security Administration reports and the 1978 Survey of the Elderly.

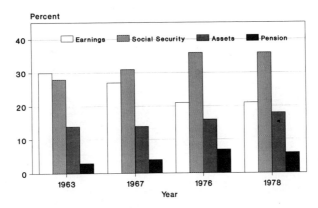

Fig. 1.10A   Composition of the income of the elderly 65 and older, selected years, excluding Medicare and Medicaid

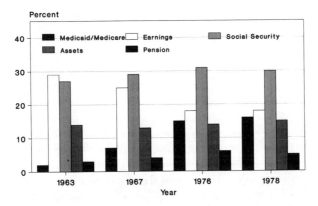

Fig. 1.10B   Composition of the income of the elderly, including Medicare and Medicaid

putations include an estimate for the user cost of housing and an estimate for the income equivalent of Medicare and Medicaid insurance (valued at cost). According to their numbers, the proportion of the income of the elderly derived from their own earnings declined from 29 to 18 percent between 1963 and 1978. Over the same period, the proportion from SS, firm pension plans, and government medical insurance increased from 32 to 51 percent. The proportion of income from assets remained roughly constant. The Hurd and Shoven data are based on *mean* income by category. Data from Venti and Wise (1991) based on *median* income by category, make it clear that the vast majority of the income of most elderly families comes from Social Security and pension benefits (see figs. 1.6A–C above).

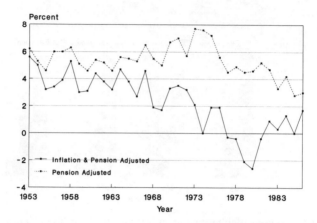

Fig. 1.11   Personal saving as a percentage of disposable private income, 1953–87

Personal Saving

Changes in personal saving may also affect retirement decisions. Personal saving declined from 3 to 6 percent of disposable private income in the 1950s to around 1 percent in the early 1980s, according to computations made by Summers and Carroll (1987) and reproduced in figure 1.11. These numbers are adjusted for inflation and exclude saving by employers through defined-benefit pension plans.[10] Without the inflation adjustment, the downward trend begins only after 1973. It is clear from papers by Venti and Wise (1990, 1991), for example, that there is a very large range in personal saving rates, with a large proportion of the population saving virtually nothing except in the form of housing equity. Thus, the extent to which the aggregate data reflect a reduction in saving that could impinge on the retirement decisions of an important proportion of employees is not clear. In any case, less personal saving, holding other income sources constant, would typically be associated with later retirement, clearly not the dominant force in the current trend.

Summary

The trends discussed above are summarized in figure 1.12. The labor force participation of older Americans has declined dramatically since 1940. Social Security and pension benefits have become the major source of income for the majority of older persons, and the total income of persons over 65 has increased enormously, over threefold between 1963 and 1978 alone. (Real annual earnings of the typical employee are about the same now as they were in

---

10. The national income accounts include firm contributions to defined-benefit pension plans under *personal saving.* Inflation-adjusted saving is measured saving minus the inflation rate (the GNP deflator) times net interest-bearing assets.

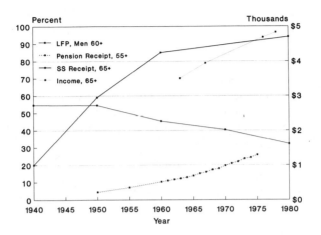

Fig. 1.12   Summary of trends

the early 1960s.) These forces have clearly dominated longer life expectancy and lower personal saving, which would be expected to prolong labor force participation. In addition, a fall in real wages since 1970 may have contributed to earlier retirement in more recent years. Without some change in labor force participation rates of older persons, the prospect is that a smaller segment of working persons will support an increasingly larger group of retirees.

1.3   The Incentive Effects of Public and Private Retirement Plans

The foregoing discussion highlights the correlates of the reduction in the labor force participation rates of older Americans and suggests the conclusion that the reduction was induced by the introduction of SS and firm pension plans. The implication is that the adoption of public and private entitlements to retirement benefits made early retirement possible; it increased the income available to support retirement consumption. The discussion below emphasizes the incentive effects inherent in the provisions of public and private plans, independent of the retirement wealth that they represent.

The 1980s have witnessed a marked shift in government policy toward promoting the labor supply of the elderly. The government has virtually eliminated mandatory retirement, and it has scheduled a gradual increase in the Social Security retirement age from 65 to 67. It has limited somewhat the Social Security earnings test that reduces Social Security benefits for "retired" workers earning more than an "exempt amount," it eliminated the earnings test after age 70, and it is increasing the actuarial incentive to delay the receipt of Social Security benefits beyond age 65.

The change in the government policy is responsive to the major demographic swing that is under way and its important implications for retirement finances in the next century. Given Social Security's pay-as-you-go method of finance, the projected increase in the ratio of beneficiaries to contributors means either significant cuts in future benefits or significant future increases in the Social Security payroll tax.

Reversing the trend toward early retirement represents an important alternative for addressing the demographic transition. Additional labor supply of the elderly would relieve Social Security's finances as well as offset a potential shortage in the supply of labor relative to that of other productive factors. In addition, it is argued that prolonging labor force participation would mean more fulfilling lives for many elderly.

What has gone largely unrecognized is that, notwithstanding recent changes in Social Security regulations intended to prolong work, private pension plan provisions operate powerfully in the opposite direction. The most prominent theoretical explanations for the firm behavior rest on the proposition that the efficient structure of the age-wage profile is such that older workers are paid more than their worth to the firm and must therefore be encouraged to retire (see, e.g., Lazear 1979). Whether this is in fact the reason has not been demonstrated. Conversations with pension managers reveal that, in some instances, the incentives of the plans are not fully understood and that many plans have been introduced without consideration of their effects on retirement. Some special early retirement incentives (temporary "window" plans) have been introduced to relieve the firm of older workers so that younger workers could be promoted or simply as a means of reducing the size of the firm's workforce.

Many researchers have pointed to the Social Security system's high benefit levels and work disincentives as a major contributor to the continuing trend toward early retirement, and a great deal of research has focused on the effect of Social Security benefits on labor force participation. Recent examples are Blinder, Gordon, and Wise (1980), Burkhauser (1980), Hurd and Boskin (1981), Burkhauser and Quinn (1983), Burtless and Moffitt (1984), Hausman and Wise (1985), Burtless (1986), and Gustman and Steinmeier (1986, 1991). With few exceptions—Hurd and Boskin (1981) and, to some extent, Hausman and Wise (1985)—these studies attribute only a modest portion of the early retirement trend to the effect of Social Security provisions, although the findings may reflect, to some degree, problems of misspecification in accounting for its effects. In contrast, there has been very little work relating retirement behavior to the retirement incentives provided by pension plans.[11] The apparent reason for this neglect has been the difficulty in obtaining data that combine the retirement choices of older workers with information about their past earnings and the specific provisions of their pension plans.[12]

More recent work of Kotlikoff and Wise (1985, 1987, 1989), Stock and Wise (1990a, 1990b), and Lumsdaine, Stock, and Wise (1991) suggests that

---

11. The most closely related work considers the effect of pension plans on job mobility (Clark and McDermed 1988; Gustman and Steinmeier 1993; Allen, Clark, and McDermed 1988, 1993) but not retirement.

12. Exceptions are Burkhauser (1979), Fields and Mitchell (1982), Lazear (1983), Kotlikoff and Wise (1987), and Hogarth (1988).

the provisions of private pension plans are typically much more important than SS provisions as determinants of the retirement behavior of workers covered by such plans. Their detailed analysis of the provisions of private defined-benefit pension plans, which account for roughly three-quarters of all pension plan recipients, indicates that a large proportion of these plans provide very large incentives to retire early. Virtually all defined-benefit plans incorporate stiff financial penalties for working past the age of 65, and a very sizable fraction have similarly stiff penalties for working past the plan's early retirement age, often as young as 55. Similar evidence is presented by Bulow (1981), Lazear (1983), Clark and McDermed (1986), Fields and Mitchell (1984), and Frant and Leonard (1987). Working an additional year often involves losing, in expected present value of future pension benefits, an amount equivalent to half a year's nonpension earnings, if not more. These retirement incentives in many, if not most, instances are significantly greater than those ascribed to Social Security.

We consider first the incentive effects inherent in the SS rules and then the incentive effects of private pension plans.

1.3.1   Social Security (SS)

The SS benefit amount is based on past individual earnings, although the relation between benefits and earnings is not linear. Benefits are a much larger proportion of the past earnings of low-wage than of high-wage workers. The initial benefit is based on nominal earnings indexed to age-60 dollars using the consumer price index (CPI). After retirement (receipt of benefits), the benefits are indexed to the CPI. The SS normal retirement age is 65. But benefits can be taken as young as 62, with the benefit amount actuarially reduced to reflect the increase in the expected number of retirement years over which benefits will be received. That is, if the benefit entitlement is not changed because of a change in earnings, the expected present value of future benefits is the same irrespective of the age, between 62 and 65, at which benefits are first received. After age 65, however, the increase in benefits is much less than actuarial. It is now 3 percent per year, but it was only 1 percent per year until 1981.[13]

The easiest way to understand the incentive effects of the benefit structure is to consider the relation between the present value of future benefits and the age of retirement. Such relations are shown in figure 1.13A for two representative workers, one a low-wage and the other a high-wage employee. The top part of the graph represents nominal earnings by age (age-50 earnings arc in 1980 dollars). The bottom part of the graph represents the accrual (SSA) of SS wealth (SSW). It is the change in the present value of SS benefits between one year and the next. That is,

$$SSA_t = SSW_t - SSW_{t-1}(1 + r),$$

---

13. Although the change from 1 to 3 percent was the result of a 1977 law, it applied to those who would be 65 in 1981 and later years.

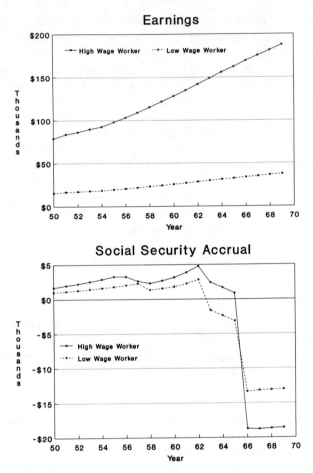

Fig. 1.13A   Social Security accrual and earnings, representative low- and high-wage workers

where in this case r is a nominal discount rate taken to be 9 percent. Thus, the figure represents two forms of compensation: one is wage earnings; the other is the increase in the entitlement to future SS benefits.

Social Security accrual is a small proportion of wage earnings for the high-wage worker but can be a significant proportion for the low-wage worker, as shown in figure 1.13B. It is about 6 percent of the wage earnings of the low-wage worker at age 50 and increases to almost 10 percent at age 62. If the low-wage worker continues to work from 62 to 65, the accrual is *negative* (10 percent of the wage at 64). The *loss* in the present value of SS benefits would be about 39 percent of wage earnings if the person continued to work past age 65. Thus, the reduction in total wage and SS compensation between 62 and 66 would be about 50 percent, were the low-wage worker to continue to work.

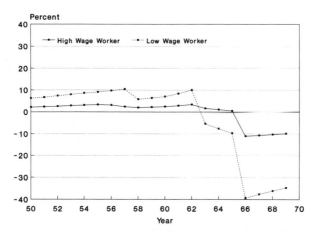

Fig. 1.13B   Real Social Security accrual as a percentage of real earnings, low- and high-wage workers

The reduction in total compensation for the high-wage worker would be about 14 percent. Thus, the SS inducement to leave the labor force at age 65 is inversely related to wage earnings.

1.3.2   Firm Pensions

Roughly three-quarters of all persons participating in private pension plans are enrolled in defined-benefit plans where benefits are determined according to a specified formula. The remainder are enrolled in plans where benefits are directly related to contributions made on behalf of the employee and to the performance of the plan's investment portfolio. Because most workers are covered by defined-benefit plans, and because they are likely to have the greatest effects on labor market behavior, the discussion here emphasizes the incentive effects of this type of plan. The evidence is presented in three sections. The first section discusses the "average" incentives of a large number of plans. The second section discusses the incentives of the plan of a single large firm and relates these incentives to departure rates from the firm.

The Incentive Effects of Typical Plans

Kotlikoff and Wise (1985, 1987) considered the retirement incentive effects inherent in typical defined-benefit plans and have analyzed the provisions of a large number of firm plans. As with Social Security, it is easiest to exhibit the potential retirement incentive effects of defined-benefit pension plans by describing the accrual of vested benefits. Figure 1.14 is taken from Kotlikoff and Wise (1987). It shows the average accrual rates (weighted by plan membership) for U.S. defined-benefit plans with selected early and normal retirement ages. The pension accrual in a year is the increase (or decrease) in the expected

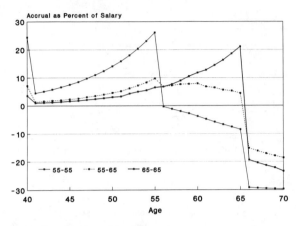

Fig. 1.14   Weighted average pension accrual as percentage of wage earnings for percentage of earnings plans with ten-year cliff vesting, for selected early and normal retirement ages

discounted value of future pension benefits that results from working that year. It is the value of deferred compensation analogous to current wage compensation. Pension accrual is shown as a percentage of wage compensation (the accrual ratio or accrual rate). The data come from a random sample of approximately 2,500 plans from the Bureau of Labor Statistics Level of Benefits Survey.[14] For each plan, accrual rates are calculated assuming average wage-tenure profiles in the industry and occupation to which the plan pertains, based on current population survey data (see Kotlikoff and Wise 1985).

Consider first plans with early and normal retirement at the same age, 55, a plan stipulation that is common in the transportation industry, for example. The average decline in the rate of pension wealth accrual at 55 is equivalent to about 30 percent of wage earnings. If the typical person covered by such a plan were to continue to work through age 65, pension accrual would be negative and equivalent to approximately 30 percent of wage earnings. Whereas at age 54 the pension benefit accrual is equivalent to about 30 percent of wage earnings, after age 65 continued work means a loss in pension wealth equivalent to about 30 percent of wage earnings. Thus, between these two ages, the decline in the rate of pension wealth accrual is equivalent to a 60 percent wage reduction!

The more common plans with early retirement at 55 and normal retirement at 65 typically exhibit an increase in pension wealth accrual to age 55 with a decline thereafter. Again, continued work past age 65 is associated with a substantial loss in pension wealth, with the decline in accrual equivalent to

---

14. Similar calculations have been made by Lazear (1983) on the basis of the Bankers Trust Survey of large pension plans.

approximately 20 percent of wage earnings. The pension wealth of persons covered by plans with both early and normal retirement at 65 increases continuously until 65 and then declines by approximately 40 percent, from a positive accrual of about 21 percent of salary to a negative accrual of about 19 percent.

Thus, on the basis of industry-wide earnings profiles, continued employment with the plan sponsor after the age of early retirement and, in particular, after the age of normal retirement typically involves a substantial reduction in total annual compensation because of declines in pension wealth accrual.

While figure 1.14 highlights the average characteristics of plans, it is important to understand that there is a very wide range in plan provisions, even among plans with the same early and normal retirement ages. This is demonstrated in figure 1.15, also taken from Kotlikoff and Wise (1987). The figure shows average accrual rates for the 513 plans of figure 1.14 with early retirement at 55 and normal retirement at 65, together with upper and lower 5 percentile levels. The lower 5 percentile level for any age group is that accrual rate below which 5 percent of plans fall. The upper 5 percentile level is defined analogously. Consider the accrual ratio at vesting. While the average vesting ratio for this sample is .071, the median is .021, the maximum is .383, and the minimum is 0. The ratio at the lowest 5 percentile point is 0, while it is .201 at the largest 5 percentile level. A similarly large dispersion in annual accrual ratios is indicated for each of the ages 40–70. The average accrual rates between ages 55 and 65 are positive, but for many plans the rates by 65 are very negative.

Thus, while the average plan may provide positive pension accrual at a particular age, the accrual rate may be substantially negative for some plans. Even a small proportion of plans that provide a strong incentive to leave the labor

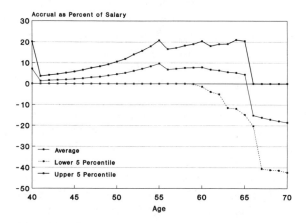

Fig. 1.15   Weighted average accrual rates and upper and lower 5 percentile levels for percentage of earnings plans with ten-year cliff vesting, early retirement at 55 and normal retirement at 65

force could have a very substantial effect on observed average labor force participation rates. Thus, it is important to base judgments about the labor force participation incentive effects of pension plans on more than average accrual rates.

The Plan of a Large Firm

Whether incentive effects like those described above have an effect on retirement decisions is a second question. Kotlikoff and Wise (1985, 1989) have addressed this question by considering the relation between pension plan provisions and retirement rates in a large Fortune 500 firm, referred to as Firm I. That work is summarized in this section. The analysis of the firm data shows a very strong relation between the plan provisions and departure rates from the firm.

The plan. The plan normal retirement age is 65; the early retirement age is 55. Vesting occurs after ten years of service. The plan is integrated with Social Security, with benefits being reduced (offset) by some proportion of SS benefits. Figure 1.16A summarizes the incentive effects inherent in the plan provisions. The figure shows the pension accrual between ages 50 and 70 of male managers hired by the firm in 1960, at age 30. By 1980, they were 50 and had twenty years of service with the firm. The accrual of Social Security benefits and predicted wage earnings for each year are also shown. The wage predictions are based on actual average earnings of firm employees. All the numbers are in real 1985 dollars.

At age 50, the typical male manager has wage earnings of about $48,446 per year. Compensation in the form of pension accrual is $2,646, or about 6 percent of wage earnings. If the manager were to retire at this age, he would be entitled to benefits at 65, based on his earnings in the seven or eight preceding years. The benefits would not be available until age 65 and thus have a relatively low present value at age 50. Normal retirement benefits could be taken earlier, as early as age 55, but they would be reduced actuarially in such a way that the present discounted value of the benefits remains unchanged. The reduction in the benefit would be just enough to offset the fact that benefits would be received for more years.[15]

If the person remains in the firm until age 55 and then retires, however, benefits are available immediately, and the reduction in benefits for early retirement is less than the actuarial reduction. In addition, the worker who remains until age 55 and then retires is eligible to receive a supplemental benefit until age 65 equal to his Social Security offset. Thus, there is a very large increase in pension wealth at age 55, $72,527, corresponding to the large spike in the graph. In effect, there is a bonus of $72,527 for remaining in the firm from age 54 to age 55.

---

15. Not accounting for any real rate of time preference.

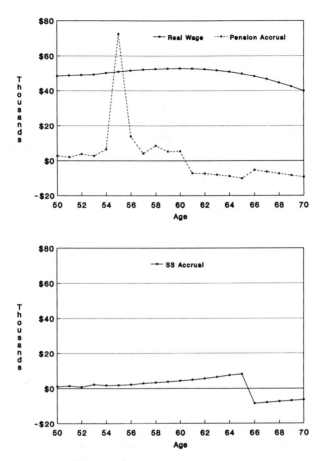

Fig. 1.16A   Wage earnings, pension accrual, and Social Security accrual, representative person in Firm I

After age 55, pension accrual falls, to about 10 percent of the wage at age 60.[16] Pension accrual is in fact negative beginning at age 61. The loss in compensation between age 60 and age 61 is equivalent to a wage cut of about 14 percent. Between age 61 and age 65, the loss in pension benefits is equivalent to about 20 percent of annual wage compensation. Workers who have thirty or more years of service at age 60 are eligible for full retirement benefits; the early retirement reduction factors no longer apply.[17]

16. The plan provisions stipulate that an additional year of service adds 2 percent to normal retirement benefits per year of service before age 55 but only 1 percent per year of service after age 55.
17. Thus, no increase in benefits will result for working another year from the application of one less year of early retirement reduction, as was the case before thirty years of service. In addi-

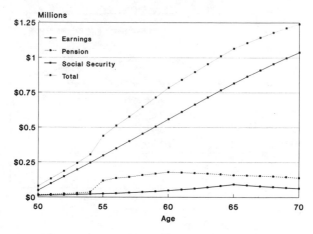

Fig. 1.16B   Cumulative earnings, pension wealth, and Social Security wealth, representative person in Firm I

Social Security accruals range from about $1,000 to $8,000 between age 50 and age 65. After 65, Social Security accrual becomes negative, about −$8,500 at age 66. At 66, the loss in private pension benefits and Social Security benefits together amounts to about 32 percent of wage earnings at that age. (For some groups of employees in the firm, the loss in pension and Social Security wealth together after age 65 is equivalent to 95 percent of wage earnings: if these employees continue to work, it is essentially without compensation.)

The data in figure 1.16A are shown in the standard budget constraint form in figure 1.16B. Total compensation, including wage earnings, Social Security wealth, and pension wealth, is graphed against age, beginning at age 50. There is a discontinuous jump in the graph at age 55, the age at which early retirement benefits are available on an advantageous basis.

The firm departure rates. Departure rates by age and years of service suggest the effect of pension plan provisions on retirement. They are shown for salesmen by age and years of service in table 1.1. The yearly departure rate is the proportion of those employed at the beginning of the year that retires—more strictly speaking, leaves the firm—during the forthcoming year. Several as-

---

tion, for each year that benefits are not taken between ages 55 and 65, the receipt of benefits for a year without the Social Security offset (reduction) is forgone. This advantage is lost at age 65. Thereafter, the loss in benefits from working an additional year is smaller because this opportunity is no longer available; it was available only until age 65. The accruals also depend to a small extent on the updating of the years used in the calculation of "final" earnings. "Final" earnings are used to determine the pension benefit.

Table 1.1   **Departure Rates for Salesmen by Age and Years of Service**

Age	< 10	11–15	16–20	21–25	26–30	31–35	36+
			Years of Service				
< 50	19	9	5	4	3	. . .	. . .
50–54	14	7	4	3	3	2	0
˙55	11	14	9	11	12	15	. . .
56–59	14	13	9	11	. 11	14	. . .
60	11	12	14	19	14	29	35
61	13	12	13	13	19	32	28
62	12	27	32	38	36	52	35
63	20	28	33	36	47	48	56
64	0	37	36	30	36	38	28
65	34	56	51	50	49	47	43
66	17	28	10	34	18	16	12
67	20	16	25	21	8	5	18

pects of the data stand out. (1) Before 55, departure rates are typically around 3 percent for vested employees; they are substantially larger for those with fewer than ten years of service, who are not vested. At 55, the early retirement age, they jump to 10 percent or more, but only for vested employees, those with at least ten years of service. It is important to notice that the departure rates stay at that level until age 60, when there is another jump in the rate of departure. (2) At age 60, the departure rates increase very precipitously, especially for persons with over thirty years of service. For this group, full benefits are available because there is no longer an early retirement reduction according to the plan's rules. For this group, subsequent pension accrual is negative. (3) When Social Security benefits become available at 62, the departure rates again increase very sharply, but only for those who are vested in the firm plan. (4) Finally, there is a large increase in departure rates at 65, the SS normal retirement age. Both pension and SS accruals are negative if the employee continues to work beyond age 65.

To understand the potential importance of the early retirement benefits, suppose that, if it were not for this inducement, the departure rates would remain at 3 percent until age 60 instead of the 10 or 12 percent rates that are observed. Departure at 3 percent per year means that 14 percent of those who were employed at 55 would have left before age 60; at 11 percent per year, 44 percent would leave between 55 and 59.

Cumulative departure rates for all employees are shown in table 1.2 for three years, together with the rates by age. The cumulative rates are one minus the percentage who have departed. Given employment at age 50, the cumulative rates show the percentage still employed at older ages. On the basis of the 1981 and 1983 departure rates, only 48 percent of those employed at 50 would still

Table 1.2   **Cumulative and Yearly Departure Rates by Calendar Year, Years of Service (YOS), and Age**

| | Yearly | | | | Cumulative, 11+ YOS | | |
| | 8–10 YOS, | 11+ YOS | | | | | |
Age	1980	1981	1982	1983	1981	1982	1983
50	7	3			97	97	97
51	9	3			94	94	94
52	3	5	5	5	89	89	89
53	0	4	4	4	85	86	86
54	4	3	4	2	83	83	84
55	5	11	12	10	74	73	75
56	4	12	14	10	66	63	68
57	2	9	12	11	60	56	61
58	5	10	14	12	54	48	54
59	2	11	20	10	48	38	48
60	4	17	29	17	40	27	40
61	0	17	32	18	33	18	33
62	8	36	48	31	21	10	23
63	14	37	54	37	13	5	14
64	11	29	49	26	10	2	11
65	25	53	58	45	5	1	6

be employed at 60, and then 17 percent of these would leave. Only 10 percent would remain until age 65, and then about 50 percent of these would leave.

These data also show the effect of a special early retirement incentive (a "window plan") that was in effect in 1982 only. For employees who were eligible for early retirement in 1982, the incentive program provided a bonus of up to one year's salary. It is clear that the effect of the incentive was large: while the departure rates for 1981 and for 1983 are virtually identical, the 1982 rates were much higher. For example, the departure rate for 60-year-olds was 17 percent in 1981 and 1983 but 29 percent in 1982. Of those employed at age 50, 40 percent would still have been employed after age 60, based on the 1981 and 1983 departure rates. Only 27 percent would remain after age 60, based on the 1982 rates. Even under the normal plan, only 10 percent of those employed at age 50 would still be employed at 65. Only 2 percent would remain until 65 with the special incentive.

1.4   An Option Value Model of Retirement

The previous section demonstrates the large incentive effects inherent in the provisions of defined-benefit pension plans and shows that these incentives have very substantial effects on firm retirement (and other departure) rates. An additional goal of research in this area is to predict the effect on retirement rates of changes in firm pension plan and SS provisions. This section discusses an econometric model of retirement and simulations based on this model.

1.4.1   The Model

Two basic approaches, in addition to least squares regression, have been used in recent years to analyze retirement behavior. The first is the method of estimation developed to analyze the choices of individuals who face discontinuous or kinked budget constraints. The central feature of this method is a lifetime budget constraint analogous to the standard labor-leisure budget constraint, but with annual hours of work replaced by years of labor force participation and annual earnings replaced by cumulative lifetime compensation. The optimal age of retirement is determined by a utility function defined over years of work (postretirement years of leisure) and cumulative compensation. A careful application of this approach to retirement is by Burtless (1986), who analyzed the effects of changes in Social Security benefits on retirement.[18] While appealing in many respects, this procedure has an important drawback. It implicitly assumes that individuals know with certainty the opportunities—like wage rates—that will be available to them in the distant future. The hazard model is the second approach. As implemented to date, it is essentially a reduced-form technique designed to capture the effects on retirement of movements in variables such as Social Security wealth. Implementations of the hazard model have not been as "forward looking" as the nonlinear budget constraint specifications.[19] On the other hand, unexpected shocks, like sudden changes in earnings, enter the analysis very naturally.

The option value model as specified by Stock and Wise (1990b) incorporates the advantages of both of the approaches described above. It allows updating of information, as does the traditional hazard model, but also considers potential compensation many years in the future, as does the nonlinear budget constraint approach.[20] The key ideas of the model can be summarized briefly. It is in-

18. An analogous model was used by Venti and Wise (1984) to describe the rent paid by low-income families faced with discontinuous budget constraints. Earlier papers that develop these techniques are Hausman and Wise (1980) and Burtless and Hausman (1978).

19. Thus, in Hausman and Wise (1985), e.g., changes from the current period to the next, in earnings, pension wealth, and the increment to pension wealth, are allowed to affect the decision to retire in the next period, but expectations of these values several years hence are not.

20. Antecedents of the Stock and Wise model begin with Lazear and Moore (1988), who argue that the option value of postponing retirement is the appropriate variable to enter in a regression equation explaining retirement. Indeed, it was their work and the analysis of military retirement rates by Phillips and Wise (1987) that motivated Stock and Wise to pursue this approach. The Stock and Wise model is close in spirit to the stochastic dynamic programming model of Rust (1989), which poses substantially greater numerical complexity than the Stock and Wise model and has not yet been estimated for retirement. In principle, Rust observes not only the individual's retirement age but subsequent consumption decisions as well. Thus, Rust's model allows the individual to optimize over age of retirement and future consumption jointly. The individual's decision is modeled as the solution to a stochastic dynamic programming problem. As in the Stock and Wise case, the individual's expectations are conditioned on current known variables such as in-

tended to capture an important empirical regularity, the irreversibility of the retirement decision. Although it is not uncommon to work—at least part-time—after "retirement," it is rare to return to the job from which one has retired. The model focuses on the opportunity cost of retiring or, equivalently, on the value of retaining the option to retire at a later date. It has two key aspects. The first is that a person will continue to work at any age if the option value of continuing work is greater than the value of immediate retirement. In effect, the person compares the best of expected future possibilities—the option value of continuing to work—with the value of retiring now. The second is that the individual reevaluates this retirement decision as more information about future earnings—and thus future retirement benefits—becomes available with age. For example, a decline in the wage between age 56 and age 57 will cause the individual to reassess future wage earnings and thus future pension benefits and Social Security accrual as well. Thus, retirement may seem more advantageous on reaching 57 than it was expected to be at age 56. Retirement occurs when the value of continuing work falls below the value of retiring.

---

come. The idea is to recover the parameters of a utility function specified in terms of these choice variables. In practice, however, Rust uses income to describe consumption (Rust 1988), with a value function similar to that of Stock and Wise, specified in terms of income. To simplify the solution to the dynamic programming problem in his model, Rust assumes that random unobserved individual components are independent over time, whereas Stock and Wise allow such terms (representing differences among individuals in health status, desire for leisure, and the like) to be correlated. In short, Rust has described a solution to a more complicated choice than Stock and Wise, but with uncorrelated errors, whereas the Stock and Wise model is a solution to a less complex problem, but with correlated errors. A "dynamic programming" model of employment behavior has also been proposed by Berkovec and Stern (1991). Berkovec and Stern's analysis is also in progress. They consider transitions among three employment states over time. To simplify the solution to their optimization problem, they assume that disturbance terms are uncorrelated over time, except for an individual-specific random effect. Their analysis is in terms of individual attributes like education, race, health status, and age. Government benefits like Social Security are not explicitly modeled, whereas these benefits, as well as firm pension benefits, play the central role in the Stock and Wise analysis. Stock and Wise estimate a discount or weighting factor, whereas they obtain estimates of other parameters conditional on an assumed discount rate. Age itself is used explicitly to estimate retirement. Age is not a direct determinant of retirement in the standard version of the Stock and Wise model. This has important implications if the model is to be used to predict the effect of changes in firm pension plan or Social Security provisions on retirement. Neither Rust nor Berkovec and Stern, however, have information on private pension plan provisions, the focus of the Stock and Wise analysis. The retirement decision rule proposed by Stock and Wise as an approximation to individual behavior is much simpler than the dynamic programming rule. A concomitant of this assumption is also much simpler econometric implementation than the burdensome calculations imposed by the dynamic programming rule. These simplifications reduce the computational requirements substantially while retaining the key forward-looking features of the dynamic programming approach. Of course, both of these models are theoretical abstractions. The important consideration is which decision rule is the better approximation to the calculations that govern actual individual behavior. The answer to this question will have to await further analysis. Stock and Wise show that the rule that they assume predicts individual choices well, but the predictive validities of the alternative decision rules have not been compared.

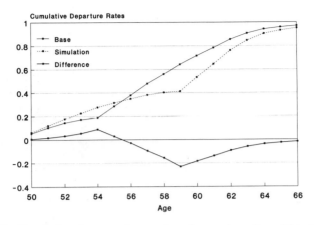

Fig. 1.17   Simulation: Increase firm early retirement age from 55 to 60

1.4.2   Simulations of the Effect of Changes in Pension and SS Provisions

To illustrate the potential to affect retirement behavior through changes in pension and SS provisions, three simulations from Stock and Wise (1990a) and one from Lumsdaine, Stock, and Wise (1991) are discussed here.

Increase the Firm Early Retirement Age from 55 to 60

The effect of increasing the firm's early retirement age from 55 to 60, leaving other provisions as they were, is shown in figure 1.17. Under the current plan, 65 percent of those employed at 50 have left before age 60. Only 42 percent would have left before age 60 if early retirement had been at 60 instead of at 55. Only 13.6 percent of employees leave between 55 and 59 if early retirement is at 60, whereas 45.5 percent leave between these ages under the current system. On the other hand, because the early retirement "bonus" is now farther in the future, more employees leave the firm between 50 and 54. This is the result of the greater weight given to current versus future income. In short, many more workers would be employed between the ages of 57 and 65 if the early retirement age were 60 instead of 55.

Increase the SS Early Retirement Reduction Factor

Social Security benefits can be taken beginning at age 62, but the current Social Security rules include a benefit reduction of ⅝ percent per month of retirement before age 65.[21] The simulated effect of increasing the reduction factor to 1 percent per month is shown in figure 1.18. It is clear that the effect of this change is small relative to the effect of the change in the firm early retirement age. This is primarily because only a small fraction of firm employees are still working at age 62—only 21 percent in the base case. The retire-

21. This reduction is intended to be actuarially fair.

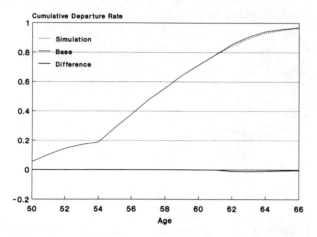

Fig. 1.18   Simulation: Increase Social Security early retirement reduction factor

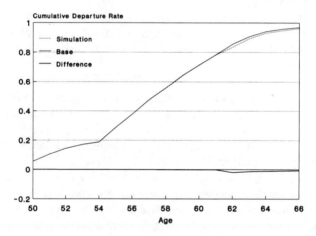

Fig. 1.19   Simulation: Increase Social Security retirement ages by one year

ment rates of those still employed at age 62, however, are considerably lower—about 14 percent—with the higher reduction factor. They are also lower at 63. Still, the net result on the employment of persons covered by the firm's pension plan is negligible.

Increase the SS Retirement Ages by One Year

Current plans are to increase the Social Security retirement age from 65 to 67 by 2027. To judge the effect of such a change on workers with pension plans like the one in this firm, Stock and Wise (1990a) simulated the effect of increasing the normal retirement age from 65 to 66 and the early retirement age from 62 to 63. The results are shown in figure 1.19. Again, the effect on the retirement rates of persons in this firm is small. This is true even though the effect on the annual retirement rates of 62- and 65-year-olds is substantial. The retirement rate of 62-year-olds is reduced from 33.9 to 25.2 percent. The rate at 65 is reduced from 28.6 to 25.1. But only a few workers remain in the firm to be affected by these changes.

The Effect of a Special Window Plan

During 1982, the firm had a special retirement incentive program (a "window" plan) that provided up to one year's salary, in addition to regular retirement benefits, for employees who retired in that year. The effects of this plan on the retirement behavior of nonmanagerial office workers were simulated by Lumsdaine, Stock, and Wise (1991) and are shown in figure 1.20. For comparison, the figure shows retirement rates in 1981 and then actual and simulated retirement rates in 1982. (Evidence on the effects of this plan is also shown in table 1.2 above.) It is clear that the plan had a very large effect. Annual departure rates were more than doubled for many age groups. In addition, the figure indicates the extent to which the option value model was able to predict the effect of this exogenous change in "retirement benefits."

1.5   Summary

The labor force participation of older Americans has declined dramatically since the inception of Social Security and the tax inducement to develop firm pension plans. Between 1937 and 1980, the participation rate of men over 60 fell from about 62 to about 32 percent, and it continues to decline. Even the rate for older women has declined since 1970. It seems evident that the decline has resulted from the retirement income made possible by these programs. The vast majority of the income of most retirees now comes from pension and Social Security benefits. Most retirement-age families have almost no personal saving other than housing wealth. Yet the average income of older families has increased dramatically in the past three decades, possibly threefold between 1963 and 1978 alone. With reference to figure 1.1 above, the retirement benefits curve has been raised. From the point of view of the individual, the wealth associated with SS and firm pension benefits encourages earlier retirement.

But it is not only the amount of the SS and pension wealth that matters. How it accumulates is also important. For example, if no benefits were available until age 70, few employees would retire at age 55. If retirement wealth accumulates rapidly between 55 and 60 and then starts to decline, employees have an incentive to retire soon after age 60. In effect, the reduction in the accumulation of retirement wealth is like a reduction in the wage; both reduce the incentive for labor force participation. In fact, the formulas determining firm pension benefits in particular tend to encourage continued employment with the firm until some age—often between 55 and 60—and provide an incentive to leave the firm thereafter—the annual addition to retirement wealth is reduced

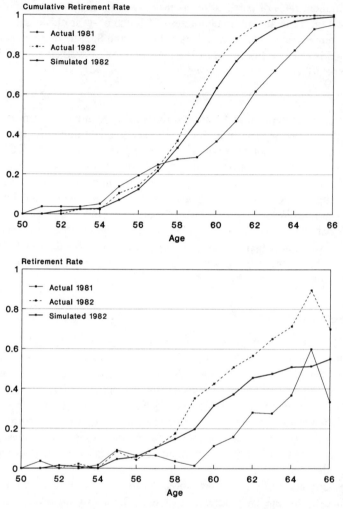

Fig. 1.20   Actual retirement rates in 1981 and 1982 vs. simulated 1982 retirement rates under the window plan, based on 1980 parameter estimates

or even negative. The addition to retirement wealth after age 65 is almost always negative. The amount of the retirement benefit is not increased enough for a person who retires one year later to offset the fact that the benefit is received for one year less.

Thus, even though individuals are living longer, *and* even though a larger fraction of the population is old, workers are leaving the labor force at younger and younger ages. The retired portion of the population is increasing; the employed portion is declining. Whether by intent or by happenstance, firm pension plan and Social Security provisions continue to encourage this trend.

References

Allen, Steven G., Robert L. Clark, and Ann A. McDermed. 1988. Why do pensions reduce mobility? In *Proceedings of the fortieth annual meeting, 1987.* Madison, Wis.: Industrial Relations Research Association.

———. 1993. Pensions, bonding, and lifetime jobs. *Journal of Human Resources* 28, no. 3:463–81.

Berkovec, James, and Steven Stern. 1991. Job exit behavior of older men. *Econometrica* 59, no. 1:189–210.

Blinder, Alan, Roger Gordon, and Donald Wise. 1980. Reconsidering the work disincentive effects of Social Security. *National Tax Journal* 33 (December): 431–42.

Bulow, J. 1981. Early retirement pension benefits. Working Paper no. 654. Cambridge, Mass.: NBER.

Burkhauser, Richard V. 1979. The pension acceptance decision of older workers. *Journal of Human Resources* 14, no. 1:63–75.

———. 1980. The early acceptance of Social Security: An asset maximization approach. *Industrial and Labor Relations Review* 33:484–92.

Burkhauser, Richard V., and Joseph Quinn. 1983. Inferring retirement behavior: Key issues for Social Security. *Journal of Policy Analysis and Management* 3, no. 1 (Fall): 1–13.

Burtless, Gary. 1986. Social Security, unanticipated benefit increases, and the timing of retirement. *Review of Economic Studies* 53:781–805.

Burtless, Gary, and Jerry A. Hausman. 1978. "Double dipping": The combined effects of Social Security and civil service pensions on employee retirement. *Journal of Political Economy* 18:139–60.

Burtless, Gary, and Robert A. Moffitt. 1984. The effects of Social Security on the labor supply of the aged. In *Retirement and economic behavior,* ed. H. Aaron and G. Burtless. Washington, D.C.: Brookings.

Clark, Robert L., and Ann. A. McDermed. 1986. Earnings and pension compensation: The effect of eligibility. *Quarterly Journal of Economics* 101:341–61.

———. 1988. Pension wealth and job changes: The effects of vesting portability and lump-sum distributions. *Gerontologist* 28:524–32.

Fields, Gary S., and Olivia Mitchell. 1982. The effects of pensions and earnings on retirement: A review essay. In *Research in labor economics,* vol. 5, ed. R. Ehrenberg. Greenwich, Conn.: JAI.

———. 1984. *Retirement, pensions and Social Security.* Cambridge, Mass.: MIT Press.

Frant, Howard L., and Herman B. Leonard. 1987. Promise them anything: The incentive structures of local public pension plans. In *Public sector payrolls,* ed. D. Wise. Chicago: University of Chicago Press.

Gustman, Alan, and Thomas Steinmeier. 1986. A structural retirement model. *Econometrica* 54:555–84.

———. 1991. Changing the Social Security rules for work after 65. *Industrial Labor Relations Review* 44, no. 4:733–45.

———. 1993. Pension portability and labor mobility: Evidence from the Survey of Income and Program Participation. *Journal of Public Economics* 50:299–323.

Hausman, Jerry A., and David A. Wise. 1980. Discontinuous budget constraints and estimation: The demand for housing. *Review of Economic Studies* 47:75–96.

———. 1985. Social Security, health status, and retirement. In *Pensions, labor, and individual choice,* ed. D. Wise. Chicago: University of Chicago Press.

Hogarth, Jeanne M. 1988. Accepting an early retirement bonus: An empirical study. *Journal of Human Resources* 23, no. 1:21–33.

Hurd, Michael, and Michael Boskin. 1981. The effect of Social Security on retirement in the early 1970s. *Quarterly Journal of Economics* 96 (November): 767–90.

Hurd, Michael D., and John B. Shoven. 1982. Real income and wealth of the elderly. *American Economic Review* 72:314–18.

Kotlikoff, Laurence J., and Daniel E. Smith. 1983. *Pensions in the American economy.* Chicago: University of Chicago Press.

Kotlikoff, Laurence J., and David A. Wise. 1985. Labor compensation and the structure of private pension plans: Evidence for contractual versus spot labor markets. In *Pensions, labor, and individual choice,* ed. D. Wise. Chicago: University of Chicago Press.

———. 1987. The incentive effects of private pension plans. In *Issues in pension economics,* ed. Z. Bodie, J. Shoven, and D. Wise. Chicago: University of Chicago Press.

———. 1989. Employee retirement behavior and a firm's pension plan. In *The economics of aging,* ed. D. Wise. Chicago: University of Chicago Press.

Lazear, Edward P. 1979. Why is there mandatory retirement? *Journal of Political Economy* 87:1261–64.

———. 1983. Pensions as severance pay. In *Financial aspects of the United States pension system,* ed. Z. Bodie and J. Shoven. Chicago: University of Chicago Press.

Lazear, Edward P., and Robert L. Moore. 1988. Pensions and turnover. In *Pensions in the U.S. economy,* ed. Z. Bodie, J. Shoven, and D. Wise. Chicago: University of Chicago Press.

Lumsdaine, Robin L., James H. Stock, and David A. Wise. 1991. Fenêtres et retraites. *Annales d'Economie et de Statistique* 20/21:219–42.

Nalebuff, Barry, and Richard J. Zeckhauser. 1985. Pensions and the retirement decision. In *Pensions, labor, and individual choice,* ed. D. Wise. Chicago: University of Chicago Press.

Phillips, Douglas, and David A. Wise. 1987. Military versus civilian pay: A descriptive discussion. In *Public sector payrolls,* ed. D. Wise. Chicago: University of Chicago Press.

Poterba, James M., and Lawrence H. Summers. 1987. Public policy implications of declining old-age mortality. In *Work, health, and income among the elderly,* ed. G. Burtless. Washington, D.C.: Brookings.

Ransom, Roger L., and Richard Sutch. 1988. The decline of retirement and the rise of efficiency wages: U.S. retirement patterns, 1870–1940. In *Issues in contemporary retirement,* ed. R. Ricardo-Campbell and E. Lazear. Stanford, Calif.: Hoover Institution.

Rust, John. 1988. A dynamic programming model of retirement behavior: Empirical results. University of Wisconsin—Madison. Mimeo.

———. 1989. A dynamic programming model of retirement behavior. In *The economics of aging,* ed. D. Wise. Chicago: University of Chicago Press.

Sandefur, Gary D., and Nancy Brandon Tuma. 1987. Social and economic trends among the aged in the United States, 1940–1985. Hoover Institution, Stanford University. Mimeo.

Stock, James H., and David A. Wise. 1990a. The pension inducement to retire: An option value analysis. In *Issues in the economics of aging,* ed. D. Wise. Chicago: University of Chicago Press.

———. 1990b. Pensions, the option value of work, and retirement. *Econometrica* 58 (September): 1151–80.

Summers, Lawrence, and Chris Carroll. 1987. Why is U.S. national saving so low? *Brookings Papers on Economic Activity* 2:607–42.

Tuma, Nancy Brandon, and Gary D. Sandefur. 1988. Trends in the labor force activity of the aged in the United States, 1940–1980. In *Issues in contemporary retirement,* ed. R. Ricardo-Campbell and E. Lazear. Stanford, Calif.: Hoover Institution.

U.S. Bureau of the Census. 1984. Projections of the population of the U.S., by age, sex, and race, 1983–2080. *Current Population Reports,* ser. P-25, no. 952, table 6.

Venti, Steven F., and David A. Wise. 1984. Moving and housing expenditure: Transaction costs and disequilibrium. *Journal of Public Economics* 23:207–43.

———. 1990. Have IRAs increased U.S. saving? Evidence from consumer expenditures surveys. *Quarterly Journal of Economics* 105 (August): 661–98.

———. 1991. Aging and the income value of housing wealth. *Journal of Public Economics* 44:371–97.

2   Social Security Benefits and the Labor Supply of the Elderly in Japan

Atsushi Seike and Haruo Shimada

2.1   Issues

In 1984, with the aim of helping the pension system remain solvent, the Japanese Ministry of Welfare proposed a major revision of the Social Security system that included reducing future benefits and raising the minimum eligibility age from 60 to 65. This proposal triggered a debate about whether the financial status of the pension system should take precedence over the employment problems of elderly workers. In fact, the employment problems of elderly workers are closely related to the strain on the Social Security system caused by the rapidly aging population; such a plan would be likely to increase the labor supply of elderly workers, thus necessitating new government policies that would create more job opportunities for this labor pool. The Ministry of Welfare ultimately decided to postpone raising the minimum retirement age, although the remainder of the proposal was approved in 1985.

In an extraordinary Diet session in the fall of 1989, the Ministry of Welfare resubmitted a proposal to raise the minimum age of eligibility for receiving Social Security benefits from 60 to 65. Although the proposal was to raise the age of eligibility gradually over a period of twenty years, it was not accepted in the Diet. The decision obviously reflected the new political situation created shortly after the election of the House of Counselors, which was a landslide victory for the Japan Socialist Party (JSP) vis-à-vis the Liberal Democratic Party. The major reason why opposition parties, led by the JSP, were opposed to raising the minimum eligibility age was that there was no prevalent employment practice or institutional guarantee that workers older than age 60 would continue to be employed up to age 65.

Atsushi Seike is professor of business and commerce at Keio University. Haruo Shimada is professor of economics at Keio University.

43

Taking this point seriously, the Ministry of Labor proposed a plan to the tripartite Employment Policy Council to be examined as a preliminary step toward formulating an actual bill. It proposed that employers should be required to keep elderly employees on the payroll up to the age of 65. This proposal met with strenuous opposition from employers. Employers assert that, since the proposal to raise the minimum eligibility age from 60 to 65 was rejected, there is no need to legislate that employers must employ elderly workers up to the age of 65. Moreover, they predict that, in the long run, they will have to employ more elderly workers in the face of an increasingly severe shortage in the young labor force. In other words, they are implying that the employment problems of elderly workers will, in the long run, be solved spontaneously by market forces. Whether employment opportunities will be redistributed adequately across different age classes through market forces, however, is certainly an interesting academic and serious policy question that has yet to be answered.

When one puts the current policy debate over modifying the Social Security system and policy interventions in employment practices into a broader and more analytic perspective, one should recognize that the debated issues should be located in a system of key variables that dictate the behavior of the relevant principal actors, namely, the labor suppliers, the employers, and the government.

The labor supply depends on the level of unearned income, on the one hand, and the availability of employment opportunities, on the other. To be more specific, the higher the level of pension benefits, the lower the likelihood of a person supplying labor, and the greater the employment opportunities in the labor market, the higher the willingness to supply labor.

Employers make employment decisions on the basis of the expected returns from employment. In other words, the employer employs a worker as long as he can expect to benefit in the form of productivity in excess of wages. The calculus of employment decisions is often based on the long term. That is, the benefit accruing from employment is calculated in terms of some sort of present value of the future stream of benefits.

In the Japanese labor market, employers display a systematic bias toward certain age classes, apparently preferring to employ young workers, not older. This bias seems to be clearly reflected in the differences among the job opening/applicant ratios compiled by the public employment service offices for different age classes.

Why are there such conspicuous differences? Is it because employers tend to avoid recruiting older workers? If so, is this because employers perceive that older workers cost more by receiving high wages but do not contribute as much in terms of productivity? Is it because employers do not expect to get as much return from their human investment in older workers as from their investment in younger workers? Or is it because of the effect of such institutional arrangements as the mandatory retirement system? Whether the distribution of employment opportunities across different age classes can be altered depends on the relative values of and relations among these economic and institutional variables.

Basically, the government has two categories of policy instrument that affect or control the demand-supply balance of elderly workers. One is public income-maintenance programs such as Social Security. Many studies of labor supply behavior suggest that, the higher the level of pension benefits, the lower the likelihood of an older person joining the labor supply. The other is what may be called an active employment policy. The Japanese government, for example, has been promoting this kind of employment policy in two ways: providing subsidies for employers who employ older workers and controlling or guiding the behavior of employers through laws or guidelines.

These two types of policy instrument—income-maintenance programs and active employment policies—are mutually dependent and closely related. For instance, the labor supply of older people depends on their perceived employment opportunities, on the one hand, and on the level of guaranteed income, on the other. The former is determined by a set of variables, as mentioned above, that dictates the behavior of employers and also by the government's employment policy. The latter is determined by the government's income-maintenance programs. The financial viability of such government programs depends on the degree to which old people work in the labor market and contribute to the funds of such programs.

When we evaluate the implications of these policy instruments, we also need to take into account dynamic changes in demand-supply balances over a long period of time. While logically we may be concerned with a likely relative excess supply of older people as a consequence of the recent revamping of the Social Security system, when put in the perspective of an increasingly diminishing supply of younger labor in the long run, that excess supply may be viewed positively, not negatively. Such an interpretation, however, would naturally depend on how flexibly the employment system and employment practices react and adapt to new external market conditions. We should also keep in mind the question of whether the distribution of employment opportunities can be justified on the grounds of securing minimum social needs for all.

Having acknowledged the issues surrounding these policy debates, we may now identify a few important and relevant research questions. One is what effect public income-maintenance programs such as the Social Security system have on the labor supply behavior of older workers. Another is whether employment opportunities for older workers will increase in the future as the result of a change in the behavior of employers. Still another question is whether, and to what extent the government's employment policy will actually create new jobs for the elderly or redistribute existing jobs among the workforce, targeting the elderly. In this paper, we confine ourselves to the question of the effect of public pension benefits on the labor supply behavior of the elderly.

One interesting observation lies in the apparent correlation between the declining labor force participation by the Japanese elderly and the increasingly high benefit payments disbursed by the Social Security system (see fig. 2.1). The labor force participation rate of elderly Japanese workers declined from 57 percent in 1960 to 36 percent in 1990, a drop of 20 percentage points. By contrast, the average monthly Social Security benefit (in 1985 yen) rose substantially during the same period, from ¥16,000 in 1960 to ¥130,000 in 1990, and the ratio of the benefit to the average wage increased from 15 to 40 percent. This suggests that the progressive rise in pension benefits may have encouraged more workers to retire early, thereby reducing the supply of elderly workers. This contrast in time trends may, however, be coincidental. To determine what effect, if any, the rise in pension benefits has had on the labor force participation of elderly workers, we undertook a rigorous cross-sectional examination of the data.

2.2   The Social Security System in Japan

In this section, we briefly describe the Japanese Social Security insurance system and the changes that this system has undergone over the past two decades. Because we are mainly interested in determining what effect the Social Security system has had on the behavior of employed people, we will be discussing Social Security for employed people.

Social Security for employed people (*Kosei-Nenkin*) in Japan is the public pension system that covers all Japanese employees who work in private businesses that employ at least five persons. As of 1990, about 32 million workers were insured through the system, and 8 million beneficiaries were collecting retirement pensions.

To be eligible to collect a pension, a worker must fulfill three criteria: (1) he must have made at least 240 months' worth of accumulated contributions to the system (or 180 months' worth, accumulated after age 40);[1] (2) he must be at least 60 years of age; and (3) his earnings must be less than the ceiling level. The third condition warrants further explanation. First, in the context of the Social Security system, the term *retirement* signifies retirement from a job specifically covered by that system. Thus, workers not paying Social Security contributions from their earnings are considered to be retired. Accordingly, a person employed at a noncovered workplace after retirement from a covered job is regarded as a retiree.[2] Second, to collect pension benefits, workers are not required to retire completely from a covered job, as long as their earnings do not exceed a certain maximum amount specified by a schedule known as the earnings test. Those workers choosing to continue in the workforce are called

---

1. In some employment categories, there are exceptions to the number of months of contributions required; e.g., for coal miners, one month of contribution is counted as four-thirds of a month.

2. It is possible for people retired from the private sector to be government employees. This situation, however, is uncommon.

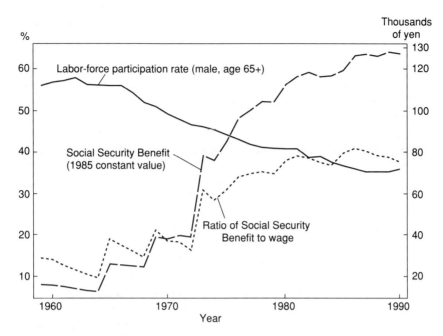

Fig. 2.1   Trends in the labor force participation rate and Social Security benefits

Table 2.1   **Benefit Reductions According to Monthly Earnings**

Age Group	Monthly Earnings (¥)	Rate of Benefit Reduction (%)
60–64	0	0
	1–94,999	20
	95,000–129,999	50
	130,000–154,999	80
	155,000+	100
65+	< 155,000	0
	155,000+	20

Source: Trends of Insurance and Pensions (Tokyo: Welfare Statistics Association, 1990).

working beneficiaries. Working beneficiaries collect only a specified percentage of their full pensions.

The ceiling level of the Social Security benefit is reduced according to the amount earned, as shown in table 2.1, with the rate of reduction varying according to the age group within which a worker falls. For workers between 60 and 64 years of age, for example, the rate of reduction can be as great as 100 percent, whereas, for workers aged 65 and older, the maximum reduction is 20 percent. This earnings test poses problems that will be discussed in greater detail below.

The dotted curve in figure 2.1 shows trends in Social Security benefits paid to beneficiaries (in 1985 yen). As a result of revisions in the pension formula, there were significant increases in benefit levels in 1965, 1969, and 1973. Of these increases, the 1973 jump was particularly noteworthy in that, after this time, pension benefits were indexed to adjust for inflation; accordingly, the real value of each benefit level increased to twice the previous value.[3] Since 1973, benefits have continued to rise steadily to compensate for the rate of inflation.

Another factor that we must examine in connection with the recent rise in pension benefits is the maturity of the Social Security pension system itself. In the past, very few workers were able to contribute to the pension system for a period sufficient to qualify them to collect regular benefits. In the late 1970s, however, the first group of workers who had contributed for the requisite number of months began to reach retirement age. Hence, the number of employee pension beneficiaries increased from 0.6 million in 1970 to 7.8 million in 1990, and the number of persons receiving the maximum benefit grew commensurately. As the benefit level rose, the ratio of the pension benefit amount to the average monthly wage also grew dramatically, increasing from 10 percent in the early 1960s to almost 40 percent in the 1980s (see fig. 2.1);[4] excluding bonus payments, which constitute as much as 30 percent of a worker's wages, the ratio is about 60 percent. The most recent major revision of the pension system, in 1985, was aimed at reducing future benefit levels in order to keep the current relative ratio constant. The Social Security benefit trend shown in figure 2.1 suggests that the Social Security system matured in the 1980s.

2.3   Analytic Framework

In this section, we discuss the empirical framework of our study. First, we estimate the standard labor supply model originally developed by Heckman (1979) and modified and expanded by others (see, e.g., the studies in Smith [1980]).

Suppose that W_r and W_m are the reservation wage and the market wage, respectively. The reservation wage is the minimum wage for which an individual will work, and the market wage is the wage offered by potential employers. We may then write the reservation wage and market wage functions as

---

3. The Employee Pension Insurance Law provides that benefits be indexed when consumer prices increase by more than 5 percent in any given year, but, as a result of political considerations, benefits have been indexed even in years when the inflation rate was less than 5 percent.

4. The Social Security system is based on the monthly wage, excluding bonuses. For example, the standard monthly wage on which the Social Security contribution is paid—and on which the benefit is calculated—is the average monthly wage for May, June, and July. Bonuses are generally paid in July and December.

(1) $W_r = \alpha X + U_r,$

(2) $W_m = \beta Y + U_m,$

where X is the vector of variables affecting an individual worker's reservation wage and includes the worker's income-leisure preference, income from non-labor sources such as pension benefits, and some institutional factors affecting the labor supply decision;[5] Y is the vector of variables affecting market earning power and includes a worker's productivity and the factors of demand for this side of the labor market; α and β are vectors of parameters; and U_r and U_m are normally distributed random errors. Thus, the condition for participation in the labor market is

(3) $W_m - W_r > 0.$

This equation means that a person will decide to participate in the labor market if the market wage offered exceeds his reservation wage.

In terms of labor supply expressed as hours worked, any person whose reservation wage exceeds his market wage has zero hours of work. Persons whose market wage is higher than their reservation wage supply a positive number of hours of work. The number of hours that a person supplies depends on the same variables in X above and on the market wage.[6] Thus, the hours-worked function is defined as

(4) $\begin{aligned} H &= \gamma X + cW_m + U_h, &&\text{if } W_m - W_r > 0, \\ H &= 0, &&\text{if } W_m - W_r < 0, \end{aligned}$

where γ and c are the vector of parameters and a parameter, respectively, and U_h is a normally distributed random error term.

Because from our data the number of hours worked and wages can be observed only for persons who are actually working, there is well-known problem of sample selectivity bias in estimating the labor supply and market wage functions, as elucidated by Heckman (1979). In order to cope with this problem, we estimate these functions using Heckman's two-stage estimation procedure.[7] In applying the estimation procedure, we first estimated the probit participation equation. The likelihood function has the form

(5) $\ln L = \sum_{1}^{N_w} \ln P_r(W_m - W_r > 0) + \sum_{N_w+1}^{N_T} \ln P_r(W_m - W_r < 0),$

where N_w is the number in the working sample, and N_T is the number in the total sample. As a by-product of the participation probit estimation, we have

---

5. The participation cost is often included in the reservation wage. In this study, we did not include this factor because our data are inadequate for this purpose.

6. Because we do not include the participation cost, the reservation-wage vector is identical to that of the hours-worked function.

7. LIMDEP, a statistical software package, was used to correct for selectivity.

the lambda variable, which corrects for selectivity bias. The market wage and hours-worked equations incorporating the lambda variable are defined as:

$$(6) \qquad \ln(W_m) = \beta Y + b\lambda + V_m,$$

$$(7) \qquad H = \gamma X + c \ln(W_m) + d\lambda + V_h,$$

where β and λ are vectors of parameters; b, c, and d are parameters; and V_m and V_h are random terms. These equations are then estimated jointly.

In the context of the analytic framework set forth above, the Social Security benefit is one component of the vector X that is supposed to affect a person's labor supply behavior both when making the decision to participate and when determining the optimal number of hours to work. Therefore, the coefficients of the Social Security benefit in the parameter vectors α and γ constitute the main targets of this paper.

In examining the magnitude of the effect of Social Security pensions on the labor supply, it is important that one check the stability of the parameters of the labor supply functions that reflect the effect of pension benefits. In order to do this, we make an inter-cross-sectional comparison by using micro data for 1980 and 1983. In this inter-cross-sectional comparison, we estimated only a reduced-form probit function for labor force participation in which the market wage rate is taken from an aggregate data source matched with the available individual characteristics of the micro data. We do this because the 1980 data lack information on working hours and wage rates. The probit function has the form

$$(8) \qquad \text{prob(work/not work)} = f(W, X),$$

where W is the market wage rate taken from aggregate data.[8]

As shown in figure 2.2, the earnings test creates a kink in the beneficiary's budget constraint. Suppose that CJ is the original budget line for a person with the market earning power of wage rate W_m and OC of nonpension, nonearnings income. If this person has the right to receive CA of the Social Security benefit and there is no earnings test, the budget line shifts from CJ to AK. The earnings test, however, results in a kinked budget line like $ABDFGJ$ for those 60–64 years old. This budget-constraint kink is substantial for eligible workers between 60 and 64. The budget-constraint kink means that, for a given market wage rate, those supplying more labor must give up a greater proportion of their Social Security benefits.

This gives rise to the problem of a simultaneity bias in estimating the coefficient of Social Security benefits in the labor supply functions (i.e., the participation and hours-worked functions). The estimated coefficient of the Social Security benefit may have a negative bias because it reflects not only the effect

---

8. The studies of Boskin (1977) and Quinn (1977) estimate the same kinds of reduced-form logit functions derived from a simple individual equilibrium model.

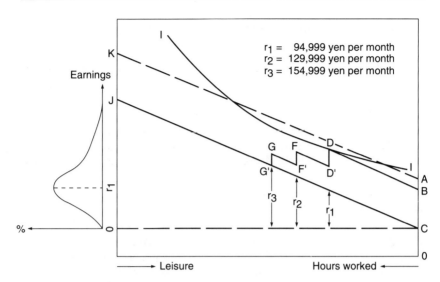

Fig. 2.2   The individual equilibrium at the kinked point of budget constraint and earnings distribution

of the pension benefit on the labor supply but also the effect of the quantity of labor on the benefit level.[9] In order to estimate the influence of the Social Security benefit on labor supply behavior without introducing this bias, we used a dummy variable for Social Security eligibility that should be independent of labor supply behavior.

In order to examine the effects of the earnings test on the distribution of earnings, we directly observe the distribution of earnings of workers who were and were not eligible for a pension. With the caveat noted above, we would expect working beneficiaries to select equilibrium points such as D in figure 2.2 so that their earnings are concentrated around the ¥94,999 ceiling.[10]

9. A rigorous investigation of the nonlinear effects of the Social Security earnings test on the labor supply would require the estimation of maximum likelihood models similar to those of Hausman (1980) and Zabalza, Pissarides, and Barton (1980). Unlike the U.S. or British cases in which the budget constraint is kinked, the Japanese earnings test creates notch-like budget lines similar to those illustrated in fig. 2.2. This difference arises because the Japanese earnings test takes the form of a lump-sum tax rather than a change in the marginal tax rate. Furthermore, this notched budget constraint makes possible the existence of dual equilibria; e.g., at one of the peak points (D) as well as at a point on $D'F$, the slope of the adjoining segment of the budget line depending on the level of benefits. Incorporating these features of the Japanese Social Security earnings test into a maximum likelihood model is complex and beyond the scope of this paper.

10. Although for eligible workers age 60–64 the ranges ABD and part of $G'J$ of the budget constraint could be the equilibrium points in the cases shown in fig. 2.2, part of $D'F$ and part of $F'G$ become possible equilibrium points if the benefit is small. The theoretically impossible range for the equilibrium is at the trough of the constraint line shown next to point D. According to our data, shown in sec. 2.6 below, people do in fact have earnings corresponding to this range, which suggests that workers do not have complete freedom to choose their working hours because of demand-side constraints.

2.4   Data and Variable Definitions Data

The data used in this analysis were extracted from the Employment Status Survey of the Elderly, which was conducted by the Japanese Ministry of Labor. The sample population surveyed was chosen to be representative of persons 55–69 years of age.

The most important feature of this data set is that it is the only collection of micro data in Japan that contains information on the employment status of elderly workers, including data with which to estimate labor supply and market wage functions for individual workers as well as input on past and current job experience. Also available are data on Social Security, including facts about those who were collecting benefits at the time of the report as well as those who were potentially eligible to do so.

Although surveys were conducted in both 1980 and 1983, the 1980 data set lacks details on hours worked and wage rates, and therefore it is used only for estimating the reduced-form probit function of equation (8). In estimating this equation, we used the Japanese Ministry of Labor's Basic Survey of Wage Structure (BSWS), which represents aggregate wage data as the outside information about wages. The BSWS, the most detailed aggregate wage survey published to date, covers all workers in business with more than ten employees, categorizing wage rates by both worker and employer characteristics.

Since we are particularly interested in the effect of Social Security on labor supply behavior, we selected a sample population consisting of males 60 years of age and older—the eligible age range for collecting Social Security benefits. We focused on the male sample because of its trend toward declining labor force participation and also because the number of female workers participating in the Social Security system is still limited.

2.4.1   Variables

The following explanatory variables affecting the reservation wage are the elements of the variable vector X of equations (1), (4), (7), and (8); for the market wage, they are the elements of the variable vector Y in equations (2) and (6).

Age. Age is an explanatory variable for both the reservation wage and the market wage. A person's preference for leisure may shift upward with age, and diminishing physical ability may curtail his market productivity, thus reducing his market wage.

Health. Health is also an explanatory variable for both the reservation wage and the market wage. If a person has health problems, his preference for leisure may increase, and his market productivity may decrease, thus reducing his market wage. We made the dummy variable HEALTHDMY equal to one if health problems exist and zero otherwise.

Mandatory retirement. Mandatory retirement is a widespread employment practice among Japanese firms. Although mandatory retirement from a primary job does not preclude a worker's participation in the labor force, it does constitute a potent institutional barrier. At the same time, those workers who have left their primary jobs through mandatory retirement have the opportunity to engage in other jobs that allow them to work fewer hours. Mandatory retirement may have a negative effect both on the decision to participate in the labor force and on hours worked; thus, it is an explanatory variable for the reservation wage. Moreover, in the Japanese wage system, wages increase with age and length of service up to the mandatory retirement age. After a worker mandatorily retires from his primary job, his wages drop dramatically if he chooses to remain in the labor force. Therefore, mandatory retirement may also have a negative effect on the market wage. To control for these effects, we introduced an indicator variable for mandatory retirement. We made the dummy variable MANDRETDMY equal to one if the worker has experienced mandatory retirement and zero otherwise.

Nonwage income. In general, individuals with higher nonwage incomes have higher reservation wages and hence tend to work less. In this study, we divided nonwage income sources into two categories: Social Security benefits and other nonwage income (NONPEN). We did so, not only because we are particularly interested in the effect of Social Security, but also because the earnings test affects Social Security and because, since only Social Security is indexed for inflation, it may therefore be a more reliable permanent income source than other pensions.[11] As discussed in section 2.3 above, we estimated the labor supply functions with this variable to confirm the effect of Social Security on labor supply behavior without the simultaneity bias. In order to avoid the bias, we introduced an indicator variable for Social Security eligibility that is completely independent of labor supply behavior (PENELGDMY). We made the dummy variable PENELGDMY equal to one if the worker is eligible to collect Social Security and zero otherwise. This includes all those who satisfy the months-of-contribution requirements.

Education. Education is an important explanatory variable for the market wage *Y* because highly employed workers are thought to be more productive in the labor market and hence more likely to receive higher wages. Educational attainment is measured by two categorical variables: (1) completion of high school and (2) graduation from a four-year college. The reference group (omitted) consists of those who have completed the minimum level of compulsory schooling. We made the dummy variable HIGHSCHL equal to one if the worker completed high school and zero otherwise and also made COLLEGE equal to one if the person received a college degree and zero otherwise.

11. On the other hand, most company pensions are not indexed and, rather than being annuities, are limited-term (usually ten-year) pensions.

Location. Because business activities are concentrated mainly in the Tokyo metropolitan area, there is a significant difference between labor demand conditions there and in the rest of Japan. For this reason, a Tokyo metropolitan area indicator variable was introduced to control for this labor demand factor. We made the dummy variable TOKYOMETDMY equal to one if the person was living in the Tokyo metropolitan area and zero otherwise.

2.5   Empirical Results

The results of estimating the probit participation function of equation (5) are shown in table 2.2. In order to look at the magnitude of the effect of each variable, we will show the ∂ prob/∂ var instead of the probit coefficients themselves.[12] As shown in table 2.2, all coefficients are statistically significant, and all parameter signs are consistent with those predicted.

The Social Security variables are negative and highly statistically significant. The highly significant negative coefficient of the dummy variable for Social Security eligibility (PENELGDMY), which is independent of the labor supply decision, confirms the negative effect of Social Security on the participation decision. The probit coefficient of PENELGDMY implies that eligibility for Social Security reduces the participation probability by 15 percent.

Table 2.3 shows the results of estimating the market wage function of equation (6). We estimated the wage equation for the working male sample population. These estimates were corrected for sample-selectivity bias using the lambda variable estimated from the participation function reported in table 2.2 above.

All coefficients are statistically significant, and all signs are theoretically consistent. The most significant coefficients are the indicator variables related to education. Having either a high school or a college education increases the market wage of an individual even when he is in his 60s. The statistical significance of lambda indicates the importance of correcting for selectivity in estimating a wage equation for the working sample.

The results of estimating the hours-worked function of equation (8) are presented in table 2.4 in conjunction with the results from estimating the market wage function. All estimated coefficients are statistically significant, and their signs are consistent with those predicted, although the significance level of the wage rate (LOGWFIT) is low.

The coefficients of the Social Security variables are significantly negative. The negative effect of Social Security on hours worked is confirmed by the coefficient of the Social Security eligibility dummy variable.

The above results definitely show that Social Security in Japan significantly reduces the labor supply of pension-eligible older people. How stable is this

---

12. Concerning the procedure of deriving ∂ prob/∂ var from probit coefficients, see Judge et al. (1980).

Table 2.2   **Empirical Results of the Participation Function (probit estimation)**

Variable	∂ Prob/∂ Var	Variable	∂ Prob/∂ Var
AGE	−.017092***	NONPEN	−.000223***
HEALTHDMY	−.331203***	MANDRETDMY	−.177402***
HIGHSCHLDMY	.036605***	TOKYOMETDMY	.056351***
COLLEGEDMY	.087208**	Log likelihood	−3,859.3
PENELGDMY	−.152729***	Sample size	7,014

**Statistically significant at the 5 percent level.
***Statistically significant at the 1 percent level.

Table 2.3   **Empirical Results for the Market Wage Function**

Variable	Specification 2 (with lambda from participation function with EP eligibility dummy [PENELGDMY])	Variable	Specification 2 (with lambda from participation function with EP eligibility dummy [PENELGDMY])
ONE	1.26281***	TOKYOMETDMY	.21099***
AGE	−.0280409***	MANDRETDMY	−.361453***
HEALTHDMY	−.281854***	LAMBDA	.543983***
HIGHSCHLDMY	.390829***	$\bar{R}^2$	.127
COLLEGEDMY	.699679***	Sample size	4,559

Note: EP = employee's pension.
***Statistically significant at the 1 percent level.

Table 2.4   **Empirical Results for the Hours-Worked Function**

Variable	Specification 2 (with EP eligibility dummy [PENELGDMY])	Variable	Specification 2 (with EP eligibility dummy [PENELGDMY])
ONE	446.642***	NONPEN	−.03992***
AGE	−4.08734***	LOGWFIT	9.40996*
HEALTHDMY	−51.2706***	LAMBDA	51.3899***
MANDRETDMY	−24.0737***	$\bar{R}^2$	.050
PENELGDMY	−11.9709**	Sample size	4,559

Note: EP = employee's pension.
*Statistically significant at the 10 percent level.
**Statistically significant at the 5 percent level.
***Statistically significant at the 1 percent level.

Social Security effect over time? Table 2.5 compares the 1980 and 1983 reduced-form participation functions of equation (8). We estimated the function using the Social Security benefit (PENEBENFT) because the 1980 data do not include information on Social Security eligibility.

To compare the magnitude of the effect of Social Security benefits on participation behavior, we divided the wage rate and pension variables from the 1983 data by the consumer price index to convert these variables to their 1980 constant-price values.

All parameters are statistically significant, and their signs are consistent with those predicted. The magnitude of the effect of a unit change in the Social Security benefit on the probability of participation (∂ prob/∂ var), or the effect of Social Security benefits on the probability of workforce participation, is very similar in both samples: -0.0025 and -0.0022, respectively. This suggests that the effect of Social Security benefits on the labor supply was stable during the early 1980s.

2.6   The Earnings Test and Its Effects

In section 2.3 above, we showed that the earnings test associated with Social Security benefits creates a kink in the budget line of an eligible worker in this age group. With this kinked budget line, the individual equilibrium points for working beneficiaries are likely to be located at the kink points, such as peak D of figure 2.2 above. To verify this, we examined the earnings distribution of working beneficiaries. If working beneficiaries put their equilibrium point at D, their earnings will tend to be concentrated at the ceiling of the earnings range, which is ¥94,999 (see fig. 2.2).

Figures 2.3 and 2.4 show the earnings distributions of eligible and noneligible workers. To control for all conditions except eligibility for Social Security benefits, we selected a sample of workers age 60–64, without health limitations, who were employed full-time at age 55 and had experienced mandatory retirement prior to taking their current jobs. The earnings distribution of eligible workers shown in figure 2.3 is unimodal, with the peak occurring

Table 2.5   **Results of Estimating the Reduced-Form Participation Function for 1980 and 1983**

	Coefficients of the Participation Function	
Variable	1980: ∂ Prob/∂ Var	1983: ∂ Prob/∂ Var
AGE	$-.0206565$***	$-.0142349$***
HEALTHDMY	$-.3579931$***	$-.3318242$***
WAGE[a]	$.0634237$*	$.1509132$***
PENBENEFT	$-.0025636$***	$-.0022427$***
NONPEN	$-.0002293$***	$-.0003952$***
MANDRETDMY	$-.3306154$***	$-.1301065$***
Log likelihood	$-4,813.2$	$-3,749.2$
Sample size	9,118	7,014

[a]WAGE is the market wage rate taken from the *Basic Survey of Wage Structure* (Tokyo: Ministry of Labor, annual).

*Statistically significant at the 10 percent level.

***Statistically significant at the 1 percent level.

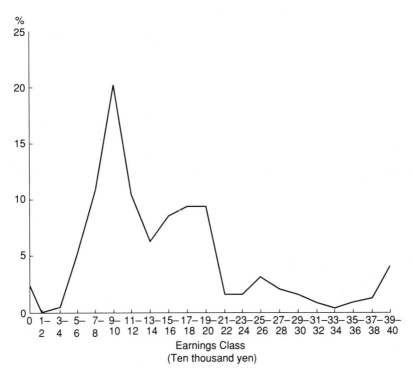

Fig. 2.3   Earnings distribution of pension-eligible workers

in the earnings class that includes the ceiling of the earnings range associated with the 20 percent reduction in benefits (less than ¥95,000). By contrast, the earnings distribution for noneligible workers (fig. 2.4) shows no such clear-cut tendency.

The observed differences in the earnings of the two groups were also sub-jected to statistical tests. We analyzed (1) the difference in the shape of the earnings distribution curves and (2) the relative frequency of the earnings class that includes ¥94,999 within the pension-eligible and -noneligible samples.

To test for statistical differences in the shape of the earnings distribution curve, we used a rank-order test.[13] In terms of the difference in the relative frequency of the earnings class including ¥94,999, we used the usual propor-tional difference test. The results of these tests, displayed in table 2.6, indicate that the shapes of the earnings distribution curves and the relative frequencies are significantly different; the chi-square test statistic exceeds the critical value in both cases. The earnings distribution of eligible workers, compared with that of noneligible workers, shows an equilibrium point at the kink in the bud-get line, a result that we attribute to the Social Security earnings test.

13. We followed the procedure presented in Takeuchi (1965).

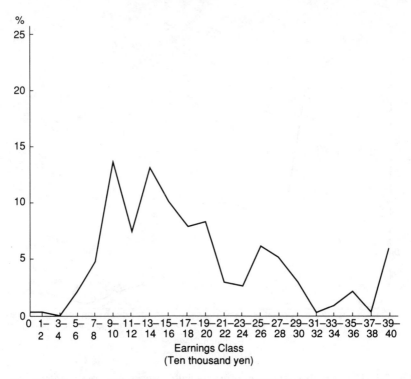

Fig. 2.4   Earnings distribution of workers not eligible for pension

2.7   Policy Implications

These findings from the above analysis may have significant implications for employment policy, particularly in connection with the recent restructuring of the Japanese Social Security system. Initially, the changes are likely to reduce, or at least curb, increases in benefit levels as the pension-eligible population grows. This may in turn cause a rapid surge in the number of elderly workers actively seeking jobs, and it may therefore be incumbent on Japanese society as a whole to provide a substantial number of job opportunities for persons in this group. As a result of the effect of the Social Security earnings test, part-time employment opportunities are likely to be especially important for elderly workers. Policymakers attempting to meet the needs of older workers should give these points serious consideration.[14]

This result of the foregoing analysis stimulates at least three policy-related questions: (1) What is the direction of ongoing policy efforts? Are they moving toward increasing the employment opportunities for elderly workers to meet

14. For a broader discussion of employment issues of the aging in Japan, see Seike and Shimada (1986).

the needs likely arising from the reforms proposed by the Japanese government? (2) What would be the long-term implications for the demand-supply balance of elderly workers? (3) What would be an appropriate and workable institutional arrangement for providing employment opportunities for the elderly, particularly in private corporations?

The answer to the first question is obviously yes. The government has been earnestly advocating (sometimes pressing private corporations by administrative guidance through employment service offices) that the age of mandatory retirement be raised in order to increase employment opportunities for the elderly. Partly as a result of this effort, and partly owing to social pressures, an increasing number of private corporations have moved back the age for mandatory retirement from 55 to 60 during the last decade. For example, while the share of corporations adopting the mandatory retirement age of 55 decreased from 39.5 percent in 1980 to 19.3 percent in 1990, those adopting the retirement age of 60 increased from 36.5 percent in 1980 to 60.1 percent in 1990.

Although the higher mandatory retirement age is meant to increase full-time employment opportunities for the elderly as opposed to part-time jobs, as suggested by the results of our analysis, this policy move will certainly more than offset short- or medium-term concerns of a shortage of employment opportunities for the elderly if the policy objectives are actually realized in the labor market.

This leads us to the second question regarding how the demand-supply balance of the labor market will be affected in the long run, particularly for the older portion of the workforce. Most long-term estimates suggest that the growth in the labor supply will be increasingly smaller in the future. (For example, the EPA [Economic Planning Agency] estimates that the average annual percentage increase in the labor force will be 0.9 percent for the period 1985–95, 0.2 percent for 1995–2000, and −0.1 percent for 2000–2010. The

Table 2.6   **Statistical Significance of the Differences in Earnings Distributions**

Type of Test	Chi Square	Critical Value
Test of differences in the shape of the earnings distributions:		
H_0: $F_p = F_{np}$	. . .	. . .
H_1: $F_p > F_{np}$	17.23	3.84
Test of differences in proportion of each sample in the earnings class ¥90,000–¥100,000:		
H_0: $P_p + P_{np}$		
H_1: $P_p > P_{np}$	.065	.052

Note: H_0 = null hypothesis; H_1 = alternative hypothesis; Fp = earnings distribution of the pension-eligible sample; F_{np} = earnings distribution of the noneligible sample; P_p = proportion of the eligible sample in the earnings class ¥90,000–¥100,000; P_{np} = proportion of noneligible sample in the earnings class ¥90,000–¥100,000.

estimates were prepared by the EPA Planning Bureau in 1989.) The expected increase in the supply of older labor may well be helpful in meeting the likely shortage of labor in the long-term future. In many areas of industry, a severe structural shortage in the labor force is already emerging. Industries such as construction, agriculture, and labor-intensive services (e.g., computer programming) are examples of this. What is needed is a reallocation of employment opportunities among different age classes of the workforce. Whether such objectives can be achieved will depend largely on the response and behavior of employers.

The third question therefore, is whether in the long run such a reallocation of employment opportunities can be effectively realized in the Japanese labor market. A critical question is whether Japanese employers will be prepared to provide good employment opportunities for elderly workers in such a way that they can both utilize their skills and experience effectively and earn a reasonable income. In most cases, the compulsory retirement system severs the relationship between the older worker and the company in which he was working. The retired worker who is still seeking other employment opportunities ends up with jobs in which he can neither utilize his skills and experience effectively nor earn a decent income. A sensible way to bridge this gap may be found in utilizing what might be termed the *quasi* or *extended* internal labor market.

This means that the worker does not stay in the company after the mandatory retirement age, but neither does he move to a totally unrelated job. The worker finds another employment opportunity in a company that is closely related to his old company so that he can utilize his skills and experience effectively and therefore has a better income than he would otherwise. In fact, utilization of the "quasi internal labor market" is increasing in the sense that an increasing number of older workers find their next jobs in companies within the same group or related groups, as networks of corporate groups develop for various reasons. If Japanese corporations will provide more jobs of this type for older workers, and if the workers in turn will be able to find more employment opportunities where they can utilize their talents effectively, then the proposed reform of Social Security may not have as disturbing an effect in distorting the demand-supply balance in the labor market over the long run as might at first be supposed. All this, however, would depend on effective government policies and the sensible adaptation of corporations to economic and social needs.

References

Boskin, M. J. 1977. Social Security and retirement decisions. *Economic Inquiry* 15, no. 1:1–25.
Hausman, J. A. 1980. The effect of wages, taxes, and fixed costs on women's labor force participation. *Journal of Public Economics* 14, no. 2:161–94.

Heckman, J. J. 1979. Sample selection bias as a specification error. *Econometrica* 47, no. 1:153–61.

Judge G. G., W. E. Griffiths, R. C. Hill, and T. C. Lee. 1980. *The theory and practice of econometrics.* New York: Wiley.

Quinn, J. F. 1977. Microeconomic determinations of early retirement: A cross-sectional view of white married men. *Journal of Human Resources* 12, no. 3:329–46.

Seike, A., and H. Shimada. 1986. Work and retirement issues in Japan. Paper presented at the Conference on National and International Implications of Population Aging, Oiso, February.

Smith, J. P., ed. 1980. *Female labor supply.* Princeton, N.J.: Princeton University Press.

Takeuchi, K. 1965. *Mathematical statistics* (in Japanese). Tokyo: Keizai.

Zabalza, A., C. Pissarides, and M. Barton. 1980. Social Security and the choice between full-time work, part-time work and retirement. *Journal of Public Economics* 14, no. 2:245–76.

3   The Economic Status of the Elderly in the United States

Michael D. Hurd

Although reliable poverty statistics for the United States do not extend very far back in time, the data that are available show that, until recently, many of the elderly (age 65 and older) were poor. For example, in 1959, 35.2 percent of persons age 65 and older were living in poverty. Because the elderly had low incomes, and because they had few responses to economic reversal, society has developed programs that transfer resources to the elderly and that shield them from risk. These programs were successful: partly as a result of them, the poverty rate of the elderly is now lower than that of the nonelderly population. For example, in 1987, the poverty rate of the elderly was 12.2 percent, as opposed to 13.5 percent in the general population.

Society's future contribution to the elderly will depend partly on demographic changes. The fraction of the population over 65 has grown substantially since the turn of the century, and it is projected to continue to grow until well into the twenty-first century. For example, about 4 percent of the population was elderly in 1900, 11 percent in 1980, and the fraction is forecast to grow to 22 percent in 2040. Combined with a long-term trend toward early retirement, the demographic changes imply that an increasing number of retirees will have to be supported by each worker. Even maintaining the current level of relative transfers will strain the system.

Whether the current level of transfers should be maintained or even increased depends on the economic status of the elderly relative to the nonelderly. Because of differences between the elderly and the nonelderly in family size and composition, needs, position in the life cycle, and so forth, it is far from straightforward to compare the economic status of the elderly and the nonelderly. Nonetheless, the goal of this paper is to provide a comparison.

Michael D. Hurd is professor of economics at the State University of New York at Stony Brook and a research associate of the National Bureau of Economic Research.

63

Two methods will be used. The first draws on government statistics to give an overview of the change and level of economic status as conventionally measured by income. That second method summarizes results from a number of research papers that adjust income to make the comparison between the elderly and the nonelderly more meaningful. Indicators of economic status will be growth in income, growth in the income of the elderly relative to the nonelderly, and a comparison of absolute levels. In addition, some data on levels and composition of wealth will be given, but, because of difficulties of interpretation and coverage, comparison of the wealth of the elderly and nonelderly is not made.

The general finding is that, as measured by adjusted income, the economic status of the elderly has improved faster than that of the nonelderly and that now the elderly are at least as well off as the nonelderly and possibly much better off. Transfer programs such as Social Security and Medicare and Medicaid can take credit for an important part of the change, especially among the less well-to-do. Because of demographic changes, however, the future is much less bright: today, about 3.3 workers support each retired Social Security beneficiary; in 2030, just 1.9 workers will support each beneficiary. Whether through the political process the workers will be willing to support the beneficiaries at their current level of economic well-being is an open question.

3.1   Demographic and Economic Changes

This section reviews government data on demographic change and income as measured by government statistics. Besides giving information on unadjusted income change, it puts into perspective the adjustments to income to be discussed in section 3.2 below.

The fraction of the population that is elderly has increased substantially since 1900, and it is forecast to increase further. As table 3.1 shows, only 4 percent of the population was 65 or older in 1900. The fraction of the very elderly (85 and older) rounded to zero. In 1980, about 11 percent were elderly, and about 1 percent were very elderly. The projections, which should be quite accurate over the next thirty years, show large increases in the size of the elderly population, especially in the oldest. By 2050, 6 percent of the population will be 85 or older (16 million people). About 8 million will be 90 or older.

The causes of the change in the age distribution of the population include a long-term decline in birthrates. Such a decline will cause a population to have a higher average age and more elderly persons than a population with a steady birthrate. On top of the long-term decline in births were the exceptionally high birthrates from 1946 to 1964, the baby boom. The cohort born in the midpoint of the baby boom, 1955, will be 65 in 2020 and 95 in 2050. Another factor is that mortality rates have declined and life expectancy has increased: in 1900, life expectancy of males and females was 46 and 49, respectively; in 1980, it was 70 and 78.

Both the probability of reaching 65 and, as shown in table 3.2, life expec-

Table 3.1   **Fraction of Population of Different Ages: Actual 1900–80 and Predicted 1990–2050 (middle series)[a]**

	% Aged							
	55–59	60–64	65–69	70–74	75+	75–79	80–84	85+
1900	3	2	2	1	1			
1910	3	2	2	1	1			
1920	3	3	2	1	1			
1930	4	3	2	2	2			
1940	4	4	3	2	2			
1950	5	4	3	2	3			
1960	5	4	3	3	3			
1970	5	4	3	3	4			
1980	5	4	4	3	4	2	1	1

	% Aged								
	55–59	60–64	65–69	70–74	75–79	80–84	85–89	90–94	95+
1990	4	4	4	3	2	2	1	0	0
2000	5	4	4	3	3	2	1	0	0
2010	7	6	4	3	2	2	1	1	0
2020	7	7	6	6	3	2	1	1	0
2030	6	6	6	6	5	3	2	1	0
2040	6	6	5	5	5	4	2	1	1
2050	6	6	6	5	4	3	3	2	1

Source: U.S. Bureau of the Census, "Projections of the Population of the U.S., by Age, Sex, and Race, 1988–2080," *Current Population Reports,* ser. P-25, no. 1018 (January 1989), table 4.

[a]The middle series (series 14) is based on intermediate assumptions about fertility, mortality, and immigration.

tancy conditional on reaching 65 have increased. The latter is forecast to be 2.9 years higher for males and 3.8 years higher for females in 2050 than in 1985. The increase in life expectancy after 65, along with earlier retirement (to be discussed below), has had, and will continue to have, important effects on Social Security and pension plans and on the ability of the elderly to finance their retirement years through their own savings: earnings from a shorter work life must be used to finance consumption over a longer lifetime.

Table 3.2 shows that the conditional life expectancy of females has been, and should continue to be, much greater than the conditional life expectancy of males. Beyond the more obvious effects on Social Security and pensions, the differences in life expectancy mean that most of the very old are widows. Furthermore, because the very old must finance a long lifetime of consumption, it is likely that they will have few assets toward the end of their lives. Therefore, in the absence of social programs, differential mortality makes almost inevitable high rates of poverty among elderly widows, and that is, in fact, what is found in the data.

Incomes of the elderly have increased both absolutely and relative to the rest

Table 3.2   Actual and Predicted Life Expectancy at Age 65

	Male	Female		Male	Female
Actual:			Predicted:		
1900	11.3	12.0	1990	14.9	19.2
1910	11.4	12.1	2000	15.6	20.1
1920	11.8	12.3	2010	16.0	20.6
1930	11.4	12.9	2020	16.3	21.0
1940	11.9	13.4	2030	16.7	21.5
1950	12.8	15.1	2040	17.0	21.9
1960	12.9	15.9	2050	17.4	22.4
1970	13.1	17.1	2060	17.7	22.8
1980	14.0	18.4	2070	18.1	23.3
1985	14.5	18.6	2080	18.5	23.7

Source: Social Security Bulletin 51, no. 2 (February 1988), table 14.

of the population. Table 3.3 shows that their household income, as measured in the Current Population Survey (CPS), increased by about 28 percent in real terms between 1970 and 1987. The mean income of the entire population increased by only 10 percent, with the result that the income of the elderly relative to the entire population rose from 0.54 to 0.63. However, as will be discussed below, the income comparison is somewhat misleading because the income measures are not what economists would call full income measures; furthermore, they make no provision for differences in household size.

The income growth was accompanied by rather large changes in the source of income, as shown in table 3.4. In 1967, 29 percent of the income of the elderly was from earnings; by 1986, only 17 percent was from earnings. Correspondingly, the fraction of income from Social Security and from assets increased. The fraction from pensions was constant.

The decrease in the importance of earnings is reflected in changes in labor force participation, which, for the elderly, is practically synonymous with retirement. The changes in participation were large: between 1950 and 1987, the participation rate of elderly men fell from 46 to 16 percent. In the population, however, the participation rate rose from 60 to 66 percent, owing mainly to the increasing participation of women.

Detail by age and sex is shown in table 3.5. The normal retirement age of men, which at one time was 65 or even older, is now substantially younger than 65, and many men retire in their late 50s. Among women, two opposite trends—earlier retirement and higher lifetime participation rates—have kept the participation rates of 60–64- and 65–69-year-olds approximately constant.

The decrease in the fraction of income from earnings in table 3.4 above is broadly representative of the experience of many of the elderly, but the increase in income from assets shown in that table is somewhat misleading as a representation of the experience of a typical elderly household because of the skewed distribution of wealth. Table 3.6 gives the distribution of elderly house-

Table 3.3   **Mean Household Income of the Elderly and of the General Population (1983 dollars)**

Year	Mean 65+	Mean All	Ratio
1970	13,901	25,660	.54
1975	16,188	26,580	.61
1980	15,268	25,467	.60
1985	17,411	26,919	.65
1987	17,849	28,217	.63

Source: U.S. Bureau of the Census, "Money Income of Households, Families and Persons," *Current Population Reports,* ser. P-60 (various years).

Table 3.4   **Distribution of Sources of Income (%)**

	1967	1976	1984	1986
Earnings	29	23	16	17
Social Security	34	39	38	38
Pensions and other retirement	15	16	15	16
Assets	15	18	28	26
Public assistance	4	2	1	1
Other	3	2	2	2
Total	100	100	100	100

Source: U.S. House of Representatives (1987); *Income of the Population Aged 65 and Over* (Washington, D.C.: Social Security Administration, 1986).

holds according to the fraction of each household's income from various sources. For example, in 1971, 69 percent of elderly households had no earnings, 16 percent had from 1 to 49 percent of their income from earnings, and 15 percent had from 50 to 100 percent of their income from earnings. The table shows that, by 1986, 81 percent of elderly households had no income from earnings and that just 8 percent had more than half their income from earnings.[1] The percentage of households having no income from Social Security dropped from 13 percent in 1971 to 8 percent in 1986. This change is partly due to increasing coverage of Social Security. It is also due to earlier retirement: under the Social Security law, few full-time workers would have had Social Security benefits, so, as participation rates fell, the fraction receiving Social Security benefits rose. The importance of Social Security to most elderly can hardly be overstated: 57 percent had more than half their income from Social Security, and 24 percent had more than 90 percent.

Although the fraction of the elderly with income from private pensions and annuities (almost all pensions) has increased, private pensions remain modest

1. A household is classified as elderly if the "householder" is elderly; earnings can come from a nonelderly spouse.

Table 3.5   Labor Force Participation Rates (%)

	Men					Women				
Year	55–59	60–64	65–69	70–74	75+	55–59	60–64	65–69	70–74	75+
1957	91.4	82.9	52.6	a	a	38.2	30.3	17.5	a	a
1965	90.2	78.0	43.0	24.8	14.1	47.1	34.0	17.4	9.1	3.7
1970	89.5	75.0	41.6	25.2	12.0	49.0	36.1	17.3	9.1	3.4
1975	89.4	65.5	31.7	21.1	10.1	47.9	33.2	14.5	7.6	3.0
1980	81.7	60.8	28.5	17.9	8.8	48.5	33.2	15.1	7.5	2.5
1985	79.6	55.6	24.5	14.9	7.0	50.3	33.4	13.5	7.6	2.2
1987	79.7	54.9	25.8	14.7	7.1	52.2	33.2	14.3	6.8	2.4

Source: Labor Force Statistics Derived from the CPS, 1948–1987, Publication no. 2307 (Washington, D.C.: U.S. Department of Labor, Bureau of Labor Statistics, August 1988).
[a]Not available.

for most. In fact, in 1986, 74 percent had no private pension income. By combining the private and public pension data, one can roughly calculate that no more than 39 percent of elderly households had pension income in 1986. Even among those with pension income, few households had a large fraction of their income from pensions: just 7 percent of households had more than 50 percent of their income from either private or public pensions.

Table 3.6 confirms that asset income (which does not include any imputed income to housing equity) has become more important, yet, in 1986, 40 percent of households had no income from assets. This accords with findings to be reported later that many households retire with practically no financial savings. Seventy percent of households had less than 20 percent of their income from assets. Although asset income was 26 percent of total income (table 3.4 above), most households had modest amounts from assets.

The data discussed in this section show large changes in the demographic structure of the population and in the income, labor force participation, and living arrangements of the elderly. The elderly have gained with respect to the nonelderly, but they still have lower household incomes. Results to be given in the rest of the paper will make adjustments to income that will make income comparisons more valid.

3.2   Economic Status

The most commonly used measure of economic status is income. But the simple income statistics discussed in the last section are not very well suited to the measurement of economic status. They need to be adjusted to account for income flows from nonmoney sources such as housing, Medicare and Medicaid, taxes and underreporting of income, and family size and composition. The aim of this section is to give some evidence about the economic status of the elderly based on adjusted income.

Table 3.6   **Percentage Distribution of Elderly Households by Importance of Income Source**

	1971	1980	1986
Earnings:			
Total (%):	100	100	100
0	69	78	81
1–49	16	12	11
50–100	15	10	8
90–100	5	2	2
Social Security:			
Total (%):	100	100	100
0	13	9	8
1–49	38	32	35
50–100	49	59	57
90–100	17	23	24
Private pensions and annuities:			
Total (%):	100	100	100
0	83	79	74
1–19	6	10	13
20–49	8	9	11
50–100	3	2	2
Government pensions:			
Total (%):	100	100	100
0	94	89	87
1–49	3	7	8
50–100	3	4	5
Income from assets:			
Total (%):	100	100	100
0	51	41	40
1–19	27	33	30
20–49	15	17	18
50–100	7	9	12

Sources: Income of the Population Aged 60 and Older (Washington, D.C.: Social Security Administration, various years); *Income of the Population Aged 55 and Over* (Washington, D.C.: Social Security Administration, various years).

3.2.1   Trends in Income

Before one can find trends in the real income of the elderly or compare trends in the income of the elderly and the nonelderly, one must find an appropriate price index for the elderly. That an index specifically tailored for the elderly might differ from the CPI can be seen by comparing budget shares of the elderly and nonelderly and the inflation rates in the components of the CPI. For example, in the 1972–73 Consumer Expenditure Survey, 70–74-year-olds spent 8.3 percent of their budgets on medical care, compared with 4.9 percent among the nonelderly; they spent 4.5 percent on clothing, compared with 7.0 percent among the nonelderly (Boskin and Hurd 1985). Between 1961 and 1981, the average annual rate of inflation of medical care was 6.4 percent and of apparel 3.6 percent. One might well imagine that a Laspeyres index based

Table 3.7   Growth in Average Real Family Unit Income

| | Annual Income Growth (%) | | |
	1967–79	1979–84	Income in 1984[a]
No size adjustment:			
Under 65	1.0	−.4	27,464
65+	1.5	3.4	18,279
Size adjustment:			
Under 65	1.7	.5	16,293
65+:	2.2	3.7	14,160
65–69	1.8	3.8	16,496
70–74	2.1	4.2	14,401
75–79	3.0	3.1	12,617
80–84	2.9	3.3	11,469
85+	2.7	5.5	11,825

Source: Radner (1987).
[a]Measured in 1982 dollars.

on the elderly's consumption patterns could differ from the CPI. That, however, turns out not to be the case. According to a Laspeyres index based on consumption patterns by age, the average annual rate of inflation of 21–54-year-olds from 1961 to 1981 was 5.08 percent. For 65–69-year-olds it was 5.10 percent, for 70–74-year-olds it was 5.11 percent, and for those 75 and older it was 5.10 percent (Boskin and Hurd 1985). These annual rates are almost identical, which is remarkable in view of the great variability in the annual rate of inflation of the CPI during the twenty-year period.[2] Because of the similarity of the two indices, the CPI is an adequate index for calculating real income changes.

Table 3.7 has annual growth rates in income and the level of income in 1984 adjusted for household size according to the official poverty index. In this scaling, one nonelderly person has a weight of 1.024, two nonelderly persons 1.322, three persons (either elderly or nonelderly) 1.568, and so forth. Elderly persons are given slightly smaller weights (about 8 percent smaller). Size-adjusted income (income per equivalent person) is household income divided by the household weight. The scaling implies substantial returns to scale in household consumption: a two-person household requires only 29 percent more income than a one-person household. This scaling yields income measures that are closer to income per household than to income per person: income per household has an implicit weight of 1.0 for all households, whereas income per person is based on assigning a weight of 1.0 to each person.

2. Bridges and Packard (1981) and Clark et al. (1984) come to the same conclusion. An additional reason for constructing a price index for the elderly has come from the use of the CPI to adjust Social Security benefits to inflation: it is periodically argued that the elderly face higher rates of inflation than the nonelderly and that the CPI-based Social Security adjustment is therefore inadequate.

The average elderly family unit is smaller than the average nonelderly family unit (1.7 persons per household vs. 3.0 persons in 1980), so the size adjustments will raise the income measure of the elderly relative to the nonelderly. In table 3.7, the ratio of incomes of the nonelderly to those of the elderly was 0.67 in 1984 with no size adjustment and 0.87 with the size adjustment. Average family size has decreased over time, but it has decreased more for the nonelderly than for the elderly. Therefore, the size adjustment will produce a larger increase in income per equivalent person of the nonelderly than of the elderly. For example, the size adjustment increased the annual rate of growth of income between 1979 and 1984 by 0.9 percent for the nonelderly but by just 0.3 percent for the elderly.

By either the unadjusted or the adjusted income measure, the elderly had much higher rates of growth of income than the nonelderly. These differences cumulate over a number of years to give quite different income changes. For example, the total income changes from 1967 to 1984 are shown in table 3.8. The growth of income of the nonelderly has come from increased work effort,[3] whereas income from earnings and labor force participation of the elderly fell sharply.

Table 3.7 above shows that, in most cases, income growth increased with age. This is partly due to the aging of younger, more wealthy cohorts and partly due to increases in Social Security, which are relatively more important to the very old. Still, as measured in table 3.7, by 1984, the incomes of the most elderly were still lower than the incomes of any age group shown in the table.

Some may find the growth in income of the elderly surprising in view of the high rates of inflation during the 1970s: at one time, it was generally thought that the elderly lived on fixed incomes and were vulnerable to inflation. It appears, however, that a substantial fraction of both income and wealth of most elderly is effectively indexed. Consider real incomes (in 1982 dollars) of the cohort born in 1898–1902, shown in table 3.9.

In 1967, when this cohort was 65–69 years old, its mean real income was $10,730. Between 1967 and 1972, Social Security benefits increased substantially owing to changes in the law, and, over the same years, some of the cohort retired. The net effect was an increase in both mean and median real income. After 1972, there were no legislated changes in Social Security benefits and little change in earnings because almost all the cohort would have already retired. Yet real income of the cohort was stable between 1972 and 1982, a period over which the average annual inflation rate was 8.4 percent.

Just why income should be effectively indexed is not apparent from the distribution of income by source shown in table 3.4 above. Although ad hoc adjustments are sometimes made to private pensions during periods of high inflation (Allen, Clark, and Sumner 1986), at least part of pension income and

---

3. In 1984, average hourly real nonagricultural earnings were almost exactly the same as in 1967 (*1988 Economic Report of the President,* table B-44).

Table 3.8   Income Change, 1967–84 (%)

	No Size Adjustment	Size Adjustment
Nonelderly	10.7	26.7
Elderly	42.4	54.7

Table 3.9   Real Income, Cohort Born 1898–1902 (1982 dollars)

Year and Age	Mean Income	Median Income
1967; 65–69	10,730	7,820
1972; 70–74	11,360	8,330
1977; 75–79	11,210	8,060
1982; 80–84	11,560	8,560

Source: Radner (1986).

part of asset income are not indexed, with the result that total income is not completely indexed. Another method of investigating inflation vulnerability will be discussed later in connection with wealthholdings. It is based on a detailed classification of wealth, and it verifies that the elderly are, on average, not particularly vulnerable to inflation.

3.2.2   Income Comparisons

The aim of income comparisons is to understand better the economic status of the elderly compared to that of the nonelderly. Its method is to bring income measures closer to welfare measures by scaling for family size and by adjusting income for nonmoney components, underreporting, and taxes.

No adjustment for household size is universally accepted, but, as discussed previously, a common method is based on the poverty line: household income is divided by the poverty line for that household (after normalization) to produce a measure of income per adult equivalent (Smeeding 1989). For example, if a single elderly person is assigned an adult equivalent weight of 1.0, in the poverty-line scaling an elderly couple is assigned a weight of 1.26 and a nonelderly three-person household a weight of 1.47. Therefore, if each household had an income of $20,000, the poverty-line scaling would assign the single elderly household an income of $20,000, the elderly couple an income of $15,873, and the three-person household an income of $13,605. This scaling implies large returns to scale in consumption: a couple needs only 26 percent more income than a single person.

An alternative scaling is based on observed consumption behavior in the 1972–73 Consumer Expenditure Survey (van der Gaag and Smolensky 1982). This scaling implies more modest returns to scale: for example, a couple needs 37 percent more than a single person. It has a firmer foundation than the poverty scaling, which is ad hoc, because it is based on observed behavior rather than on arbitrary assumptions; therefore, at least in principle, it is superior to the poverty-line scaling.

Table 3.10 gives the ratio of the size-adjusted income of the elderly to the size-adjusted income of the nonelderly in 1986 for the poverty-line scaling and the budget-share scaling. The ratio of income, which was 0.64 in 1986 before size adjustment, is 0.79 under the poverty scaling and 0.91 under the budget-share scaling. Because the tax rate of the elderly is lower than the tax rate of the nonelderly, an adjustment for taxes increases the ratio further, as shown in the second line of table 3.10. The last adjustment in the table adds an imputed return to housing equity, which increases the incomes of the elderly more than the incomes of the nonelderly because the elderly hold more housing equity. By the budget-share scaling, the elderly had incomes about 4 percent higher than the nonelderly in 1986.

The adjustments shown in table 3.10 are probably not controversial and, by the budget-share scaling, show that the incomes of the elderly and nonelderly were about the same in 1986. According to a validation study of the 1973 CPS, the elderly underreport their incomes by 37 percent, mainly because of the underreporting of financial asset income, and the nonelderly by 3 percent. Were incomes to be adjusted for underreporting by these percentages, the income of the elderly would be greater according to the poverty scaling and substantially greater according to the budget-share scaling. Because financial assets are very highly concentrated, an adjustment for underreporting may be valid for mean incomes, but it would not reflect the economic status of most households.

Adjusting for nonmoney transfers (income in kind) is also controversial; but the transfers are large and surely of value to the recipient, so they should be taken into account when assessing consumption opportunities. The most common method of valuing income in kind is market valuation, the cost to the provider. Some people object that recipients value in-kind transfers, particularly Medicare, at less than the market value. An alternative method that, although arbitrary, has some plausibility assigns a "fungible value" to in-kind transfers. The fungible value is zero if the household income is so low that it

Table 3.10   **Mean Household Income of the Elderly Relative to That of the Nonelderly, 1986**

Income Concept	Poverty Line	Budget Share
Gross money income	.79	.91
After-tax money income	.84	.99
After-tax money income plus housing	.90	1.04

Source: Author's calculations from U.S. Bureau of the Census (1988).

Note: Figures given in the table represent the ratio of the mean household income of the elderly to the mean household income of the nonelderly.

cannot purchase the minimum necessary amounts of food and housing. At higher income levels, income in kind frees money income that would have otherwise been spent on the good that has been transferred. This liberated income can then be spent as desired, so it is valued as ordinary money income, and it is the fungible value of the in-kind transfer. Fungible value probably understates the value of the transfer to the recipient because it places no value on the transfer for households with low income levels.

In 1986, according to a "fungible value" measure, the elderly received $2,560 in nonmoney transfers, mostly Medicare. This was 12 percent of their before-tax, unadjusted household income. The nonelderly had nonmoney transfers of $886, which was just 3 percent of their before-tax, unadjusted household income. For the elderly, the fungible value is substantially below the market value of the transfers and may well be an underestimate of the value to the recipients: in 1984, 72 percent of elderly households had some form of private supplementary medical insurance. To the extent that the insurance was freely purchased and took roughly the same form as Medicare insurance, market valuation is appropriate, not fungible value. Even so, if the fungible value of nonmoney transfers were added to the incomes of the elderly and nonelderly, the elderly would be better off than the nonelderly even by the poverty-line measure.

The conclusion of the comparison of income levels is that, regardless of the exact magnitudes of the adjustments made for underreporting and the value of nonmoney transfers, on average the elderly were as well off (as measured by fully inclusive after-tax income adjusted by the budget-share scaling) as the nonelderly in 1986. Making modest adjustments for underreporting or income in kind implies that they were at least as well off under poverty scaling and better off under budget-share scaling. Adjusting fully for underreporting and income in kind makes them substantially better off under either scaling.[4]

It should be emphasized that the full income comparisons are not utility comparisons. The adjustment for nonmoney transfers puts a monetary value on the transfers to an individual that yields a monetary measure of the economic position of the individual. It aims to answer the question, What money income would make the individual as well off as the combination of actual money income and nonmoney income transfers? Although actual measurement may pose difficulties, the concept is clear, simple, and well supported in economic theory. The main difficulty arises in comparing incomes (whether adjusted for income in kind or not) across individuals or households because the comparison of income is not a welfare comparison. The utility functions of the individuals would have to be the same to make a utility comparison, but it is unreasonable to suppose that they are, especially in the case of a comparison between the elderly and the nonelderly because of different needs, in particular

---

4. Adjusting for underreporting, market value of nonmoney transfers, and taxes gives an income ratio of 1.48 for the budget-share measure (Hurd 1990).

different medical needs. The important issue is not, as some people believe, the valuation of nonmoney transfers but rather the use of an income measure to make cross-person or cross-household welfare comparisons.

3.2.3   Distribution of Income

Table 3.4 above showed that, on average, the most important income sources of the elderly are Social Security and asset income. Social Security acts strongly to reduce income inequality through the progressivity of the benefit schedule from lifetime earnings to benefits, whereas asset income acts to increase income inequality owing to the highly skewed distribution of assetholdings. The net effect appears to be that the income of the elderly is more unequally distributed than that of the nonelderly. Table 3.11 has Gini coefficients of income and the percentage of income going to the highest income quintile. Although there is some variation by year, data set, and income measure, both inequality measures show more income inequality among the elderly than among the nonelderly. The results from the 1973 Consumer Expenditure Survey and the 1979 CPS are based on the same income measure, and they are about the same. The adjustments to income in the 1979 CPS reduced income inequality because the well-to-do have higher tax rates and the poor receive a large fraction of their budgets from nonmoney transfers. The differences between the unadjusted and the adjusted inequality measures are greatest among the elderly because of the importance of Medicare and Medicaid. The last three rows of table 3.11 are based on consistent methods of measuring income in the CPS; they have the poverty scale size adjustment for household size discussed earlier. They indicate increasing inequality from 1979 to 1984, especially among the nonelderly.

3.2.4   Poverty

The poverty rate is the fraction of a population whose incomes fall below the poverty line, which varies by age and household composition. It is a widely used measure of income inequality and an indicator of the need for social policy. In 1987, the poverty line was $5,447 for a single elderly person and $6,871 for an elderly couple.

Table 3.12 shows that, as the income of the elderly rose, their poverty rate fell. By 1984, the rate was lower than the poverty rates of the nonelderly, and it remained lower through 1987.[5] The decline was largest for the oldest, yet their poverty rate remains high.

As discussed earlier, putting a value on nonmoney income increases income measures of the elderly considerably, which should lead to a large reduction in poverty rates, as shown in table 3.13. Adjusted income includes capital gains,

---

5. In 1987, the poverty rate of the elderly was 12.2 percent and that of the general population was 13.5 percent.

Table 3.11   Distribution of Income

	Gini Coefficients		% of Income to Upper Income Quintile	
Year, Data, and Income Measure	Age < 65	Age ≥ 65	Age < 65	Age ≥ 65
1973 Consumer Expenditure Survey[a]	.36	.44	40.4	49.8
1979 CPS[b]	.35	.43	40.6	49.5
1979 CPS, adjusted[c]	.31	.35	37.2	42.8
1967 CPS, family size adjustment[d]	.36	.42	41.6	51.6
1979 CPS, family size adjustment[d]	.36	.40	41.3	47.1
1984 CPS, family size adjustment[d]	.40	.42	44.2	48.1

[a]Danziger et al. (1984). Household income.
[b]Smeeding (1989). Household income.
[c]Smeeding (1989). Household income adjusted for nonmoney income, taxes, and employment-related income.
[d]Radner (1987). Family unit income. Size adjustment based on poverty scale.

Table 3.12   Poverty Rates of Family Units (%) Based on Family Unit Money Income

Age	1967	1979	1984
Under 65	11.8	11.1	14.5
65+	28.1	15.1	12.4
65–69	21.9	12.2	9.4
70–74	25.8	13.4	11.5
75–79	33.8	17.9	13.7
80–84	38.2	19.4	17.7
85+	38.9	22.7	18.5

Source: Radner (1987, 19).

Table 3.13   Poverty Rates, 1986 (%)

	Elderly	Nonelderly
Measured income	12.4	13.8
Adjusted income	5.7	10.9

Source: U.S. Bureau of the Census (1988).

nonmoney income (measured as fungible value), and taxes. Even as calculated by measured income, the poverty rate of the elderly was lower than that of the nonelderly. This is a considerable social accomplishment: in 1959, 35.2 percent of the elderly were in poverty. Social Security can take much of the credit for the improvement. For example, in 1984, 78 percent of the income of households in the lowest income quintile came from Social Security.

The poverty rate of elderly widows has also declined, but it remains considerably higher than the poverty rates of the general population and of the rest of the elderly. Some of the poverty is undoubtedly due to the high fraction of the very elderly that are widows: ceteris paribus, one would expect the very elderly to be poor simply because they must finance a longer lifetime of consumption from a given lifetime wealth. Table 3.14 shows, however, that the explanation is more complicated. It is true that widows age 72 and older had higher poverty rates than widows age 65–71, but younger widows had poverty rates at least as high.

One explanation is differential mortality by income and wealth level: husbands in poor families die sooner than husbands in wealthy families. For example, in the Retirement History Survey (RHS), the poverty rate in 1969 of couples who survived intact during the entire ten years of the RHS (1969–79) was 7.6 percent. The poverty rate in 1969 of couples in which the husband eventually died during the ten years of the RHS was 11.7 percent (Holden, Burkhauser, and Myers 1986). One might think that the difference in poverty rates is caused by health expenditures in the several years before the husband's death, but the association with poverty in 1969 and eventual widowhood lasts over many years. For example, the poverty rate in 1969 of couples in which the husband died between 1977 and 1979 was 9.2 percent, again compared with 7.6 percent for couples intact between 1969 and 1979.

Beyond differential mortality, the transition to widowhood itself seems to induce poverty. Table 3.15 gives poverty rates from the RHS by marital transition between 1975 and 1977 for the entire sample of 1975 couples and for the 1975 couples not in poverty in 1975. The table shows that the couples in which the husband died between 1975 and 1977 had somewhat but not greatly higher poverty rates than the other couples in the years before the husband's death. However, in the first survey year after the husband's death, the poverty rate of the surviving widow rose to 42 percent, while the poverty rate of the intact couple was just 7 percent. Other calculations (not given here) show that the average increase in poverty following the husband's death was 30 percent. The increase is partly due to income mismeasurement associated with the husband's death, but mostly due to permanent changes in economic resources

Table 3.14   **Poverty Rates of Widows**

			65 and Over		
Year	60–61	62–64	Total	65–71	72+
1971	. . .	. . .	35.1	. . .	. . .
1976	22.8	22.9	23.3	21.7	24.0
1981	26.2	27.2	25.4	23.9	26.1
1984	27.6	25.5	20.1	18.3	20.9
1987	22.0	22.8	19.1	17.3	19.9

Sources: U.S. Bureau of the Census, *Current Population Reports,* ser. P-60 (various years).

Table 3.15   **Poverty Rates (%)**

Year	Entire Sample		Not Poor in 1975	
	Couple to Couple	Couple to Widow	Couple to Couple	Couple to Widow
1969	5	8	3	5
1971	7	11	4	7
1973	8	8	4	4
1975[a]	8	9	0	0
1977[a]	7	42	4	37
1979	10	32	6	26

Source: Calculations of Hurd and Wise (1989) from the RHS.

[a]Husband in "couple to widow" columns died between these years.

(Burkhauser, Holden, and Myers 1986). The two right-hand columns give poverty rates before and after the transition years over couples that were above the poverty line in 1975. Thirty-seven percent of the surviving widows, none of whom had been in poverty in 1975, were in poverty in 1977.

One might well imagine that much of the increase in poverty at the husband's death is due to the termination of his earnings. Apparently, however, this is not the case: using RHS data, Burkhauser, Holden, and Feaster (1988) studied the determinants of the hazard of poverty of widows. Only 10.1 percent of the transitions into poverty were associated with the loss of the husband's earnings. About two-thirds of the cases were associated with widowhood itself and with a decline in nonwage income, particularly Social Security. Even after the husband's retirement (so that he had no earnings), the probability that the widow became poor when the husband died is high (Holden, Burkhauser, and Feaster 1988)

The causes of the high rates of poverty among elderly widows are varied and complex. Some families reach retirement already poor or close to becoming poor. Were the husband to survive, the family would have a high risk of poverty, but, because husbands in poor families tend to die sooner than husbands in wealthy families, often the widow inherits the family's poverty. In addition, some sources of income drop when the husband dies, and some wealth is reduced. How much poverty is due to age itself is not clear. Cross-sectional poverty rates have cohort effects; one would want to observe panels over, say, twenty years to observe the life-cycle effects.

3.2.5   Wealth

Table 3.16 has average net wealth from the 1975 RHS and the 1979 RHS. Most of the heads of households were 64–69 years old in 1975 and 68–73 years old in 1979, so the table shows wealth near the beginning of retirement. In fact, future earnings accounted for only 6 percent of wealth in 1975 and 3 percent in 1979, so, practically speaking, the sample had retired by 1979. Financial

Table 3.16   **Average Household Wealth and the Distribution of Wealth by Source, 1975 and 1979 RHS Sample**

	1975		1979		Lowest Wealth Decile 1979	
	Wealth	%	Wealth	%	Wealth	%
Housing	22.4	14	26.9	18	1.4	4
Business and property	11.0	7	11.6	8	1.1	3
Financial	23.2	15	22.5	15	.7	2
Pensions	23.2	15	18.0	12	1.6	4
SSI, welfare, and transfers	2.7	2	2.3	2	3.6	10
Medicare-Medicaid	15.8	10	17.7	12	11.9	34
Social Security	48.4	31	44.0	30	14.2	40
Future earnings	9.6	6	3.9	3	1.0	3
Total	156.3	100	146.7	100	35.5	100

Source: Hurd and Shoven (1985).

Note: Wealth in thousands of 1979 dollars. Based on 7,483 (1975) and 6,610 (1979) observations from the RHS. Farm families and farm wealth excluded.

wealth includes stocks and bonds, savings accounts, and so forth. Flows (all but the first three entries) are converted to stocks through actuarial discounting, either real or nominal, depending on the flow. SSI is Supplemental Security Income, a means-tested old-age welfare program. Transfers includes transfers from relatives and children. Medicare and Medicaid is the expected present value of the per household transfer through the Medicare and Medicaid program evaluated at cost, the market value discussed earlier.[6]

The average wealth levels are reasonably high and consistent with independent measures of income and wealth.[7] Most people, however, would be surprised at how little saving is in the conventional form of business and property and financial wealth: about 22 percent in 1975 and 23 percent in 1979. Adding in housing equity to find the fraction of saving that takes place at the household level brings these figures to 36 percent and 41 percent. Pensions and Social Security, which represent saving by firms and society on behalf of the household, accounted for 46 percent in 1975. Both in levels and as percentages of total wealth, the sum of pensions and Social Security fell between 1975 and

6. This is the method used by Smeeding (1989) and Clark et al. (1984).

7. For example, Smeeding (1989) calculates the full income of the elderly to be $13,423; if the wealth in 1979 were annuitized at a 7 percent interest rate and a 4 percent mortality rate, it would yield $16,137. Given that this applies to 68–73-year-olds who are more wealthy than older cohorts, the figures seem quite consistent. Radner (1989) reports mean financial and housing wealth of 65–74-year-olds from the Survey of Income and Program Participation to be $99,800, which is $69,700 in 1979 dollars. The comparable wealth figure in the 1979 RHS, when most heads of households were 68–73, is $71,100.

1979 because of higher mortality discounting at the RHS sample aged and, in the case of pensions, because inflation reduced the real value. Undoubtedly, for the same reasons discussed earlier in connection with the valuation of the income flow from Medicare and Medicaid, the most controversial entry is the wealth value of Medicare and Medicaid.[8] It accounted for 10 percent of wealth in 1975 and 12 percent in 1979.[9] Its value rose between 1975 and 1979 despite the aging of the RHS population (the actuarial discounting is higher at greater ages) because the growth in Medicare and Medicaid transfers was much higher than the inflation rate.

The level of wealth in the lowest wealth decile is low indeed and consists almost entirely of wealth from public programs. Any underreporting is not likely to be substantial because most underreporting is associated with financial assets, but, even allowing for some, it is clear that many elderly reach retirement with very little.

3.2.6   Inflation Vulnerability

Although the elderly may be reasonably well off as measured by either income or wealth, their economic status could be eroded by inflation. As noted earlier, however, incomes of the elderly maintained their purchasing power during the 1970s and early 1980s despite high inflation rates, which suggests that they are not particularly vulnerable to inflation. This suggestion was verified by Hurd and Shoven (1985), who used the wealth data in the RHS to calculate an index of inflation vulnerability. All assets and income flows were classified as real or nominal. Under the assumption that the nominal interest rate varies one for one with the rate of inflation, the value of a nominal asset such as a bond will vary with changes in the inflation rate in a way that depends on the maturity of the bond. Neither the value of a real asset, such as a house, nor the present value of a real income flow, such as Social Security, will vary with inflation. Nominal income flows such as private pensions or a stream of mortgage payments will vary with inflation owing to a change in the nominal discount rate.

Table 3.17 has measures of inflation vulnerability for the RHS sample calculated according to these assumptions. The table gives the percentage change in wealth associated with an increase in the inflation rate of 0.01 from the base inflation rate, which is given in parentheses. For comparison, the change in the value of a consol bond is given for the assumption that the nominal interest

8. The market valuation for most elderly may be fairly accurate: many elderly purchase additional medical insurance beyond Medicare and Medicaid. This indicates that, from Medicare and Medicaid alone, they are not at a corner solution in their demand for medical coverage and that, apart from wealth effects, market valuation is appropriate. This argument would not hold for the poor elderly, many of whom do not purchase additional medical coverage (U.S. Senate Special Committee on Aging 1988).

9. These fractions are very close to the fraction of income from Medicare and Medicaid (10 percent) in Smeeding (1989).

Table 3.17   **Median % Wealth Change**

Year[a]	Bond	All	Lowest Decile	Highest Decile	SS Vulnerable
1969 (.057)	10.3	.03	.00	.32	3.7
1975 (.058)	10.4	.06	.00	.25	2.3
1979 (.113)	6.5	.09	.00	.23	1.7

Source: Hurd and Shoven (1985).
[a]The base inflation rate is given in parentheses.

rate is 0.03 higher than the inflation rate. Thus, if the inflation rate changed from 5.7 to 6.7 percent, the value of a consol would change by 10.3 percent. Because the assumed change of 0.01 in the inflation rate is a smaller fraction of the inflation rate in 1979 than in 1969, the percentage wealth change of the consol will be smaller in 1979 than in 1969. The interpretation of the first row is that, if the inflation rate had changed in 1969 from 5.7 to 6.7 percent, the medial total wealthholding of the RHS population would have declined by 0.03 percent. In the lowest wealth decile, there would have been no change. Even in the highest wealth decile, just 0.32 percent of wealth would have been lost. As a practical matter, these estimated changes are zero. The importance of the indexing of Social Security is shown in the last column: it gives the wealth loss under the assumption that Social Security benefits are not indexed (vulnerable to inflation). The loss would be 3.7 percent of wealth. Because of the importance of Social Security to households in the lower part of the wealth distribution, the loss in the lowest decile would be even greater: 4.5 percent of total wealth in 1969 (not shown).

The conclusion to be drawn from table 3.17 and from observed income over periods of high inflation is that the elderly are not particularly vulnerable to inflation.[10] The indexing of Social Security is responsible for a considerable part of this income and wealth stability.

3.3 Conclusion

On average, the elderly in the United States are at least as well off as the nonelderly and possibly substantially better off. The averages, however, conceal considerable income inequality, as reflected in the Gini coefficient of income and in the high poverty rate of widows. In fact, it may well be that the Gini coefficient of all the elderly is simply a reflection of the low incomes of widows.

Not only are the elderly well off on average, but they are substantially protected from uncertainty. Indeed, one reason that they gained with respect to the nonelderly is that, since the early 1970s, real wage rates have been constant

10. For a similar conclusion, see also Clark et al. (1984) and Burkhauser, Holden, and Feaster (1988).

yet real Social Security benefits have increased substantially. Most of the elderly are well protected against inflation changes. Medical costs, however, remain a major source of uncertainty.

The future economic status of the currently retired seems well assured. The baby boom generation, moving into their prime earning years, will be contributing to the Social Security trust funds more than enough for the funds to meet their obligations. The elderly hold substantial stocks of housing and other assets. When they decide to convert those assets to consumption, there will be an ample number of buyers in the younger generations who will be saving for their own retirements.

The more distant future of the elderly does not seem as bright. When the baby boom generation retires, there will be fewer workers to support each retired person. This has negative implications for the Social Security and Medicare systems, of course, but also for the pension systems and for private savings. Firms will have to support larger numbers of retirees. When the retired want to sell and consume their financial assets, they will have fewer buyers. This implies that their consumption relative to the consumption of workers will be lower than it is today. Whether it will be absolutely lower than it is today depends on the future course of productivity in the economy. Productivity, in turn, depends on how the large bulge in Social Security contributions and retirement savings of the baby boom generation is used.

In principle, the world economy could help relieve the stress caused by the aging of the U.S. population. By purchasing claims today to the future output of other countries, the United States could prefund future consumption. This would require an export surplus. Of course, exactly the opposite has happened: other countries are accumulating claims on future U.S. production because the United States has a trade deficit. Because many developed countries have roughly the same demographic problem as the United States, it is likely that they will want to redeem those claims just when the United States has a high ratio of retirees to workers. This will, of course, make it even more difficult to support the consumption of retirees in the distant future.

References

Allen, Steven, Robert L. Clark, and Daniel Sumner. 1986. Postretirement adjustments of pension benefits. *Journal of Human Resources* 21, no. 1:118–37.
Boskin, Michael J., and Michael D. Hurd. 1985. Indexing Social Security benefits: A separate price index for the elderly? *Public Finance Quarterly* 13, no. 4 (October): 436–49.
Bridges, Benjamin, and Michael Packard. 1981. Price and income changes for the elderly. *Social Security Bulletin* 44, no. 1:3–15.
Burkhauser, Richard, Karen C. Holden, and Daniel Feaster. 1988. Incidence, timing,

and events associated with poverty: A dynamic view of poverty in retirement. *Journal of Gerontology* 43, no. 2 (March): S46–S52.

Burkhauser, Richard V., Karen C. Holden, and Daniel A. Myers. 1986. Marital disruption and poverty: The role of survey procedures in artificially creating poverty. *Demography* 23, no. 4:621–31.

Clark, Robert L., George Maddox, Ronald Schrimper, and Daniel Sumner. 1984. *Inflation and the economic well-being of the elderly.* Baltimore: Johns Hopkins University Press.

Danziger, Sheldon, Jacques van der Gaag, Eugene Smolensky, and Michael Taussig. 1984. Implications of the relative economic status of the elderly for transfer policy. In *Retirement and economic behavior,* ed. H. Aaron and G. Burtless. Washington, D.C.: Brookings.

Holden, Karen, Richard Burkhauser, and Daniel J. Feaster. 1988. The timing of falls into poverty after retirement and widowhood. *Demography* 25, no. 3:405–14.

Holden, Karen, Richard V. Burkhauser, and Daniel Myers. 1986. Income transitions at older stages of life: The dynamics of poverty. *Gerontologist* 26, no. 3:292–97.

Hurd, Michael D. 1990. Research on the elderly: Economic status, retirement, and consumption and saving. *Journal of Economic Literature* 28 (June): 565–637.

Hurd, Michael D., and John B. Shoven. 1985. Inflation vulnerability, income and wealth of the elderly, 1969–1979. In *Horizontal equity, uncertainty, and economic well-being,* ed. Martin David and Timothy Smeeding. Chicago: University of Chicago Press.

Hurd, Michael D., and David A. Wise. 1989. The wealth and poverty of widows: Assets before and after the husband's death. In *The economics of aging,* ed. D. Wise. Chicago: University of Chicago Press.

Radner, Daniel, 1986. *Changes in the money income of the aged and nonaged, 1967–1983.* Studies in Income Distribution, no. 14. Washington, D.C.: Office of Research and Statistics, Social Security Administration.

———. 1987. Money incomes of aged and nonaged family units, 1967–84. *Social Security Bulletin* 50, no. 8 (August): 9–28.

———. 1989. The wealth of the aged and nonaged, 1984. In *The measurement of saving, investment and wealth,* ed. Robert E. Lipsey and Helen Stone Tice. Chicago: University of Chicago Press.

Smeeding, Timothy, 1989. Full income estimates of the relative well-being of the elderly and the nonelderly. In *Research in economic inequality,* vol. 1, ed. D. Bloom and D. Slottje. Greenwich, Conn.: JAI.

U.S. Bureau of the Census. 1988. Measuring the effect of taxes and income on poverty: 1986. *Current Population Reports,* Ser. P-60, no. 164-RD-1.

U.S. House of Representatives. Committee on Ways and Means. 1987. Retirement income for an aging population. Washington, D.C.: U.S. Government Printing Office.

U.S. Senate Special Committee on Aging. 1988. *Aging America, 1987–88 edition.* Washington, D.C.: U.S. Department of Health and Human Services.

van der Gaag, Jacques, and Eugene Smolensky. 1982. True household equivalence scales and characteristics of the poor in the U.S. *Review of Income and Wealth* 28 (March): 17–28.

4 Household Asset- and Wealthholdings in Japan

Noriyuki Takayama

For most nations, data on household asset- and wealthholdings are not available, and Japan is no exception. The most recent comprehensive data on Japanese household assets are reported in the Economic Planning Agency's 1970 National Wealth Survey. Since then, the Family Savings Survey has reported only household monetary assets each year, and data on household real assets are not available. Some macro data on household net worth are available, however, from the Annual Report on National Accounts series.

In 1986 and 1987, stock and land values rose sharply, and their total capital gains came to exceed GNP.[1] This increased people's interest in stock variables considerably. A debate over the effects of wealth on consumption ensued, and some voiced concerns over the growth of asset differentials.

In Japan, the debate over equity has centered mainly on the distribution of income. If the relation between income and wealth is not parallel, the current debate would be severely undermined. Specifically, Japan's Social Security system will be in crisis in the near future. Intergenerational transfer programs in Japan need to be reformed. In redesigning these programs, it is fundamental to have relevant information not only on income and consumption but also on the wealthholdings of different cohorts.

What assets does each household in Japan have today? How big is the asset differential? How does the Japanese level of assetholdings or wealth inequality compare with that of other countries? If the amounts of household assethold-

Noriyuki Takayama is professor of economics at the Institute of Economic Research, Hitotsubashi University.

This paper is largely based on the work of the Economic Planning Agency research project on the economics of Social Security, directed by Noriyuki Takayama. The author is grateful to Michael Hurd, Laurence J. Kotlikoff, and Edward Lazear for their valuable comments.

1. In 1986 and 1987, respectively, GNP stood at ¥331 and ¥345 trillion, capital gains on land at ¥245 and ¥371 trillion, and capital gains on stock shares at ¥121 and ¥106 trillion.

ings are estimated, it may be possible to give answers to such fundamental questions. It may also be possible to present concrete figures for the above-mentioned debate over the effects of wealth or the expanding asset differential. Such estimation is also essential to an examination of the life-cycle hypothesis of consumption and to a detailed understanding of intergenerational transfers.

In this paper, I estimate household asset- and wealthholdings. The data come mainly from the National Survey of Family Income and Expenditure (NSFIE). The discussion is organized as follows. The next section explains my procedures for estimating assetholdings, while the estimated results for 1984 are outlined in sections 4.2–4.4. In section 4.5, longitudinal changes in assethold-ings are discussed. Section 4.6 takes up the housing and living arrangements of the elderly. The final section gives concluding remarks.

4.1   Estimation Procedures for Household Asset- and Wealthholdings

In this paper, only real and monetary assets are considered. Although human capital is a household asset, it is not discussed here.[2] Only residential land, housing structures, rental property, and consumer durables are considered real assets. Precious metals, drawings, and antiques are not included among real assets.

Monetary assets include demand deposits, time deposits, life insurance, bonds, trusts, investment trusts, stock shares, in-company deposits, etc. Premiums on life and damage insurance of the nonsaving type and golf club membership certificates are not included. Net monetary assets are calculated by subtracting liabilities from total monetary assets. Net worth is obtained by adding real assets to net monetary assets.

For monetary assets and liabilities, the figures recorded (as of the end of November) in the NSFIE are used directly. However, real assetholdings are not recorded in the NSFIE. Thus, it is necessary to estimate each of the four asset components stated above independently. Each estimation procedure is described below.

4.1.1   Equity in the Residential Site for Owner-Occupied Housing

Households may have land for owner-occupied housing, land for a shop or workshop, land for rent, land for cultivation, or mountain and forest land. In this paper, only residential land for owner-occupied housing and/or for rent is examined. *Real rental assets* includes both the rental housing site and the physical building. The assets referred to as *land assets* in this paper are the sites for

---

2. Takayama et al. (1990) estimate household asset- and wealthholdings, including human assets, and describe their structure. It may be interesting that couples in their early 60s participating in the KNH (Kosei-Nenkin-Hoken, a Social Security system for employees in the private sector in Japan) had gross Social Security wealth around ¥44 million (in median value) in 1984.

owner-occupied housing. Land assets are estimated by multiplying land area by land price.

The size of residential land is unfortunately not reported in the NSFIE. Figures on the floor space of owner-occupied housing, however, can be obtained directly from the NSFIE. It is thus necessary to estimate separately the floor/area ratio (i.e., total floor space divided by site size). The floor/area ratio is estimated as follows.

First, the average floor/area ratio is obtained, using micro data from the Current Survey of Construction with separate figures by construction date, prefecture (cities, rural counties, ten major cities), type of building (exclusively residential or residence and shop), construction material (wood, fireproof wood, block, ferroconcrete, etc.), and number of floors.

Next, I estimated the parameters of the floor/area ratio function using micro data in the Housing Survey and used these parameters to correct the average floor/area ratio obtained above. These corrections cover only *residential wooden houses* (including hereinafter fireproof wooden houses) owing to the limitations of the data (see Takayama et al. 1989; and Takayama 1992).

The Land Price Survey assembled by the Land Management Agency is used to obtain land prices. I checked the distribution of the officially announced prices of *residential land* by cities and rural counties of each prefecture and adopted the median price as of 1 January of the following year. Data on rural counties, however, are scant. Some rural surveys also select land prices that are high compared with nearby cities. In such cases, the first decile or the first quartile of neighboring urban land prices is used.

4.1.2   Value of Housing Structures Net Depreciation

The value of housing structures used for owner-occupied housing is obtained by estimating reconstruction costs in 1984 as total floor space times the inflated average construction cost per square meter, minus depreciation. In so doing, the cost figures reported in the Current Survey of Construction, which are broken down by construction dates, by prefectures (urban, rural counties, ten major cities), and by housing materials, are used as the average construction costs. The construction deflator is derived from the fixed capital formation matrix in the 1980 Industrial Input-Output Table (compiled by the Management and Coordination Agency, Tokyo, in 1984) and from the wage and wholesale price indices.

In estimating the depreciation of housing structures, I assume the service life to be twenty-four years for wooden houses, twenty-two years for wooden houses with fireproofing, sixty years for ferroconcrete houses, and forty-five years for block houses, assumptions based on the *Ministry Ordinance on Service Lives of Depreciable Assets* issued by the Ministry of Finance, Tokyo, in 1984. In this paper, therefore, the value of housing structures is depreciated at a constant rate of 9.2, 9.9, 8, and 5.5 percent per year according to the respective service life.

4.1.3 Rental Property

The NSFIE includes data on housing and land rent as sources of income. Multiplying this coefficient by the reciprocal of the annual rate of return on rental housing property yields the estimated value of rental property. The rate of return on rental housing property was estimated for private rental houses and apartments for each prefecture from the 1983 Housing Survey. The value of land and housing assets for private rental houses and apartments is estimated in the same manner as that for owner-occupied homes.

4.1.4 Value of Consumer Durables

The NSFIE reports the quantity of each major consumer durable held and the quantity purchased during the survey year. For each item, the quantity held is multiplied by the unit purchase price in 1984, and the depreciation is subtracted. The mean price reported in the NSFIE is used. In the few cases in which the prices of consumer durables are not explicitly reported in the survey, I estimated them, using the Machinery Survey and the Miscellaneous Goods Survey (both compiled annually by the Ministry of International Trade and Industry and published by Tsusho-Sangyo-Chosa-Kai, Tokyo) and other industry-specific statistics (see Takayama et al. 1989; and Takayama 1992).

In order to estimate the amount of depreciation of consumer durables accurately, it is necessary to know when each item was purchased. But the year of purchase of those items bought prior to 1984 is not given in the 1984 survey. The number of years since purchase is assumed to be half the service life for all items.

4.2 Estimates of 1984 Household Asset- and Wealthholdings

Table 4.1 shows my estimates of 1984 household assetholdings. Multimember households, including farm households, are covered in the estimation. Figures for single-member households are not estimated.

The estimated mean household net worth is ¥28 million, and the median is ¥20 million.[3] Overall, the net worth/income ratio is 5.0 in 1984. In this estimation, those households with zero holdings of respective assets are included. As a whole, real assets account for 85 percent of net worth, and landholdings (¥15.41 million on the average) account for an especially large proportion at 56 percent. On the other hand, monetary assets amount to ¥6.76 million gross and ¥4.09 million net (mean values in both cases).

It is estimated that the amount of household assetholdings in Japan is at an extremely high level, in international comparisons. U.S. Department of Commerce, Bureau of the Census (1986), is useful for reference. According to the Census Bureau's report, the mean net worth of U.S. households is $101,900

---

3. At the end of 1984, ¥1 million was worth about U.S.$4,000.

Table 4.1   **Estimates of Household Assets- and Wealthholdings (all households)**

Asset Category	Holdings per Household (¥10,000)	
	Mean	Median
1. Residential land	1,541	1,151
2. Home buildings	307	146
3. Rental property	323	0
4. Consumer durables	199	187
5. 1 + 2 + 3 + 4	2,371	1,783
6. Monetary assets (gross)	676	414
7. Liabilities	268	15
8. Monetary assets (net)	409	265
9. Net worth (= 5 + 8)	2,779	1,972

Source: The 1984 NSFIE and others.
Note: Multimember households (including farm households).

and the median $50,100 in 1984 (married-couple households). Only vehicles are included in consumer durables in the U.S. data, and the value of furniture and jewelry is not covered in net worth. Homeowner households account for 77 percent of the total number of households in the United States, while the mean equity in the home is $53,200 dollars and the median $42,600.

As for the estimated value of assets by each household category, the following can be observed:

1. The mean value of land assets held by homeowners (accounting for 74 percent of the total households) is ¥20 million, the median is ¥16 million, and the mode is in the ¥10–¥15 million range. The value of land accounts on average for nearly 60 percent of net worth. The mean gross monetary assets held by this group are ¥7.70 million, with a median value of ¥4.80 million, considerably higher than the values for home renters. Homeowners also have, on average, liabilities of ¥3 million, a figure considerably larger than the ¥770,000 in liabilities held by home renters. In home-renter households, real assets naturally account for a small part of net worth (only 40 percent on average).

2. By age group, the homeownership rate generally increases as the household head gets older (30 percent or less for those in their late 20s, 66 percent for those in their late 30s, roughly 80 percent for those 45 years old or so, and 90 percent for those 55 years or older). Consequently, average landholdings (including those households with zero holdings) get larger with age. But landholdings get larger with age even if we exclude households with zero holdings. This is true because older household heads acquired their land earlier; therefore, the size of their holding is somewhat larger (see table 4.2). In addition, older people have enjoyed capital gains. Land assetholdings as a whole account for 50–60 percent of net worth, and this proportion does not vary much by age group. From age 40 to age 60, however, this proportion decreases a little, and

Table 4.2   **Residential Land Space of Owner-Occupied Housing by Age (unit: m^2)**

Age	Mean	Median
<24	187	163
25–29	187	161
30–34	218	186
35–39	222	183
40–44	238	198
45–49	247	208
50–54	283	240
55–59	320	260
60–64	344	275
56–59	364	269
70–74	336	265
75+	314	258
All	271	218

Source: The 1984 NSFIE and others.

instead the proportion of monetary assetholdings increases. Gross monetary assetholdings tend in general to increase with age, reaching a peak at 60 years of age. Incidentally, the monetary assetholdings of those households with household heads between 60 and 65 have a mean of ¥11 million, a median of ¥7.10 million, and a mode of ¥2 million. In net terms, after deducting liabilities, monetary assetholdings are in general very poor (not reaching ¥2 million even on average), especially in younger households. Many households are capable of increasing net monetary assets only after reaching age 45 (fig. 4.1). The net worth of households between 60 and 65 has a mean of ¥44 million, a median of ¥32 million, and a mode of ¥21 million.

3. The assetholdings of households living in the Keihin metropolitan zone (the greater Tokyo area, which accounts for 25 percent of total households) are larger than those of households living in the rural regions (regions other than the three metropolitan zones, which account for 54 percent of the total number of households). The only exception is the stockholdings of consumer durables, including cars. The median ratios of the assetholdings of the two groups are 1.6 for land, 1.3 for monetary assets (in gross terms), and 1.3 for net worth when the assetholdings of rural households are set at 1. Homeownership rates are 69 percent in the Keihin metropolitan zone and 78 percent in the rural regions. If only homeowner households are compared, the mean difference in land assetholdings between the two groups is roughly on the order of two.

4. When workers' households (accounting for 63 percent of all households) and nonworkers' households (excluding jobless households) are compared, the latter group exceeds the former in the holding of every asset item. The ratios of the two groups' holdings, in terms of median value, are 1.7 for land, 1.2 for housing (buildings only), 1.5 for total real assets, 1.3 for monetary assets (in

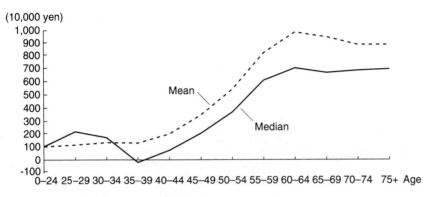

Fig. 4.1 Monetary assetholdings (in net terms)
Source: The 1984 NSFIE

gross terms), and 1.7 for net worth (when the assetholdings of workers' households are assumed to be 1). Such differences in asset ownership may be thought of as due mainly to differences in average age (42 years old for workers' households, 51 years old for nonworkers' households) and in the homeownership rate (67 percent for workers' households, 87 percent for nonworkers' households). The net worth of nonworkers' households has a mean of ¥40 million and a median of ¥27 million.

5. By income group, those households with higher incomes generally have more assets in both mean and median values.

4.3   Distribution of Household Asset- and Wealthholdings

Lorenz curves by each asset item are shown in figs. 4.2, 4.3, and 4.4. Multimember households, including farm households, are covered.

The value of the Gini coefficient is the index used to measure the degree of inequality.[4] The Gini coefficient of household net worth was 0.52 in 1984.[5] This figure is highly dependent on the Gini coefficient of real asset distribution, as real assets (especially land) account for a large proportion of net worth. The Gini coefficient is decomposed by asset component,[6] and the Gini coeffi-

---

4. Consider a society S of n households. Let the amount of assetholdings of household i be A_i. Then the asset distribution is given by vector $A = (A_1, A_2, \ldots, A_n)$. Provided that $A_1 \leq A_2 \leq \ldots \leq A_n$, the Gini coefficient of asset distribution is given by

(i) $$G = 2 \sum_i (n + 1 - i)(\mu - A_i)/(\mu n^2),$$

where μ is the mean value of assetholdings. The Gini coefficient is a normalized weighted sum of the gaps in assetholdings of every household in S, the weight being equal to the ranking of assetholdings from the top. The Gini coefficient is equivalent to two times the area enclosed by the Lorenz curve and the forty-five-degree line. For details, see Takayama (1979).

5. The figures for the Gini coefficient in this paper are more or less *underestimated* since mean and median values are used instead of direct observations of real assetholdings.

6. The method used to decompose the Gini coefficient for net worth (G) by the Gini coefficients for the asset components is given by Rao (1969):

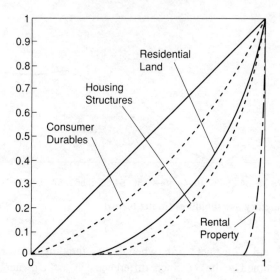

Fig. 4.2   Lorenz curves of real assets
Source: The 1984 NSFIE and others

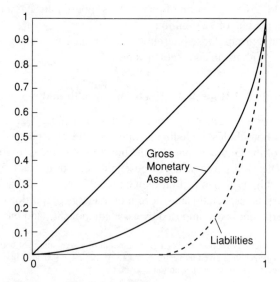

Fig. 4.3   Lorenz curves of monetary assets
Source: The 1984 NSFIE and others

(ii)
$$G = \sum w_j \times \tilde{G}_j$$

where w_j indicates the ratio of the aggregate amount of the jth asset component to the total sum. $\tilde{G}_j$ is called the *pseudo–Gini coefficient* and is calculated by rearranging the distribution of asset component j into the order of net worth and then formally applying eq. (i).

cient for total real assets could explain 82 percent of the overall Gini coefficient.

The Gini coefficient for the distribution of total real assets is 0.5. The Gini coefficient for land is 0.55, whereas that for housing (buildings only) is 0.62. The Gini coefficient for rental property is rather high at 0.97 since households with those assets account for a very small proportion of total households (8.8 percent). Consumer durables are owned by all households, on the other hand, and the distribution is rather even (the Gini coefficient is 0.27).

The Gini coefficient for the distribution of monetary assetholdings, in gross terms, is 0.54. This figure is almost the same as the Gini coefficient for land distribution. On the other hand, those households with positive liabilities account for 57 percent of total households, and the Gini coefficient for liabilities is relatively high at 0.78. Many households incur liabilities when they purchase their own home. Younger families with relatively small assetholdings use consumer loans extensively. Consequently, the pseudo–Gini coefficient for monetary assets in net terms exceeds 1. This is because some households (22.5 percent of all households) own negative monetary assets.

I have also calculated the Gini coefficient for wealth distribution for each household group. Some central points are as follows.

For homeowner households, the Gini coefficient for land distribution is 0.40, and the Gini coefficient for net worth remains at 0.42. The asset distribution of home-renter households is determined mainly by the distribution of

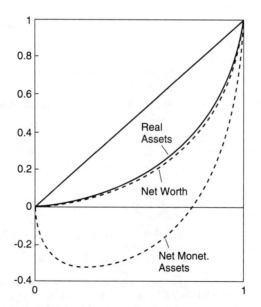

Fig. 4.4   Lorenz curves of net worth
Source: The 1984 NSFIE and others

gross monetary assets. The Gini coefficient of net worth is 0.53 within this household group.

By age group, the Gini coefficient for net worth within the age group gets smaller up to the 50–55 age group. For those over 55, however, this Gini coefficient hardly changes. This is in all likelihood related to the homeownership rate, which increases with age.

When the land distribution among households living in the Keihin metropolitan zone is compared with that among households living in rural regions, the former shows a somewhat higher degree of inequality (the Gini coefficients being 0.57 and 0.50, respectively). As a result, the former group shows a higher level of inequality in the distribution of net worth as well.

When we compare workers' and nonworkers' households, the former group shows a higher degree of inequality in land distribution, but there is hardly any difference between the two groups in the inequality of net worth or total real assets. This is in part due to the relatively large proportion (19 percent) of aggregate net worth constituted by rental properties in nonworkers' households (the rental property ownership rate is 16 percent).

As for the distribution of net worth by income group, higher income groups generally have smaller Gini coefficients, at least for income groups between ¥2 and ¥10 million. The Gini coefficient of net worth is 0.41 for the ¥8–¥10 million income group.

Income and wealth distributions do not necessarily overlap. As is clear from table 4.3, there are wide gaps in assetholdings even among those households belonging to the same income group. Flow and stock do not necessarily run parallel. Income and wealth are different, and an argument based on only one of the two is incomplete.[7] Wealth is generally more widely dispersed than income. Consumption expenditures, however, are less widely dispersed than income (see fig. 4.5).[8] And comparing the wealth distribution in Japan with wealth distributions in Europe and the United States, we can say without exaggeration that, in 1984, inequality in Japan was comparatively low.[9]

Variance analysis is one means of understanding the factors governing wealth inequality. In this paper I shall calculate the coefficient of variation (the square of the coefficient of variation divided by 2; call it T) as an index of inequality (see Toyoda 1980). This index can also be decomposed by constituent groups:

$$T = T_b + \Sigma_k w_k \times T_w(k),$$

7. This is a true statement when income is defined on an actual cash income basis. If the service flow of real assets is included in income, the statement is expected to change.

8. The 1984 Gini coefficients are 0.52 for net worth, 0.30 for annual income, and 0.26 for consumption expenditures.

9. According to Wolff (1987) and Atkinson and Harrison (1978), the Gini coefficient for net worth was 0.72 in the United States in 1983 and 0.78 in Great Britain in 1972. The wealth share of the top 5 percent was 49 percent in the United States in 1983 and 55 percent in Great Britain in 1972. On the other hand, the share in Japan was only 25 percent in 1984. It must be borne in mind, however, the the NSFIE is not necessarily the most suitable data source for examining the top wealthholders in Japan.

Table 4.3   **Distribution of Net Worth by Annual Income (%)**

	Annual Income (million yen)						
	< 1.99	2.0–3.99	4.0–5.99	6.0–7.99	8.0–9.99	10.0+	Total
Household							
distribution	5.1	27.8	33.5	18.1	8.5	7.0	100.0
Homeownership rate	64.9	61.5	72.3	85.2	90.3	92.7	74.2
Net worth (million yen):							
< 4.99	32.6	31.3	16.7	7.0	3.4	2.2	17.7
5.0–9.99	13.2	13.2	14.7	8.5	4.5	1.8	11.3
10.0–19.99	24.9	22.5	24.6	21.8	16.0	7.5	21.6
20.0–29.99	14.2	15.3	19.1	23.7	21.0	12.3	18.3
30.0–49.99	11.1	12.0	16.8	23.7	29.4	26.0	18.1
50.0–99.99	3.7	4.9	6.7	12.4	19.9	29.9	9.8
100.0–199.99	.2	.7	1.3	2.5	4.8	14.2	2.5
200.0+	.0	.1	.1	.3	1.0	6.2	.6
Gini coefficient	.53	.53	.47	.42	.41	.47	.52

Source: The 1984 NSFIE and others.

Note: The distribution of net worth is given by % in the column.

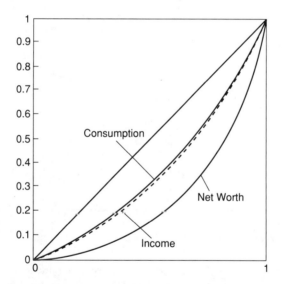

Fig. 4.5   Lorenz curves of income, consumption, and net worth
Source: The 1984 NSFIE and others

where T_b represents the between-group coefficient of variation. The number $T_w(k)$ the within-group coefficient of variation. The number w_k is a weight that is equal to the aggregate wealth share of each population multiplied by the average ratio of net worth (the denominator being the average net worth of the total population).

Table 4.4 presents a T decomposition of the wealth distribution in 1984.

Table 4.4   **Factors Governing Wealth Inequality**

Household Category	Household Distribution (%)	Share in Aggregate Net Worth (%)	Net Worth (¥10,000)		T_w	T_b
			Mean	Median		
Total	100.0	100.0	2,779	1,972	.923	
Homeowner	74.2	95.0	3,558	2,613	.656	
Homerenter	25.8	5.0	536	396	1.256	.113
Age:						
< 24	.7	.2	651	249	1.400	
25–29	4.7	1.5	865	410	.890	
30–34	11.9	6.0	1,405	803	.704	
35–39	16.2	11.4	1,953	1,392	.771	
40–44	15.4	13.5	2,429	1,888	.642	
45–49	13.4	13.9	2,878	2,172	.643	.077
50–54	12.0	14.1	3,255	2,449	.587	
55–59	10.4	15.1	4,042	2,923	.701	
60–64	6.7	10.6	4,416	3,223	.592	
65–69	4.5	7.5	4,617	3,256	1.513	
70–74	2.6	4.0	4,289	3,204	.528	
75+	1.5	2.4	4,438	3,076	.558	
Keihin metropolitan	24.5	32.3	3,665	2,434	.933	
Chukyo/Keihanshin metropolitan	21.6	23.1	2,968	2,157	1.189	.021
Rural	53.9	44.6	2,301	1,813	.574	
Worker	63.2	48.9	2,152	1,617	.611	
Nonworker	30.9	44.7	4,017	2,707	.953	.047
Jobless	5.9	6.4	3,015	2,485	.424	
Annual income (million yen):						
< 1.99	5.1	2.9	1,557	1,142	.580	
2.0–3.99	27.8	17.7	1,774	1,227	.659	
4.0–5.99	33.5	27.1	2,251	1,762	.488	
6.0–7.99	18.1	20.3	3,116	2,497	.424	.147
8.0–9.99	8.5	12.8	4,197	3,261	.392	
10.0+	7.0	19.2	7,604	5,016	.788	

Source: The 1984 NSFIE and others.

Note: Multimember households (including farm households).

Homeownership, age, region, income, and workers'/nonworkers' households are taken up as inequality factors. Simple comparisons of the estimated figures may be misleading since the number of groups used in each classification is different for different factors. Let us begin with factors that can be broken down into two or three groups. First, homeownership affects the wealth differential considerably. While homeowner households account for 74 percent of total households, their aggregate net worth accounts for 95 percent of total net worth. The average net worth of homeowner households is 6.6 times that of home-renter households. Second, the regional differential in the 1984 data is not very large. Twenty-five percent of all households live in the Keihin metropolitan zone. The aggregate net worth owned by those households amounts to ¥262 trillion, or 32 percent of the total. If we divide households into six income groups, we find that income differences may explain 16 percent of the wealth difference.

It should be noted, however, that wealth differentials *within* subpopulations are far larger than those *between* subpopulations. Further analysis is necessary to understand the determinants of wealth inequality fully.

4.4   Distribution of Net Worth by Asset Component

Table 4.5 shows the distribution of net worth by asset component in 1984 for multimember households, including farm households, grouped by assetholdings. Ownership rates and average amounts of each component of assetholdings get larger as net worth increases. Almost all households own consumer durables and monetary assets, however. The most important determinant of the size of assetholdings is whether a household is homeowner or -renter.

For the group with less than ¥10 million in assets, the homeownership rate is extremely low, at 22 percent. For those households with a net worth of ¥10 million or more, the homeownership rate is close to 90 percent; for those with more than ¥20 million, the rate is almost 100 percent.

The modal value of net worth is around ¥17 million. The typical distribution of net worth is such that land accounts for 60 percent, housing structures for 20 percent, consumer durables for 13 percent, and net monetary assets for 7 percent. On the other hand, the assetholdings of the so-called middle-middle class may be shown by the median value. These holdings amount to about ¥20 million in 1984 (fig. 4.6). Land accounts for 60 percent of median net worth, housing structures for 20 percent, monetary assets for 10 percent, and consumer durables for 10 percent.[10]

Average net worth is about ¥28 million, which corresponds roughly to the sixty-seventh percentile. Its distribution is as follows: equity in the home accounts for almost two-thirds, monetary assets for 15 percent (close to 25 percent in gross terms, but liabilities amount to about 10 percent of total net worth), rental property for 10 percent or so, and consumer durables for 7 percent. To move up from the "middle-middle" class, it generally seems necessary to increase monetary assets and/or to acquire rental properties.

Those households having a net worth of ¥100 million or more account for only 3 percent of the total in 1984. They generally have a considerable amount of rental property (the ownership rate is a little less than 70 percent). They have, on average, at least ¥65 million in rental property, which in many cases

10. The median is defined here as the mean value of assetholdings ranked above 45 percent and below 55 percent in the data divided into 100 percentiles.

Table 4.5   **Distribution of Net Worth**

	Net Worth (million yen)									
Asset Category	< 4.9	5–9.9	10–19.9	20–29.9	30–49.9	50–99.9	100–199.9	200+	Total	Median
Distribution of households (% in the row)	18	11	22	18	18	10	2.5	.6	100.0	9.3
Distribution of net worth (% in the column):										
1. Residential land	32.7	38.3	58.7	61.6	61.9	58.5	45.2	30.8	55.5	61.6
2. Home buildings	22.3	19.7	20.3	15.3	11.3	7.4	4.6	2.1	11.0	17.8
3. Rental property	1.7	1.0	1.1	1.9	3.2	11.1	31.3	57.8	11.6	1.6
4. Consumer durables	68.0	22.5	12.5	8.6	6.1	3.8	2.1	1.0	7.2	10.3
5. Real assets (= 1 + 2 + 3 + 4)	124.7	81.4	92.6	87.3	82.6	80.8	83.2	91.6	85.3	91.2
6. Monetary assets (gross)	90.1	55.3	29.4	23.6	23.4	22.5	18.9	10.9	24.3	23.7
7. Liabilities	114.8	36.7	22.0	10.9	6.0	3.3	2.1	2.5	9.6	15.0
8. Monetary assets (net)	−24.7	18.6	7.4	12.7	17.4	19.2	16.8	8.4	14.7	8.8
9. Net worth (= 5 + 8)	100.0	100.0	100.0	100.0	100.0	100.0	100.0	100.0	100.0	100.0

Source: The 1984 NSFIE and others.

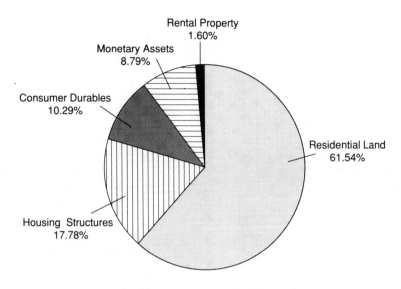

(median net worth = 19.87 million yen)

Fig. 4.6   Distribution of net worth
Source: The 1984 NSFIE and others

exceeds the equity in their own home. This group has, on average, ¥25 million
or so in monetary assets (in net terms).

Table 4.6 presents the distribution of new worth by age group. The aged
households have a mean net worth of around ¥45 million, much larger than
that for younger households. It is questionable, however, whether the elderly
decumulate their assets; table 4.6 is classified by the age of the householder.
The ownership rate of rental property increases with age, and about 15 percent
of those in their early 60s own it.

Overall, the distribution of net worth in elderly households is such that housing equity accounts for nearly 60 percent, rental property for 14–18 percent,
and gross monetary assets for 20 percent.

4.5   Longitudinal Changes in Assetholdings

4.5.1   Longitudinal Changes

How much has each household increased its wealthholdings in recent years?
Here, the 1979 and 1984 estimates are compared. For reference purposes, the
1987 estimates are also examined. The 1987 figures are based on the 1984
NSFIE; only land and share prices are replaced by 1987 data. I used the official
land prices in the Land Price Survey as of 1 January 1988 for land prices.
The mean price/earnings ratio from the end of November 1984 to the end of

Table 4.6   **Distribution of Net Worth by Age (1984)**

Asset Category	< 24	25–29	30–34	35–39	40–44	45–49	50–54	55–59	60–64	65–69	70–74	75+	Total
Mean net worth (10,000 yen)	651	865	1,405	1,953	2,429	2,878	3,255	4,042	4,416	4,617	4,289	4,438	2,779
Median net worth (10,000 yen)	245	415	878	1,439	1,908	2,148	2,407	2,810	3,069	3,094	2,980	2,991	1,987
Distribution of net worth (% in the column):													
1. Residential land	43.4	46.1	56.3	59.0	60.1	57.0	55.0	52.4	52.9	52.3	53.7	54.6	55.5
2. Home buildings	15.9	17.7	17.4	16.7	14.5	12.2	10.2	8.1	6.9	5.5	5.6	5.3	11.0
3. Rental property	4.0	2.3	3.8	7.6	9.0	11.6	11.8	13.9	13.8	18.3	16.8	17.4	11.6
4. Consumer durables	22.0	20.1	13.0	10.0	8.2	7.4	6.8	5.6	4.5	3.7	3.6	3.1	7.2
5. = 1 + 2 + 3 + 4	85.3	86.3	90.6	93.3	91.9	88.2	83.8	80.0	78.0	79.8	79.7	80.4	85.3

Age

December 1987 is used to increase shareholdings uniformly by a factor of 2.0101.

In the 1979 NSFIE, farm households are not included. For an intertemporal comparison, therefore, farm households are excluded from the 1984/1987 figures in the following analysis.

Table 4.7 summarizes the longitudinal changes in assetholdings of multimember households. In the five years from 1979 to 1984, the aggregate amounts of household net worth grew from ¥406 to ¥718 trillion, increasing 1.8 times. During the same period, aggregate net worth increased by ¥312 trillion, which is equivalent to 2.0 times aggregate disposable income (¥156 trillion) in 1984. Capital gains from land between 1984 and 1987 were ¥252 trillion. Adding ¥14 trillion of capital gains from stock shares, household net worth, including only land and shares, increased by ¥266 trillion over the past three years. This amount is equivalent to 1.7 times the level of 1984 disposable income.

4.5.2   Expansion of Wealth Differentials

How much has the wealth differential expanded in Japan recently? Table 4.7 shows the figures for Gini coefficient. According to the table, the Gini coefficient for net worth increased from 0.51 in 1979 to 0.53 in 1984 and 0.60 in 1987. This expansion of the wealth differential is confirmed by the Lorenz curves drawn in figs. 4.7 and 4.8.

The influence of the Gini coefficient for landholdings on the Gini coefficient for net worth has increased. This is because landholdings as a fraction of aggregate net worth have increased from 41 percent in 1979 to 54 percent in 1984 and 65 percent in 1987. Consequently, the Gini coefficient for landholdings alone explains 72 percent of the Gini coefficient for net worth in 1987. The distribution of landholdings is thus of particular interest. The Gini coefficient for landholdings decreased from 0.59 to 0.57 from 1979 to 1984. Inequality as measured by the coefficient of variation (T) changed from 0.79 to 0.81. It is known that Lorenz curves cross each other when two different inequality indexes show opposite movements.

The homeownership rate of multimember households, excluding farm households, increased from 68.3 percent in 1979 to 72.8 percent in 1984. The reduction in the Gini coefficient reflected this increase in the homeownership rate. Meanwhile, the distribution of land among homeowners grew more uneven during the same period. This increased disparity was reflected in the movements of the coefficient of variation.

From 1984 to 1987, the inequality of landholdings expanded rapidly. In terms of the Gini coefficient, inequality jumped to 0.68 from 0.57. The median value of landholdings changed little during the same period. This means that those households ranked high in terms of landholdings further expanded the gap between themselves and those ranked in the middle or lower. The share of aggregate landholdings in the hands of the top 1 percent increased from 8.1 to

Table 4.7   **Longitudinal Changes in Household Asset and Wealthholdings**

Asset Category	Aggregate Sum of Asset Holdings (trillion yen)	Net Worth (10,000 yen)		Gini Coefficient
		Mean	Median	
1979				
1. Residential land	168	706	514	.590
2. Home buildings	53	220	80	.673
3. Rental property	72	303	0	.911
4. Consumer durables	36	150	139	.268
5. = 1 + 2 + 3 + 4	329	1,379	1,033	.535
6. Monetary assets (gross)	118	496	306	.524
7. Liabilities	41	170	4	.812
8. Monetary assets (net)	78	326	220	1.027
9. Net worth (= 5 + 8)	406	1,705	1,216	.513
1984				
1. Residential land	391	1,456	1,081	.566
2. Home buildings	82	306	143	.626
3. Rental property	83	309	0	.967
4. Consumer durables	53	196	185	.266
5. = 1 + 2 + 3 + 4	608	2,268	1,715	.537
6. Monetary assets (gross)	183	682	415	.537
7. Liabilities	73	273	15	.773
8. Monetary assets (net)	109	408	264	1.168
9. Net worth (= 5 + 8)	718	2,676	1,878	.526
1987 (reference)				
1. Residential land	643	2,397	1,211	.675
5. = 1 + 2 + 3 + 4	861	3,209	1,866	.621
6. Monetary assets (gross)	197	736	424	.558
8. Monetary assets (net)	124	463	272	1.118
9. Net worth (= 5 + 8)	985	3,671	2,082	.597

Source: The NSFIE and others.

Note: Multimember households (excluding farm households). The number of households estimated is 23.82 million in 1979 and 26.82 million in 1984 (1987).

16.4 percent. The share of the top 5 percent (10, 20 percent) increased from 27 percent (36.8, 55.7 percent) to 37.7 percent (51.9, 68.7 percent).

Whereas those households (including farm households, but excluding single-member households) with ¥100 million or more of landholdings numbered only 153,000 in the whole country in 1984, they had reached 1.15 million (5.3 percent of the total) by 1987. Those households with ¥50 million (¥30 million) or more of land assets increased from 1.24 million (96 million) in 1984 to 26 million (6.24 million), and their fraction of the total number of households reached 15 percent (30 percent). The modal value of landholdings per homeowner household was ¥10–¥15 million in both 1984 and 1987. The median increased little, growing from less than ¥16 million to about ¥18 million. However, the mean value increased rapidly from ¥21 million to ¥33 mil-

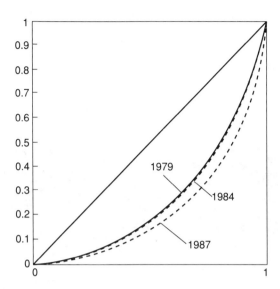

Fig. 4.7   Changes in Lorenz curves (net worth)
Source: The 1984 NSFIE and others

lion over the same three years.[11] This skyrocketing of land prices occurred only in the metropolitan zone surrounding Tokyo.

Those households residing in Toyko or in the three prefectures surrounding Tokyo (Kanagawa, Saitama, and Chiba) account for 23 percent of the total number of households in Japan. The aggregate residential land area held by the households residing in that same area is less than 15 percent of the national sum, but their share of the aggregate value of landholdings rapidly increased from 34 percent in 1984 to 54 percent in 1987. Land prices in Tokyo and the three prefectures overall increased by 2.5 times over this period, and home-owner households in these regions earned capital gains of about ¥230 trillion from residential land. This is a concrete example of the so-called Tokyo-centrism.[12]

The recent wave of skyrocketing land prices swept through the metropolitan zone surrounding Tokyo but did not expand to other regions until 1987.[13] Land price inflation has further distorted asset distribution and simultaneously expanded the regional gap between the metropolitan zone and the rest of the country considerably. This has been one of the reasons for the current situation known as "urban dissatisfaction and rural anxiety."

One aspect of urban dissatisfaction relates to the feelings of employed

11. At the end of 1987, ¥1 million was worth approximately U.S.$7,700 and, in the spring of 1988, nearly U.S.$8,000.
12. Tachibanaki (1989) argues the same point.
13. From 1988 to 1989, that wave expanded to the other two metropolitan zones (Osaka-Kyoto and Nagoya). According to the 1989 NSFIE, the Gini coefficient for home equity was 0.666.

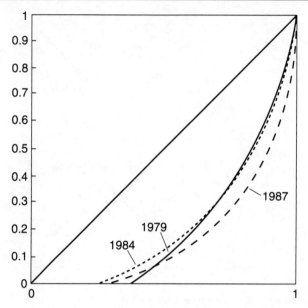

Fig. 4.8   Changes in Lorenz curves (residential land)
Source: The 1984 NSFIE and others

people under 40 living in the metropolitan zone. A good number are from rural areas. If they cannot depend on their parents for land, they must buy their home with their own earnings. Roughly speaking, they cannot afford more than ¥40 million for their own home, but, with this amount, it is almost impossible to buy residential land in the suburbs of Tokyo. Many of them failed to "get aboard," and this contributes to their frustration.[14]

Average landholdings per homeowner household in Tokyo exceeded ¥100 million to reach ¥130 million in 1987. Even the median amounted to ¥91 million, far larger than in the other prefectures. The median residential site of homeowner households in Tokyo is 113 square meters. This is the smallest, together with that in Osaka, and is only half the national median.

4.6   Housing and Living Arrangements of the Elderly

Roughly 90 percent of the elderly in multimember households are homeowners in Japan. It should be noted, however, that the households are classified by the age of the householder; thus, the elderly persons who reside in households that have a younger householder are not included in the elderly group.

The majority of the elderly in single-member households are homeowners, too, although their homeownership rate is not as high; it was around 65 percent

14. *Urban serfs* is the new name given by *Business Week* (9 August 1988) to the employed people in the Tokyo metropolitan zone who do not own their homes. It should be noted that children can expect private transfers, including home equity, from their parents through gifts or bequests.

in 1984 (see Takayama and Arita 1987). It may be safe to say that the share of homeowners with housing liabilities falls sharply with age.

Table 4.8 presents the living arrangements of the elderly in Japan. It shows that a majority of the elderly are living with their sons or daughters. About 60 percent of the population aged 65 and older were living with their children in 1990. Their numbers are showing a gradual increase, from 7.4 million in 1980 to 7.8 million in 1985 and 8.6 million in 1990. The percentage of the elderly population living with their children, however, decreased rapidly during the same period, and, in the near future, the elderly living with their children will become a minority in Japan. Increasingly, there has been a trend for the elderly to live alone as singles or couples, although the percentage who do so was still 37 percent in 1990.[15]

Table 4.9 gives the headship status of the elderly in Japan in 1986. *Headship* refers to the principal income recipient of the household in the Basic Survey of Japanese Living Conditions. It indicates that, overall, 44 percent of the elderly are living as household heads and 17 percent as spouses of household heads. Specifically, 30 percent of the elderly living with their married sons or daughters are heads or spouses of heads, and nearly 70 percent of those living with their unmarried children are living as heads or spouses of heads. Consequently, the majority of the elderly are now living with their children, but they are not always secondary individuals.

Table 4.10 exhibits the number of the elderly living with their children, classified by the annual income of the elderly person on an individual basis. It indicates that the decision to live with the children depends on income. The higher the annual income of the elderly, the less likely they are to live with their children.[16] It is interesting to study the elderly who live with their children and what determines the various living arrangements of the elderly. An intensive study in this field using micro data remains for the future.

4.7   Concluding Remarks

The Japanese are now living longer. At present, one out of every two males and two out of every three females have a life expectancy of over eighty years.

Previously, Japan's elderly population was regarded as uniformly poor and dependent on welfare. Today, however, the living conditions of the elderly are changing. Although the number of the elderly blessed with high incomes and considerable assets is still small, it is steadily growing. Home equity is the major asset of most elderly households. They are "home rich but cash poor." There is a need to liquidate their home assets by using equity conversion

15. Table 4.8 excludes the elderly in the institutionalized population, who amounted to 202,000, or 1.6 percent of the population aged 65 and older, in 1985.

16. It might be interesting to consider the children's income as another determinant of the living arrangement.

Table 4.8   **Living Arrangements of the Elderly (65 and older)**

	1980	1985	1990
Total number (millions)	10.7	12.1	14.5
Single (%)	8.5	9.3	11.2
Couple (%)	19.6	23.0	25.7
Living with:			
Married children (%)	52.5	47.9	41.9
Unmarried children (%)	16.5	16.7	17.8
Living with relatives other than children (%)	2.8	2.8	3.3
Others (%)	.2	.2	.2
Total (%)	100.0	100.0	100.0

Source: Basic Survey of Japanese Living Conditions (Ministry of Health and Welfare).

Table 4.9   **Headship Status of the Elderly (65 and older)**

	Elderly (1,000) (1)	Household Head (1,000) (2)	His/Her Spouse (1,000) (3)	(2)/(1) (%)	(3)/(1) (%)
Total	12,626	5,529	2,132	43.8	16.9
Single	1,281	1,281	...	100.0	...
Couple	2,784	1,717	1,066	61.7	38.3
Living with:					
Married children	5,897	1,218	624	20.7	10.6
Unmarried children	2,219	1,122	390	50.6	17.6
Living with relatives other than children	409	176	50	43.0	12.2
Others	37	14	1	37.8	2.7

Source: 1986 Basic Survey of Japanese Living Conditions (Ministry of Health and Welfare).

schemes such as reverse annuity mortgages. The elderly are better off than the young or middle aged in terms of assets held. Owing to the recent rise in the value of land, the difference in assetholdings has widened between generations. In the current situation, even young people who work all their lives will never be able to buy their own homes in the suburbs of Tokyo if they cannot depend on their parents for land. Thus, there seems to be a dispersion occurring in the former goal of equity in the distribution of income.

In the past, the elderly could be said to be riding on the top of "a portable shrine." From now on, they will be required to play a different role. The elderly can no longer just be the recipients of Social Security and social services. They will also have to start contributing to Social Security within their means. The increased wealth/income ratio will require changes in the present tax balance

Table 4.10   **Number of the Elderly Living with Their Children by Income Class (65 and older)**

Annual Income (million yen)	Number of the Aged Having Their Children (1,000) (1)	Living with Their Children (1,000) (2)	Living Separately but in the Same Residential Site as Their Children (1,000) (3)	(2)/(1) (%)	(3)/(1) (%)
0	2,000	1,764	40	88.2	2.0
0.1–0.3	2,605	2,103	54	80.7	2.1
0.4–1.1	2,288	1,451	65	63.4	2.8
1.2–1.7	1,103	650	51	58.9	4.6
1.8–2.3	741	433	43	58.4	5.8
2.4–3.5	736	413	38	56.1	5.2
3.6–4.9	312	177	26	56.7	8.3
5.0–9.9	261	132	22	50.6	8.4
10.0+	101	54	4	53.5	3.9
Total	10,147	7,177	344	70.7	3.4

Source: 1986 Basic Survey of Japanese Living Conditions (Ministry of Health and Welfare).
Note: Annual income is that of the elderly on an individual basis.

of income, wealth, and consumption, with lower taxes on income and higher taxes on wealth and consumption.[17]

References

Atkinson, A. B., and A. J. Harrison. 1978. *Distribution of personal wealth in Britain.* Cambridge: Cambridge University Press.
Rao, V. M. 1969. Two decompositions of the concentration ratio. *Journal of the Royal Statistical Society,* Ser. A, 132, no. 3:418–25.
Tachibanaki, T. 1989. Japan's new policy agenda: Coping with unequal asset distribution. *Journal of Japanese Studies* 15, no. 2:345–69.
Takayama, N. 1979. Poverty, income inequality, and their measures: Professor Sen's axiomatic approach reconsidered. *Econometrica* 47, no. 3:747–59.
———. 1992. *The greying of Japan: An economic perspective on public pensions.* Tokyo: Kinokuniya; Oxford: Oxford University Press.
Takayama, N., and F. Arita. 1987. Economic aspects of pension beneficiaries in Japan (in Japanese). *Hitotsubashi Review* 97, no. 6:805–27; 98, no. 1:39–68.
Takayama, N., F. Funaoka, F. Ohtake, M. Sekiguchi, and T. Shibuya. 1989. Household

17. Takayama and Kitamura (1994) show changes in wealthholdings in Japanese households from 1979 to 1989, using the micro data from the 1979, 1984, and 1989 NSFIEs, clarifying how much the three factors flow savings, capital gains, and intergenerational transfers contributed to the wealth increase during these years.

assetholdings and the saving rate in Japan (in Japanese). *Keizai Bunseki* (Economic Planning Agency), no. 116:1–93.

Takayama, N., F. Funaoka, F. Ohtake, M. Sekiguchi, T. Shibuya, H. Ueno, and K. Kubo. 1990. Household assetholdings including Social Security wealth in Japan (in Japanese). *Keizai Bunseki* (Economic Planning Agency), no. 118:1–73.

Takayama, N., and Y. Kitamura. 1994. Household saving behavior in Japan. In *International savings,* ed. J. Poterba. Chicago: University of Chicago Press.

Toyoda, T. 1980. Decomposability of inequality measures. *Economic Studies Quarterly* 31, no. 3:207–16.

U.S. Department of Commerce. Bureau of the Census. 1986. "Household Wealth and Asset Ownership: 1984." *Current Population Reports: Household Economic Studies,* Ser. P-70, no. 7.

Wolff, E. N. 1987. Estimates of household wealth inequality in the U.S., 1962–1983. *Review of Income and Wealth* 33, no. 3:231–56.

5   Problems of Housing the Elderly in the United States and Japan

Daniel L. McFadden

The main issues in housing the elderly in the United States are *affordability* and *suitability*. In the aggregate, there are a sufficient number of housing units for the population, and sufficient capacity in the construction industry, to meet any foreseeable increases in demand. However, sharp increases in housing costs in the past two decades, fueled by rising urban land prices and a reduction in government support for low-income housing, have created distributional problems in housing the poor at prices they can afford. The most graphic evidence of this problem is the well-publicized plight of "homeless" households. Changing population demographics are also creating distributional problems. The "graying" of the United States, with a rising share of the population over 65 years of age and an increasing number of the very old, creates new demand for small housing units, with such amenities as level entries and first-floor bathrooms that are suitable for frail or disabled individuals. The demand for these units concentrates in Southern and Western areas favored by retirees. In addition, there is a rapidly growing demand for "quasi-institutional" housing that provides health and living assistance, such as "congregate" housing, nursing homes, and "aided living" in private housing units.

The gross demographics of the U.S. population are responsible for much of the strain on the housing market and are also an important factor in the evolution of housing costs. Table 5.1 gives population statistics through 1985 and "middle-series" projections of the U.S. Bureau of the Census through 2030. The percentage of the population age 65 and older has risen sharply since 1970 and will continue to rise rapidly for the next forty years. While the annual growth rate (AGR) of the total population is less than 1 percent from 1970 to

Daniel L. McFadden is professor of economics at the University of California, Berkeley, and a research associate of the National Bureau of Economic Research.

This research was supported by a grant from the National Institute on Aging to the National Bureau of Economic Research. Chunrong Ai provided research assistance. Miki Seko provided much of the data for comparisons of the United States and Japan.

Table 5.1   U.S. Population by Age

	Total Pop. (mil.)	Pop. 65+ (mil.)	% of Total	Pop. 75+ (mil.)	% of Total	Ratio of 75+ to 65+
1970	205.1	20.1	9.8	7.6	3.7	37.9
1975	216.0	22.7	10.5	8.8	4.1	38.7
1980	227.8	25.7	11.3	10.1	4.4	39.1
1985	239.3	28.5	11.9	11.5	4.8	40.4
1990	249.7	31.7	12.7	13.7	5.5	43.1
1995	259.6	33.9	13.1	15.4	5.9	45.4
2000	268.0	34.9	13.0	17.2	6.4	49.4
2005	275.9	37.0	13.4	18.0	6.5	48.8
2010	284.0	39.2	13.8	18.8	6.7	48.2
2015	290.2	44.9	15.5	20.2	7.0	45.0
2020	296.6	51.4	17.3	21.7	7.3	42.1
2025	300.6	57.6	19.2	25.5	8.5	44.2
2030	304.6	64.6	21.2	30.0	9.9	46.5
AGR (%):						
1970–90	.99	2.30		2.99		
1990–2010	.64	1.07		1.59		
2010–30	.35	2.53		2.36		

Source: U.S. Bureau of the Census, *Current Population Reports,* ser. P-25, no. 952.
Note: AGR = average growth rate.

2030, the AGR of the population 65 and older over the same period is almost 2 percent. The population 75 and older has an even more rapid growth rate of 2.3 percent over this period. A particular feature of the demographics is the large cohort of "baby boom" individuals born between 1945 and 1960, who swell the 65 and over population starting in 2010 and the 75 and older population starting in 2020.

In the aggregate, there have been sharp increases in real housing prices in the United States since 1970 and correlated changes in the net cost of shelter. Table 5.2 gives indices of the real price of housing (calculated from components of the GNP implicit price deflator and reflecting the cost of new residential construction) and the price of shelter (calculated from components of the consumer price index and reflecting both rental costs and the cost of purchasing new and existing residences). Both indices increased rapidly in the years around 1980 and since then have generally maintained the higher level. Explanations that have been given for the price increases include (1) a substantial demographic shift in the demand for housing, owing to the baby boom generation reaching the age of household formation and home purchase, (2) significant foreign investment in real estate, particularly from Hong Kong and Japan, which escalated land prices, and (3) speculative bubbles fueled by these fundamentals.

It is a matter of considerable speculation as to whether the current high costs of shelter will be relatively permanent or will reverse quickly as the "baby boomers" pass beyond the stage of acquiring their first house. The two possibilities have quite different economic implications for the elderly. At present, many elderly households have out-of-pocket shelter costs that are a relatively high fraction of current income but also considerable wealth generated by capital gains on residential property. One housing policy issue has been whether, in light of the relatively high transactions costs associated with moves, the financial market provides adequate instruments for elderly households to convert equity in residences to cover operating costs. Reverse annuity mortgages have been tested as a mechanism for providing this liquidity. Related policy initiatives involve deferral of out-of-pocket costs, such as property taxes, until the residence is sold.

The baby boom cohort will face a more difficult situation in old age than the current generation of elderly. Their real estate purchases will have been of fully appreciated property in many cases. If housing prices fall, their out-of-pocket costs will be lower, but their wealth will be substantially reduced by capital losses. If housing prices stay high, they will face substantial out-of-pocket costs without a cushion of capital gains–created wealth.

The housing needs of the elderly, in terms of geographic location, size, and amenities, are likely to create pressures that increase their shelter costs relative to the overall housing market. Demographic shifts of the elderly from the Northern and Eastern United States to the South and West have been strong and are likely to continue, driving up the price of Sun Belt "retirement" homes relative to Midwestern "family" homes. The increasing numbers of older elderly, who are disabled or frail, create demand for dwellings with features such as access to shopping, absence of steps, and availability of home and health care assistance. The effect of elevated housing prices is partially mitigated for the elderly by some structural characteristics of their demand—they need less space, and they can relocate in areas or regions with lower housing costs.

Table 5.2　　　　　**Real Price of Housing, United States**

	GNP Implicit Price Deflator	CPI Residential Shelter Cost		GNP Implicit Price Deflator	CPI Residential Shelter Cost
1970	.881	.911	1980	1.043	.979
1971	.878	.910	1981	1.028	.991
1972	.886	922	1982[a]	1.000	1.000
1973	.905	.908	1983	.984	.991
1974	.923	.897	1984	.985	.997
1975	.914	.903	1985	.977	1.016
1976	.919	.901	1986	.975	1.052
1977	.960	.902	1987	.987	1.063
1978	1.006	.924	1988	.989	1.071
1979	1.036	.945			

Source: The GNP implicit price is the ratio of the residential fixed investment deflator and the GNP deflator. The CPI shelter price is the ratio of the total shelter index and the CPI index. The first series is from July issues of the *Survey of Current Business;* the second series is from *Monthly Labor Review.*

[a]Base.

The information in this paper on the housing and economic status of the elderly is drawn primarily from the 1984 wave of the Panel Study on Income Dynamics (PSID). This panel was started in 1968 with approximately 5,000 households and has since interviewed these and split-off households annually. My analysis is based on 2,089 households that had a household member aged 35 or older in 1968. Of these, 960 had a household member aged 50 or older, and 193 had a member aged 65 or older, in 1968. The original panel oversampled the poor and minorities. Table 5.3 describes some of the demographic features of the PSID sample, with U.S. population statistics shown for comparison. The effects of oversampling the poor and minorities are minor, and the panel appears to be fairly representative of U.S. households.

Section 5.1 of this paper outlines the methodology used to measure wealth and shelter costs, taking into account the contribution of transactions costs and the rather complex system of tax entitlements and offsets enjoyed by homeowners in the United States. Section 5.2 summarizes information on aggregate holdings of various assets by the elderly; sections 5.3 and 5.4 discuss the distribution of these holdings. Section 5.5 provides information on user costs and the distribution of shelter burdens that they imply for elderly households. Section 5.6 gives data on features of the dwellings occupied by the elderly and discusses mobility. Section 5.7 examines the effects on user costs and shelter burdens of several of the tax policies that have been adopted, or are under discussion, in the United States, Section 5.8 compares the housing problems of U.S. and Japanese elderly along several dimensions. Section 5.9 concludes.

5.1   Household Wealth and Shelter Costs: Methodology

An initial picture of the economic and housing status of the elderly can be obtained from statistics on current income and assets, out-of-pocket housing costs, and physical characteristics of dwellings. I summarize some of these statistics, from government sources and from the PSID. Going beyond these statistics, I try to account for the effects on economic well-being of mobility with its associated transactions costs, tax treatment of home ownership, and expectations about mortality, health, income, and housing out-of-pocket costs.

5.1.1   Income and Wealth

First consider the wealth of elderly households. This will include not only the net worth of current real and financial assets but also the expected present value of the future stream of non-asset-generated income (i.e., labor income, Social Security and other transfers, and employer-provided pension income). To account for differences in life expectancy across households and differences in expected present value of nonasset income expectations, I convert assets and the nonasset income stream into life annuities.[1]

---

1. For a couple, a double life annuity is calculated that provides a flat income stream as long as one of the two individuals survives.

Table 5.3   **Characteristics of the Elderly Population, Age 65 and Older**

	PSID	Population
Individuals age 65+:[a]		
% 75+	36.7	38.2[b]
% white	81.3	90.2[b]
% female	59.8	58.7[b]
% married, spouse present	59.9	53.5[b]
% widowed or divorced	38.1	39.6[b]
Households age 65+:[c]		
% 75+	47.0	41.1[d]
% homeowners	65.9	75.0[e]
% of owners mortgage free	80.4	83.0[e]
Median house value, owners, 1983 ($)	48,600[f]	48,800[d]
% of income on shelter:		
Age 65–74	. . .	36.6[g]
Age 75+	. . .	35.5[g]
Monthly household income ($):		
Age 65–74	1,362[f]	1,164[h]
Age 75+	1,189[f]	828[h]
Net worth total ($):		
Age 65–74	78,598[f]	63,597[h]
Age 75+	81,639[f]	55,178[h]
Net worth excluding home equity ($):		
Age 65–74	47,546	19,979[h]
Age 75+	28,374	17,025[h]

[a]PSID, $N = 1,054$.

[b]1986 proportions: Current Population Survey, 1987.

[c]PSID, $N = 823$.

[d]1983 means from U.S. Bureau of the Census, "Financial Characteristics of the Housing Inventory," *Current Housing Reports,* ser. H-150-83 (1983).

[e]1983 means from U.S. Bureau of the Census, *Current Population Reports,* seri. P-60, no. 152 (1986).

[f]PSID, 1984, sample tabulations.

[g]1984 means from U.S. Bureau of the Census, "Consumer Expenditure Survey: Interview Survey, 1984," Bulletin no. 2267 (Washington, D.C., 1986).

[h]1984 medians from U.S. Bureau of the Census, "Household Wealth and Asset Ownership, 1984," *Current Population Reports,* ser. P-70, no. 7 (1986). A median family income of $1,518 per month, units age 65 and older, excluding unattached individuals, in 1984 is given in *Current Population Reports,* ser. P-60. The Survey of Consumer Finances gives 1983 net worths as follows: 65–74: mean, $125,184; median, $50,181; 75+: mean, $72,985; median, $35,939.

The 1984 PSID provides an inventory of assets. However, expectations of the future nonasset income stream must be modeled. I assume that income expectations are determined by current income and demographic characteristics. The method, described in detail in Ai et al. (1989), assumes that a household forms expectations using the historical relative income streams of other households from the past that were then the same demographically as this household is now. I assume that there is no information available to the household that is not available to the econometrician, that there were no macro shocks through the period of the PSID panel that make the life-cycle income patterns observed therein unrepresentative, and that relative income expectations are stationary once trends are accounted for. Then, the ex post distribution of relative incomes for older households in the PSID coincides with the ex ante expectation of younger households. I estimate this ex post distribution for total income and for income components: labor, transfer, and nonasset.

The income profiles starting from year t with a head of age A_t are assumed to have the form

$$(1) \qquad y_{t+s} = y_t \exp\left\{\sum_{j\in J} \theta_j \left[d_j(A_{t+s}) - d_j(A_t)\right]\right\}$$

where $s = 1, 2, \ldots$ denotes future years, the θ_j are coefficients, and the $d_j(A)$ form a quadratic spline that permits a flexible description of the life-cycle income profile. This system is log-linear in parameters and is estimated using PSID data stacked by household, and by year within household, conditioned on all income variables appearing in the regression being positive. The cases of zero income almost all correspond to nonsurvival, and for these the regression conditioning corresponds to the conditional forecast needed.

This formulation of the life-cycle income profile and estimation method differs from more common autoregressive forecasting models in that I use a direct s-period-ahead forecast rather than an s-step-ahead iterative forecast. The reason I do this is that I anticipate the existence of persistent individual effects, which can be approximated in an autoregressive model only with a lengthy lag. A second variation on conventional analysis is that I combine labor and pension income and do not condition on retirement. Thus, this model gives unconditional income profiles that incorporate sample information on retirement patterns and their interdependence on earnings and pension profiles. This approach circumvents the necessity of specifying a correct structural model of the retirement process and is robust to the nature of this structure. One drawback is that I am unable to do policy analysis of housing behavior response to structural changes in retirement programs or to forecast housing demand in a future where structural changes in retirement programs have occurred.

Income forecasts from the model are conditioned only on initial household demographics, not on survival of individual household members. Thus, they incorporate the expected effect on income on nonsurvival of head or spouse. This avoids structural modeling of, say, income conditioned on the event of future widowhood. However, in order to estimate the model using the eleven-year window from 1974 through 1984 in which the PSID has consistent income data and associated demographics, I assume that households treat their initial demographic state as time invariant. For example, a household consisting of a couple with head aged 60 is postulated to assume that changes in its income profile between age 80 and age 90 will resemble the changes over a decade of *couples* that start with head age 80. In fact, there is a substantial probability that this head will die before age 80, and the household's income profile in this future decade will more closely resemble that of widows that start at age 80. Hence my assumption is not very satisfactory. A better solution would be to use data on full life cycles in which future income profiles could be constructed conditioned on demographic status at each age.

5.1.2   Net Shelter Costs

The first component in a calculation of the expected present value of user cost of housing is a stream of out-of-pocket costs that will be incurred as long as the current dwelling is occupied. For renters, this is simply rent plus utilities. In a few states, there is some state income-tax offset for rental expenses. For homeowners, the out-of-pocket costs include mortgage payments, real estate taxes, utilities, maintenance, and insurance. The deductibility of homeowner interest and real estate tax expenses in federal income taxes, and some state income taxes, is an important offsetting factor in calculating out-of-pocket expenses.

The second major element in user cost is the transaction cost associated with moves, purchases, or sales. A house purchase involves loan fees, title insurance, and other closing costs. A sale involves real estate broker's fees. Moving between dwellings involves direct moving expenses, less easily measured time and money costs in setting up the household, and psychic costs of disruption.

A third component in user cost for owners is capital gains on the housing asset. An increase in the present value of net equity resulting from sale of a home at a future date, rather than immediately, is an additional component that offsets the cost of ownership. Calculation of capital gains is complicated by their tax treatment, particularly a one-time exemption for elderly households that was in effect during the period of this study. A second complication arises in the treatment of homes sold as part of the household's estate after the death of the household. In this analysis, I take the "Ricardian equivalence" view that bequests, including home equity, have utility to the household and are determined jointly with lifetime consumption. With further simplifications, this leads me to treat capital gains from sale of a house symmetrically whether the household is living or not. Alternatively, the household may treat bequests as the unintended residual of a "self-insured annuity" that contributes little to utility. This would increase the perceived cost of options in which the household owns its home until death, at least to the extent that increases in home equity are not offset dollar for dollar by decreases in liquid assets.

In calculating the present value of expected user cost of housing, important factors will be the discount rate that the consumer uses, the length of time the household stays in the current dwelling, and the likely transitions after the household leaves the current dwelling. First, the Fisherian consumer in an imperfect capital market will use a discount rate that depends endogenously on lending or borrowing status, credit limits, and instruments available in each period. The length of time the household stays in the dwelling will be influenced by largely exogenous factors such as the death of one or more household members, job changes or retirements, and changes in health status (i.e., ability to live unaided in a dwelling with specific characteristics). It will also be influenced by endogenous response to factors such as realized cost of current dwelling and alternatives and life-cycle issues involving current income, portfolio of assets including equity in owner-occupied housing, and bequest motives.

The approach taken in this paper is to calculate an annualized expected present value of user cost taking all the factors above into account, in a fashion that mimics the calculations of a representative household. However, the endogenous interactions between life-cycle income and consumption patters that enter the discount rate, and the endogenous decisions of length of stay that would enter the actual calculation of a consumer that solves a life-cycle dynamic stochastic program, are replaced by exogenous rates and probabilities based on statistical averages from a population of similarly situated individuals.

The formula that I use for calculating user cost of housing is simply the value of a life annuity that has the same expected present value as the actual stream of housing costs, including capital gains and losses on transactions during the household's lifetime, and including capital gains and losses from liquidation of the housing component of bequests on the death of the household. In this formula, future costs are discounted at a rate reflecting the market interest rate and the household's survival probability. I consider discrete choice among three dwelling sizes, as well as tenure, so that in each year the household has the alternative of not moving or of moving to one of the six possible size/tenure combinations. I incorporate a relatively complete model of the offsets resulting from federal and state treatment of property taxes, mortgage interest, and capital gains. I incorporate concrete models of expectations about future incomes, price levels, interest rates, and mobility. These models assume that households are Bayesian "imitators" who use the experiences of similarly situated households in the past to forecast the distribution of their own responses in the future. I note that these are not necessarily "rational expectations," nor in the implementation are they based solely on information available prior to the decision year.

5.2   Income and Wealth

Households in the United States enter the "postretirement" phase of their life cycle facing future income streams that are sharply lower than their life-cycle peak. Social Security income, private pensions, and public assistance programs are, however, sufficient to assure that most elderly households are not in poverty. For many households, owner-occupied housing is the only major asset. Asset holdings decline with age, but not as rapidly as life-cycle theories without strong bequest motives would suggest.

The money income of households, classified by age, is shown in table 5.4. Income levels for those over age 65 are less than 60 percent of income levels

Table 5.4   **Money Income of Households, 1984**

	All Households	55–64	65+
Mean:			
CES, urban units[a]	24,578	26,989	14,900[b]
PSID[c]		24,361[d]	13,688
CPR[e]	26,518	29,465	17,649
Median:			
CPR[e]	22,804	24,677	12,797
SIPP[f]	20,124	21,864	12,252

[a]Consumer Expenditure Interview Survey.
[b]Income per unit is $16,815 for age 65–74, $12,442 for age 75+.
[c]Panel Study of Income Dynamics, unweighted sample.
[d]Ages 50–64.
[e]U.S. Bureau of the Census, *Current Population Reports,* ser. P-60, no. 151.
[f]Survey of Income and Program Participation.

in the preceding decade of life and continue to decline with age. The lower income levels in the PSID reflect the original oversampling of poor households for this panel. The substantial rightward skew of the income distribution shows in the excess of means over medians. Figures 5.1 shows total money income plotted as a function of age, using PSID data.[2] Also shown on this graph are nonasset income (e.g., labor income, pensions, and transfers) and transfer income (primarily Social Security). Total income falls sharply until age 70. The United States has a high rate of early retirement, more than one-third by age 62, which is evident in the early decline in nonasset nontransfer income.

The assets of households and their net worth are hard to measure accurately from survey data, owing to the highly skewed distribution of assets in the population, ambiguity in the definition and valuation of assets, and reporting biases. Table 5.5 gives the net worth of households from different sources; the variations reflect some of the difficulties of measurement. The net worth figures from the PSID exclude the value of employer-provided pension funds, the major reason that these figures are lower than the other surveys. Truncation of asset responses at the upper end may also lower PSID means. Also, recall that the PSID oversamples poor households; these are not reweighted. The Survey of Consumer Finance oversamples, then reweights, wealthy households, making it more precise in determining the effect of the upper tail on mean net worth. All the sources show net worth falling with age, although not as rapidly as life-cycle consumption models without a bequest motive would suggest.

Using the method for calculation for the expected present value of nonasset income described in section 5.1, I obtain the estimates of mean and median nonasset wealth and total wealth for the PSID population that are shown in the

2. The curve is fitted using a quadratic spline with knots every five years, using all sample households in 1984 for which income data are complete.

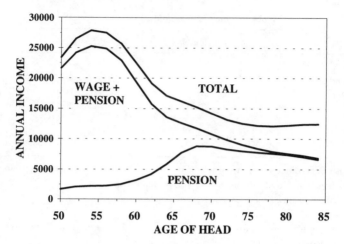

Fig. 5.1   Age profile of income (PSID, 1984)

second panel of table 5.5. Wealth is dominated by the nonasset component, which includes labor and transfer income and employer-provided pensions. The exhibit shows that, for the 50–65 age range, only 19 percent of wealth is in financial and real assets. This figure rises to 39 percent in the over-65 age range, as labor income disappears, but the largest share of wealth still comes from transfer income, primarily Social Security.

The ratio of wealth to income rises with age: the ratio of mean net worth to income, using the Survey of Consumer Finances measure of net worth and the PSID measure of income, is 4.91 for households in the 50–64 bracket and 7.75 in the over-65 bracket. A different view of household wealth is obtained by expressing it as a life annuity; this is done in the final panel of table 5.5. In the 50–64 age range, current income is substantially above the annuity value of wealth. This would then be a period of rapid accumulation for households seeking a flat or annuitized life-cycle expenditure level. In the over-65 age range, the annuity value of wealth exceeds current income, indicating that households are not disaccumulating assets rapidly enough to end their lives with zero bequests. The difference in these numbers is not large and is within the margin of error in the wealth calculation. However, other data tend to confirm the reluctance of the elderly to disaccumulate assets.

5.3   The Distribution of Income and Wealth

The United States is characterized generally by a moderately unequal income distribution and a strongly unequal wealth distribution. Inequality is reduced for the elderly compared to a younger population, primarily because of social support programs. Figure 5.2 shows the distribution of current income

Table 5.5   **Net Worth of Households ($1984)**

		Age of Head	
	Total	50–64	65+
No. of households (mil.)	86.8	12.9[a]	18.3
Mean net worth:			
SCF, 1983[b]	66,050	119,714[a]	106,016
PSID, 1984[c]		46,325	44,266
Median net worth:			
SCF, 1983[b]	24,574	55,587[a]	44,934
SIPP, 1984[d]	32,667	73,664[a]	60,266
Mean wealth:			
Nonasset, PSID		195,018	69,209
Total, PSID		241,343	113,475
Median wealth:			
Nonasset, PSID		82,852	42,622
Total, PSID		121,167	61,215
Mean wealth annuity:			
Nonasset, PSID		14,543	8,232
Total, PSID		17,104	14,840
Current income, PSID		24,361[a]	13,688

[a]Age 55–64.
[b]Survey of Consumer Finances, Federal Reserve.
[c]Panel Study on Income Dynamics.
[d]Survey of Income and Program Participation.

by age group and figure 5.3 the distribution of wealth.[3] Only 8.2 percent of households in the 55–64 age group and 7.0 percent of households in the over-65 age group are below the poverty line,[4] compared with an 11.4 percent rate for all households. However, the lowest 20 percent of the age 50–64 population receives only 3.8 percent of the income. There is greater equality among the older elderly: the lowest 20 percent of the over-65 population receives 5.1 percent of the income. Wealth is distributed almost the same for the two age groups, with the lowest 20 percent of the population holding about 2.5 percent of the wealth. The wealth definition used here, including nonasset wealth, implies far less wealth inequality than if only real and financial assets are considered.

3. Figures 5.2 and 5.3 are derived from the following sources: total household income, including transfer income but excluding income in kind, for all sample PSID households in 1984; total household wealth in 1984, including real and financial assets *and* the expected present value of future earnings and pensions, for all sample PSID households for which the income projections described in sec. 5.1 could be carried through. The income and wealth distributions are estimated using a cubic spline with knots at the deciles.

4. The poverty line, or annual need standard, varies with region and household composition, but the overall mean using the distributions of locations and demographics in the PSID is $3,166 for the 50–64 age group and $2,354 for the over-65 age group.

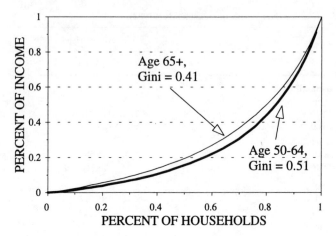

Fig. 5.2   Income distribution

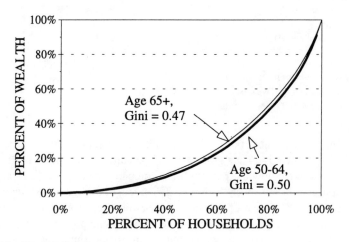

Fig. 5.3   Wealth distribution

5.4   The Composition of Income and Wealth

The primary sources of income of elderly households are Social Security, asset income, and pensions. Table 5.6 shows the percentage breakdown for the PSID sample and corresponding population statistics. The PSID sample relies substantially more on Social Security, and substantially less on earnings, than is true for the over-65 age group as a whole. This reflects the fact that this sample is poorer, and somewhat older, than the corresponding population group.

Table 5.6   Sources of Income, Households Age 65 and Older in 1984

	%	%
Social security and pensions	57.9[a]	46.9[b]
Asset income	28.1	23.7
Earnings	14.0	28.6

[a]PSID, $N = 806$ households with complete data. For the 50–65 age group, the sources are 11.8 percent Social Security and pensions, 11.5 percent asset income, and 73.9 percent earnings.
[b]U.S. Bureau of the Census, *Current Population Reports,* ser. P-60 (1984).

The composition of assetholdings is shown in table 5.7. This table gives the percentage of the population holding assets in each category and the median level among the holders of each asset. Home equity is the only major asset for many elderly households. Table 5.8 summarizes the percentage distribution of assets. In this exhibit, "cash" includes interest-bearing accounts, bonds, and other "liquid" assets.

The presence of an asset inventory along with income in the PSID data allows estimation of implicit rates of return by regressing income on assetholdings. Deviations of these implicit returns from market returns may indicate biases in reporting. The results of this regression are given in table 5.9 and are close to market rates (taking into account reinvestment of earnings).

5.5   Shelter Costs

The mean costs of housing gradually decline for older households in a cross-sectional survey. This correlation contains some cohort effect but mainly reflects the reduced needs for space of households with fewer members and adjustments to live in lower-cost areas. However, income drops much more sharply, with the result that the share of income spent on housing rises. A substantive policy question in the United States is whether there are remediable market imperfections that prevent older households from substituting consumption away from housing as income falls.

Table 5.10 gives the share of income devoted to providing shelter, by age. The CES (Consumer Expenditure Survey) share shows a clear upward trend with age. This does not occur in a measure of out-of-pocket cost share in the PSID, owing to reductions in average mortgage payments with increasing age combined with increasingly stringent selection by the income criteria. However, when annualized user cost is considered, there is an increase in housing share for the elderly. Because these annualized costs reflect future as well as current outlays, they do not change as rapidly with age as the CES measure of current expenditures. The inclusion of taxes and transactions costs in the PSID

Table 5.7   **Composition of Assetholdings**

	Total		Age 55–64		Age 65+	
	% Holding	Median among Holders (1984$)	% Holding	Median among Holders (1984$)	% Holding	Median among Holders (1984$)
Savings accounts	71.8	3,066	76.0	7,340	77.5	13,255
Bonds, insurance	8.5	9,471	11.5	13,559	11.6	18,144
Checking accounts	53.9	449	55.4	568	48.5	651
Stocks	20.0	3,892	25.5	5,662	21.1	6,882
Business assets	12.8		15.1		5.1	
Automobiles	85.8		89.1		71.4	
Equity in home	64.3	40,597	80.2	54,059	73.0	46,192
Rental property	9.5		15.4		10.8	
Other real estate	10.0		15.9		8.4	
Government bonds	15.0		18.3		11.3	
Retirement accounts	19.5	4,805	38.9	6,390	6.5	6,369
Debt			37.3	2,350	19.0	1,987
Households (mil.)	86.8		12.9		18.2	

Source: Survey of Income and Program Participation, 1984, except debt data from the PSID, 1984 (age group 50–65).

Table 5.8   **Assets of Household Age 65 and Older in 1984**

% distribution of net worth:		
Home equity	50.3[a]	38.6[b]
Other real estate	7.4	11.2
Cash	33.2	30.3
Stocks	4.1	8.6
Business	3.1	4.5
Other	1.9	6.8
Debt as a % of net worth	1.9	. . .

[a]PSID, 1984, $N = 693$ with complete data.

[b]1984 data, U.S. Bureau of the Census, "Household Wealth and Asset Ownership," *Current Population Reports,* ser. P-70.

user cost measure is apparently the reason that it gives higher shares overall than the CES.

The relative user cost of owning to renting is expected to rise with age since owning involves transactions costs that must be amortized over a shorter period. Comparing these costs for dwellings of comparable size, averaged over the PSID sample, we find that this increase does occur but that it is relatively small. The reason appears to be that remaining life expectancy is sufficiently long, even for the very elderly, to make the amortized transactions cost small relative to out-of-pocket costs. These results are given in table 5.11. Also shown in this table is the ratio of the user cost of moving versus staying in

Table 5.9   **Relation of Asset Income to Assetholdings, 1984**

		Ordinary Least Squares Dependent Variable: Asset Income	
	Independent Variable	Estimate	Standard Error
	Cash	.0504	.0029
	Bonds	.0257	.0005
	Business nonlabor income	.0259	.0037
	Real property	.0251	.0021
	Stocks	.0458	.0025

Note: $N = 823$. $R^2 = 0.840$.

Table 5.10   **Shelter Share of Income**

	50–65	65–74	75+
CES, shelter and utilities[a]	19.8	24.0	26.7
PSID out of pocket[b]	20.8	17.6	18.6
PSID user cost[c]	27.1	33.7	33.4

[a]Consumer Expenditure Survey, 1984, share of shelter plus utility expenditures. The first age group is 55–64.

[b]Panel Study on Income Dynamics, 1982, annual expenditures for shelter and utilities, for households with $5,000 or more per year income.

[c]Panel Study on Income Dynamics, 1984, annualized user cost, median share.

Table 5.11   **User Cost Ratios**

	Age Group		
	50–65	65–74	75+
PSID, mean ratio of owner to renter user cost	1.45	1.54	1.58
PSID, mean ratio of mover to stayer user cost	1.17	1.17	1.14

dwellings of comparable size. Despite the amortization of moving costs over a shorter time for the elderly, this ratio does not change significantly with age. The absence of dramatic shifts in relative prices of housing alternatives with age suggests that housing changes will be induced primarily by changing income and by changing health and demographic status.

5.6   Housing Status and Mobility of the Elderly

The majority of the elderly are homeowners, and many elderly homeowners are free of mortgage debt. Table 5.12 gives tenure by age and the proportion of homeowners with mortgages. The classification *other* includes institutional-

Table 5.12   **Housing Status of the Elderly**

	Age Group		
	50–65	65–74	75+
Tenure (%):			
Own:	71.1	64.6	64.7
% small	29.9	42.6	53.8
% medium	24.3	28.0	19.5
% large	45.8	29.4	26.7
Rent:	25.8	30.9	29.1
% small	12.0	20.1	29.5
% medium	21.4	31.8	22.4
% large	66.6	48.1	48.1
Other	3.1	4.5	6.2
Share of homeowners with mortgages (%)	52.2	26.4	10.6
Mean house value (owners)	62,309	52,558	45,509
Mean equity (owners)	52,303	48,232	43,731
% of house value	83.9	91.8	96.1
Mobility (annual rate):			
Total	10.7	6.9	7.4
Owners	4.5	3.4	2.3
Renters	24.7	11.5	16.3
% who will or might move	18.2	12.1	11.0
Work reason (% of movers)	16.0	.0	.0
More house (% of movers)	14.4	27.0	14.8
Less house (% of movers)	26.4	32.4	40.7
Tenure switch (% of movers)	18.4	5.4	7.4
Involuntary (% of movers)	24.8	35.1	37.0

Source: Panel Study on Income Dynamics, 1984.

ization, housing provided by relatives, etc. The ownership rate falls in the "postretirement" years, age 65 and older, and the *other* rate rises with age. However, even for the very elderly, the ownership rate remains high. The share of homeowners with mortgages falls sharply with age. Net equity falls with age, despite the falling percentage of mortgage debt. This is partly a cohort effect, with the older generations located in smaller, less expensive dwellings, and partly a substitution effect, with households relocating to smaller houses. However, the latter effect is necessarily small since mobility among homeowners is quite low. Mobility of homeowners falls steadily with age, while the mobility of renters falls and then turns up at the oldest ages. Since elderly renters are the most likely group to be squeezed by falling income, the increased mobility of this group may reflect income-induced adjustments to housing. The last section of table 5.12 gives the proportion of households reporting that they will or might move in the coming year; as expected, these rates exceed observed mobility rates. The most common reasons for a planned move are to reduce dwelling size or cost ("less house") or because of availability ("involuntary"). The last category includes units that become unavailable owing to demolition, condominium conversion, eviction, and so forth but, more important, also includes moves induced by health, divorce, or death of a household member. There are significant fractions of planned moves to increase dwelling size, even for the very old.

Table 5.13 gives the transition matrix of households from one housing state to another. This is an average from the PSID for the starting years 1968–83, for all households in my sample. Mobility rates are lower for owners than renters and lower for occupants of large dwellings than small ones, reflecting the positive correlation of income with dwelling size and the negative correlation of mobility with income. Among owners, there is "regression to the mean," with owners of small or middle-sized dwellings predominantly moving upward in size and owners of large dwellings predominantly moving downward. This pattern is correlated with age, with the downsizers being mostly older.

There is strong "mover-stayer" heterogeneity in mobility among households, not apparent in the one-period transition matrix in table 5.13. To see this, table 5.14 classifies the mobility histories of households in the PSID over seventeen years from 1968 to 1984. The frequency of long-term stayers is far higher than the mobility patterns implied by the "independent-trials" transition probabili-

Table 5.13   **Transition Frequencies between Housing States**

| Current State | Previous State, All Households, 1968–83 | | | | | | |
	Rent Small	Rent Medium	Rent Large	Own Small	Own Medium	Own Large	Row Total
Rent small	260	103	91	33	33	63	583
	(10.3)	(4.1)	(2.1)	(.97)	(.6)	(.5)	(1.8)
Rent medium	99	131	117	18	22	41	428
	(3.9)	(5.2)	(2.6)	(.5)	(.4)	(.3)	(1.3)
Rent large	71	144	382	10	19	89	655
	(2.8)	(5.7)	(8.7)	(.3)	(.3)	(.7)	(2.1)
Own small	30	22	34	63	27	54	230
	(1.2)	(.9)	(.8)	(1.86)	(.5)	(.4)	(.7)
Own medium	11	31	62	36	75	75	290
	(.4)	(1.2)	(1.4)	(1.06)	(1.4)	(.6)	(.9)
Own large	26	41	138	34	81	288	608
	(1.0)	(1.6)	(3.2)	(1.0)	(1.46)	(2.1)	(1.9)
Stay	2,033	2,035	3,554	3,192	5,307	13,007	29,128
	(80.4)	(81.2)	(81.2)	(94.3)	(95.4)	(95.5)	(91.1)
Column total	2,530	2,507	4,378	3,386	5,564	13,617	31,982
	(7.9)	(7.8)	(13.7)	(10.6)	(17.4)	(42.6)	

Note: This table is made over all the pairs of adjacent years starting in 1968. Figures in the table give the count, with percentages in parentheses.

Table 5.14   Mobility Patterns over Sixteen Years, PSID

	"Independent Trials" Implied Rates (%)	Observed Rates (%)
Owner, no moves	4.3	38.0
Renter, no moves	.6	14.3
One move, owner to owner	13.7	10.8
One move, owner to renter	1.1	1.8
One move, renter to owner	3.8	4.7
One move, renter to renter	3.0	4.4
Total, one move	21.6	21.7
More than one move	73.4	26.0

ties given in table 5.13 would suggest. The observed frequency of three moves is 6.6 percent, of four moves 4.0 percent, and of five or more moves 4.9 percent. The "independent-trials" model predicts a lower rate for five or more moves.

One mechanism that an elderly homeowner with low current income and house equity can use to convert equity to income is to sell the house and move to a rental unit or a less expensive house. In an analysis of PSID data, Feinstein and McFadden (1989) find that mobility of homeowners is virtually the same for low-income and high-income elderly households when wealth is held constant. Furthermore, they find that most elderly households that move from one house to another maintain or increase their equity. While the probability of actually increasing equity is positively correlated with income, they find no correlation between the probability of decreasing equity and the presence of low-income "liquidity-constrained" households. This finding is supported in the analysis of other data sets, particularly Merrill (1984) and Venti and Wise (1989, 1990) in the Retirement History Survey. For households over age 75, where the studies above have relatively few observations, there is some evidence from wealth statistics and from dwelling sale and purchase prices that, when households do move, there is significant equity extraction. Liquid assets rise by considerably less than the equity extracted; this may be a problem of asset measurement or may reflect rapid dissipation of the extracted equity for medical or estate expenses or as gifts.

There is a clear tendency of the elderly to choose smaller housing units when they do move; this is seen in the distribution of dwellings by age and size in table 5.12 above. Reduced household size is the primary factor driving these shifts, but reduced maintenance and out-of-pocket costs may also be important. The modest shifts of the elderly from owned to rented dwellings, combined with this downsizing among owners, are a net contribution to the post–housing consumption stream, even without large shifts from equity to income.

5.7   Tax Policy Effects

Analysis of the behavior of elderly households suggests that, despite a rising share of expenditures on housing with age, there does not appear to be extensive "bottled-up" demand for mechanisms that permit housing costs to be postponed and charged against the household's bequests. In addition to the evidence that mobility rates and equity adjustments are insensitive to liquidity squeezes, there is direct evidence from reverse annuity mortgage (RAM) experiments in the United States that, in most cases, elderly homeowners are not seeking transactions that increase current income or reduce current expenditures via wealth adjustments.[5] This behavior may simply be driven by bequest motives or by precautionary demand for assets to cover contingencies such as health catastrophes. A demographic factor is that the poorest households, most in need of mechanisms to augment current income, are mostly those without any home equity or other assets available for conversion. In addition, a psychological mechanism may be at work. For most households, net worth from financial and real assets is small relative to the present value of transfer income and pensions and, when annuitized, would yield only a small increase in current income. Most market mechanisms for annuitization of assets also have a significant loading penalty. Thus, the annuity appears to be a poor harvest of hard-earned savings.

To assess the potential gain or loss to elderly households from some of the tax policies that have been considered in the United States, I examined housing costs under alternative conditions. The two policies that I consider are directed toward increasing U.S. government tax receipts; the question is the magnitude of their negative effect on the elderly. The first of these is the elimination of the deductibility of mortgage interest in the calculation of taxable income. The second is the elimination of the one-time capital gains exclusion for sales of residential property by elderly households; the existing tax law on capital gains is summarized in table 5.15.

Table 5.16 shows the percentage change in the user costs of owners and renters when they choose to stay in their current dwelling in the coming year and when they consider moving to another rented or owned unit. The largest effect is on owner-stayers in the 50–65 age range, 3.4 percent, with a falling effect for older households who faced lower 1984 tax rates and had smaller mortgage balances. The effect on renter-stayers is not zero because the user cost calculation takes into account the probability of a future move to an owned dwelling.

The effects of eliminating the capital gains exclusion have been examined in detail by Newman and Reschovsky (1987), and I make only a summary calculation. The capital gains exclusion is relevant only for homeowners who

5. In a RAM, the homeowner receives monthly income in exchange for a claim by the financial institution on the homeowner's equity when the household dies and the estate is settled.

Table 5.15   **Tax on Capital Gains from Resale of Residential Real Estate**

Tax:
1974–80   0.5 × (capital gain) should be included in taxable income
1981–84   0.4 × (capital gain) should be included in taxabale income
Deduction:
1974–76   Person aged 65 or older can deduct any gains if adjusted selling price is not more
           than $20,000. Otherwise, he/she can deduct ($20,000/selling price) × capital
           gain
1977–78   Person aged 65 or older can deduct any gains if adjusted selling price is not more
           than $35,000. Otherwise, he/she can deduct ($35,000/selling price) × capital
           gain
1979–81   Person aged 55 or older can exclude $100,000 from capital gain
1982–84   Person aged 55 or older can exclude $125,000 from capital gain

Table 5.16   **Effect on User Costs of Nondeductible Mortgage Interest**

	Age Group		
	50–65	65–75	75+
Owners (%):			
Move to rental unit	.0	.0	.0
Move to owned unit	1.6	1.2	.2
Stay	3.4	2.3	.5
Renters (%):			
Move to rental unit	.0	.0	.0
Move to owned unit	.5	.2	.5
Stay	.2	.1	.0

move to a rental unit or to an owned unit with equity less than the capital gains, as the capital gains can be rolled over into a new owner-occupied dwelling without being taxed. The average amount of capital gains of homeowners who move that are not rolled over into a new dwelling and the fraction of movers with positive exposure are given in table 5.17. Households younger than age 75 do not, on average, have significant "exposed" capital gains, that is, those not rolled over into a new home. Averages disguise the upper tail of the distribution of exposed gains, where the capital gains exclusion has the most effect. Nevertheless, these figures suggest that the fraction of households in these age groups that would be substantially economically disadvantaged is small. It is possible that the exclusion provides a significant incentive for households to downsize; Newman and Reschovsky found this to be the case in their analysis. Households over age 75 have a mean exposure that is a significant fraction of their asset holdings, so the capital gains exclusion can be important. Under the 1984 tax laws, the average additional tax liability for this age group if the exclusion were revoked would be on the order of $2,900. This table also shows the effect of downsizing. For owner-to-owner moves, the gross asset value in housing increases under age 75. This is consistent with the finding that house-

Table 5.17   **Exposure of Capital Gains to Taxation**

	Age Group		
	50–65	65–75	75+
Mean exposed capital gain	1,912	−3,922	13,776
Fraction of owner-movers with exposure	52.3	51.9	70.0
Mobility rate (%)	4.5	3.4	2.3
Price differential, new versus old:			
Own to own	4,297	7,091	−20,019
Total	−20,251	−10,509	−27,833

holds in these age groups do not use moves between owned dwellings to extract equity. Over age 75, there is substantial equity extraction.

5.8   Comparisons with Japan

Papers and statistical tabulations of Seko (1984, 1989a, 1989b), Takayama (chap. 4 in this volume), and other sources (Martin 1989; Martin and Tsuya 1989; Ito 1989; and Way 1984) permit some comparisons of housing problems of the elderly in the United States and Japan. Both countries experienced high birthrates in the decade beginning in 1945 and sharply lower birthrates after 1955. Consequently, both countries face a bulge of households that will become elderly soon after the turn of the century, when the working-age populations are relatively small. Figure 5.4 shows projections of the proportion of the population exceeding age 65 in each country; the fraction of elderly in Japan rises faster, and farther, than in the United States.[6] Figure 5.5 shows the age distribution of the populations of the two countries in 1980; except for immigration, these profiles effectively determine the ratios of the elderly to the working-age population over coming decades.[7] The Japanese cohorts between age 30 and age 54 in 1980 will induce the rapid growth in the proportion of the elderly between 1990 and 2015. The fraction of elderly in the United States will grow most rapidly between 2015 and 2030. These demographic changes have dramatic implications for savings rates and labor supply and can also be expected to have major effects on housing markets.

Living arrangements of the elderly in the United States and Japan are strikingly different, primarily for cultural reasons, although geographic proximity and differences in female labor force participation rates may play a role. Figure 5.6 shows the frequencies of various arrangements.[8] In the United States, 17 percent of elderly nuclei (e.g., couples or individuals over age 65) live together

6. Figure 5.4 is derived from table 5.1 and from Japan Institute of Population Problems (1988).
7. Figure 5.5 is derived from U.S. Bureau of the Census *Current Population Reports,* ser. P-25, no. 985; and Japan Statistical Bureau (1982, table 2).
8. Figure 5.6 is derived from U.S. Bureau of the Census (1982, table 4); "Marital Status and Living Arrangements," *Current Population Reports,* ser. P-20, no. 3651; Borsch-Supan (1989, table 4.1); and Japan Statistical Bureau (1983, table 2-20).

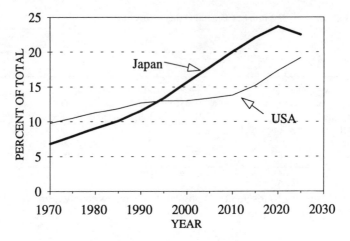

Fig. 5.4   Population age 65 and over

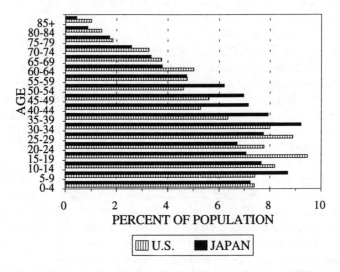

Fig. 5.5   Population age distribution (United States and Japan, 1980)

with their children; in Japan, this figure is 69 percent. One implication of these patterns is that intergenerational inequality in income and housing wealth is significantly internalized in intergenerational Japanese households. Consequently, Japan may be able to avoid some of the divisive issues of intergenerational equity that will color U.S. public policy discussions of the treatment of the elderly. However, the percentage of Japanese elderly living with children has been dropping steadily over time, from 77 percent in 1970 to 65 percent in 1985. This is creating a significant class of elderly in Japan who face the same problems in finances and care as do most U.S. elderly. A challenge to Japanese

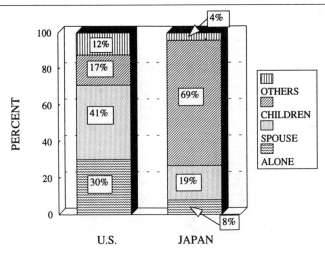

Fig. 5.6   Living arrangements (elderly nuclei, age 65 and over, in 1980)

housing policy is to make provisions for the minority of elderly living alone without introducing incentives that encourage the breakup of intergenerational living arrangements.

Homeownership and dwelling size follow contrasting patterns in the two countries, reflecting the differences in living arrangements. This is shown in figure 5.7.[9] In the United States, the fraction of owners in large units decreases with age; in Japan, the reverse is true. Similarly, the fraction of renters in small units increases with age in the United States and decreases in Japan. These differences are explained by the Japanese pattern in which the elderly and their children are joined in intergenerational households occupying relatively larger dwellings. An implication for Japan is that, as the fraction of elderly rises in the coming decades, there will be an increasing number of three-generation households, larger in size and requiring larger dwellings. By contrast, in the United States, there are likely to be increases in relative demand for small dwellings occupied by elderly living alone.

The mobility of the elderly in the two countries is compared in figure 5.8.[10] Japan shows substantially lower mobility than the United States, particularly for renters. However, mobility does not decline with age in Japan as it does in the United States. This may be a reflection of the movement of Japanese elderly into children's dwellings and of the mobility of intergenerational households.

Japan has notoriously high land prices, which translate into high housing

9. Figure 5.7 is derived from table 5.12 and the 1978 Housing Survey of Japan, Tokyo metropolitan area, tabulation by Miki Seko, Nihon University.

10. Figure 5.8 is derived from table 5.12 and the 1978 Housing Survey of Japan, Tokyo metropolitan area, tabulation by Miki Seko, Nihon University. The Japanese rates are the rates for a move in a three-year period, annualized. Thus, they understate annual mobility rates in a heterogeneous population of "movers" and "stayers." For example, an annual mobility rate of 10 percent assuming homogeneity rises to 11.9 percent in a population with 50 percent "stayers."

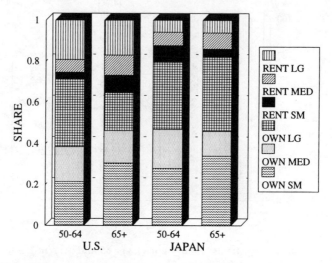

Fig. 5.7   Dwelling tenure and size

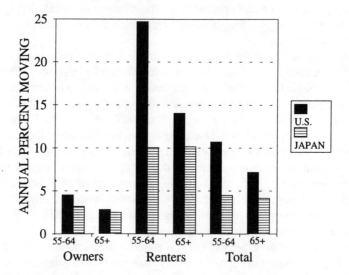

Fig. 5.8   Mobility rates

prices. This is less true in the United States but it also a factor in some major
urban areas. Figure 5.9 compares housing prices, expressed relative to annual
income of households, in two of the most expensive areas in the two countries,
Tokyo and Los Angeles.[11] In both areas, the ratio rose above 6 in the late 1970s
and, despite recent declines, has remained near this level. For comparison, the

---

11. Figure 5.9 is derived from National Association of Realtors (various years) (median sales
prices of existing dwellings, Anaheim–Santa Ana PMSA [primary metropolitan statistical area]),
U.S. Bureau of Labor Statistics (1984), and Seko (1989a, table 4-a).

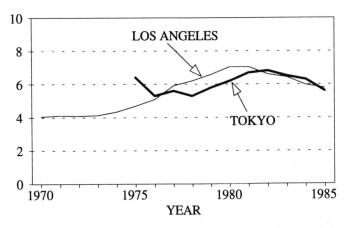

Fig. 5.9   Housing price/income ratio (median price, existing home sales)

1984 U.S. national average for the housing price/income ratio was 3.23. Housing price/income ratios above 4 are high enough to drive many younger households out of the market for first homes, unless housing capital gains are transferred to them by the elderly, via intergenerational living arrangements or bequests. As the population ages, the supply of housing from the elderly should increase, causing price/income ratios to fall. However, there is considerable repressed demand, so declines are likely to be gradual.

Another comparison of shelter costs in the two countries can be made using components of the consumer price index. Figure 5.10 gives the ratio of the shelter component (housing, utilities, and furnishings) to the nonshelter component of the CPI, with 1982 as the base.[12] These measures of the relative price of shelter have risen sharply since 1970 and more rapidly in the United States than in Japan. There are methodological issues in defining the housing component of shelter price in the CPI. The ideal starting point is a measure of the user cost of housing of the sort defined in section 5.1 above, with expected capital gains and tax offsets netted out. The price index and expenditure share would then be based on the user cost of constant-quality dwellings. The U.S. measure errs by failing to adjust for the savings component in housing expenditures. The Japanese index is based on an imputed rent concept and is closer to the ideal. The rise in the U.S. index in figure 5.10 relative to the Japanese index may be an artifact of not removing capital gains from housing expenditures in the U.S. CPI.

Income comparisons between the United States and Japan are difficult because the exchange rate does not accurately measure relative domestic purchasing power and because of different accounting conventions for treatment of income sources and expenditures and different patterns in the provision of pub-

12. Figure 5.10 is derived from the *1989 Statistical Abstract of the United States* and Japan Statistical Bureau (1989).

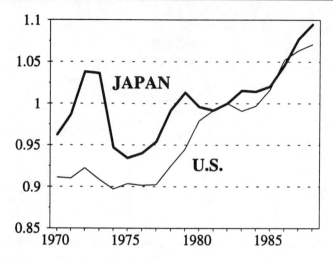

Fig. 5.10   Price of shelter (CPI shelter component)

lic services (e.g., transportation and medical services). Subject to these reservations, figures 5.11 and 5.12 show the sources of income and the patterns of expenditure in the two countries.[13] Figure 5.11 identifies three income sources: wages and salaries, including fringe benefits and bonuses; asset, business, and miscellaneous income; and Social Security income. In this figure, we see that measured income falls sharply with age in the United States, less sharply in Japan. This is due to a relatively modest decline in household wage income in Japan, in part because of the contribution of younger wage earners in intergenerational households, and in part because of the Japanese accounting conventions for pensions, which appear in wages rather than in asset income.

Figure 5.12 shows the expenditures of elderly households in the two countries. First, note that the United States has a much higher expenditure rate on shelter and a much lower savings rate than Japan, in both age categories. In part, this difference reflects different accounting conventions for imputing consumption in owner-occupied dwellings. These conventions cause the Japanese savings rate to be overstated relative to shelter cost and the U.S. savings rate to be understated relative to shelter cost. More careful analysis of savings by Hayashi (1986) suggest that, when the savings rates of the two countries are calculated using a common, economically sound method, the Japanese savings rate is substantially higher than the U.S. rate and comparable to European savings rates, but not nearly as high as measured savings in table 5.12 above would suggest. The Japanese expenditure rates on transportation and medical services are much lower than in the United States, reflecting less reliance on private automobiles, efficient provision of mass transit and medical services, and pub-

13. Figures 5.11 and 5.12 are derived from U.S. Bureau of Labor Statistics (1984) and Japan Statistical Bureau (1984).

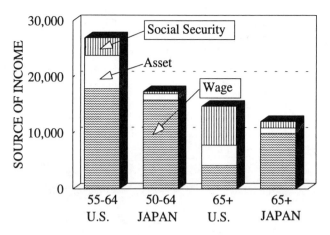

Fig. 5.11   Income by source (1984 household income, U.S. dollars)

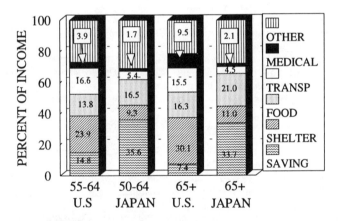

Fig. 5.12   Distribution of household expenditures

lic supply of medical services. Expenditure patterns change less with age in Japan than in the United States, partly because the categories of transportation and medical services, for which demand shifts substantially with age, have relatively low budget shares, and partly because total income is changing less.

5.9   Conclusions

This paper has provided a summary of the economic and housing status of elderly households in the United States. Despite rising housing prices and the decline of household income with age, the evidence is that, in terms of annuitized wealth, the elderly are about as well off as younger households. Housing choices made by the elderly do not suggest the presence of major market barriers that prevent their making desired transactions between nonliquid and liquid assets. The demographics of the elderly population in the United States and the age distribution of capital gains from housing price increases suggest that the baby boom generation will face more difficult economic circumstances at the end of its life cycle than the previous generation. Japan faces a similar problem of an aging population, which may, however, have markedly different implications for the housing market, owing to the high incidence of intergenerational households that internalize some of the problems of economic equity between the young and the old.

References

Ai, C., J. Feinstein, D. McFadden, and H. Pollakowski. 1990. The dynamics of housing demand by the elderly: User cost effects. In *Issues in the economics of aging,* ed. D. Wise. Chicago: University of Chicago Press.

Borsch-Supan, A. 1989. Household dissolution and the choice of alternative living arrangements among elderly Americans. In *The economics of aging,* ed. D. Wise. Chicago: Univesrity of Chicago Press.

Feinstein, J., and D. McFadden. 1989. The dynamics of housing demand by the elderly: 1. Wealth, cash-flow, and demographic effects. In *The economics of aging,* ed. D. Wise. Chicago: University of Chicago Press.

Hayashi, F. 1986. Why is Japan's saving rate so apparently high? *NBER Macroeconomics Annual,* 000–000.

Ito, T. 1989. Housing bequests and saving in Japan. Working paper. Hitotsubashi University.

Japan Institute of Population Problems. 1988. *Latest demographic statistics, 1987.* Tokyo: Ministry of Health and Welfare.

Japan Statistical Bureau. 1982. *1980 population census of Japan.* Vol. 2, *Results of the first basic complete tabulation.* Pt. 1, *Whole Japan.* Tokyo.

———. 1983. *Japan statistical yearbook.* Tokyo.

———. 1984. *Annual report on the family income and expenditure survey, 1982.* Tokyo.

———. 1988. *Annual report on the consumer price index, 1988.* Tokyo.

Martin, L. 1989. The graying of Japan. *Population Bulletin* 44:1–40.

Martin, L., and N. Tsuya. 1989. Interactions of middle-aged Japanese with their parents. Working paper. Honolulu: East-West Population Institute.

Merrill, S. 1984. Home equity and the elderly. In *Retirement and economic behavior,* ed. H. Aaron and G. Burtless. Washington, D.C.: Brookings.

National Association of Realtors. Various years. *Existing home sales.* Chicago.

Newman, S., and J. Reschovsky. 1987. An evaluation of the one-time capital gains exclusion for older homeowners. *AREUEA Journal* 15:704–24.

Seko, M. 1984. Japanese homeownership: Relative tenure prices versus demographic factors. *Nihon Daigaku Keizaikagakukenkyusho Kiyou* 8:273–89.

———. 1989a. The effect of inflation on Japanese homeownership rates: Test of capital market imperfections by time-series data. Working paper. Nihon University.

———. 1989b. Effects of subsidized home loans on housing decisions in Japan. Working Paper. Nihon University.

U.S. Bureau of the Census. 1982. *1980 census of the population: Living arrangements of the children* (PC80-2-4B). Washington, D.C.

U.S. Bureau of Labor Statistics. 1984. *Consumer Expenditure Survey results, 1984.* Bulletin no. 2267. Washington, D.C.

Venti, S., and D. Wise. 1989. Aging, moving, and housing wealth. In *The economics of aging,* ed. D. Wise. Chicago: University of Chicago Press.

————. 1990. But they don't want to reduce housing equity. In *Issues in the economics of aging,* ed. D. Wise. Chicago: University of Chicago Press.

Way, P. 1984. Issues and implications of the aging Japanese population. Staff Paper no. 6. Washington, D.C.: Center for International Research, U.S. Bureau of the Census.

6 The Cost of Aging: Public Finance Perspectives for Japan

Seiritsu Ogura

During the next forty years, the Japanese population is expected to go through a period of rapid aging. The share of those age 65 or older in our population is about 11 percent now, and the government expects it to double by the year 2010. Since most of these people will be retired, their living costs will have to be financed either by liquidating their private wealth or by private or public income transfers from the working generation.

In the early 1960s, Japan constructed a comprehensive network of public annuity and health insurance plans. Ever since the hyperinflation following the Second World War, however, the national government had to operate under a balanced-budget constraint. Under these circumstances, the fiscal authority was always wary of expanding the benefits of these plans, for they naturally meant more uncontrollable fiscal commitment. As a result, by and large, the benefits of these plans had been kept fairly modest.

Toward the end of the high economic growth era around 1970, however, the general public and politicians discovered the annuities and insurance plans as attractive political instruments. They wanted to redistribute more income to the elderly, who had not received the full benefits of economic growth, by transforming the plans into intergenerational income-transfer mechanisms. Finally, under intense political pressure, in 1973 the government made these plans pay very generous benefits to the retired without demanding commitment for the increased burden from the working generation.

In retrospect, the aging of the population had already begun in the 1970s,

Seiritsu Ogura is professor of economics at Hosei University and chief economist of the Japan Center for Economic Research.

The author wishes to thank Seimei-Kai, the Japanese Ministry of Finance, and the Japan Center for Economic Research for financial support, conference participants for valuable comments, and Takashi Irifune of the Bank of Japan for capable assistance.

and the number of those over 65 years old was increasing at the rate of 600,000 every year, an increase of 50 percent over the preceding decade. It was only a matter of time before the inconsistencies between the benefits and the premiums of these plans began to surface. After the first oil shock, the economy no longer grew 10 percent every year, and, almost instantly, the autonomous expansion of these expenditures helped send the national budget into huge deficits (figs. 6.1, 6.2). In the lower-house election of 1979, however, voters decisively rejected a major tax increase in the form of a European-style value-added tax, which might have restored the budget balance. During this time, the national debt was accumulating, and, by the early 1980s, the deficit started to feed on itself.

Finally, in the midst of an unprecedented fiscal crisis, the government was forced to announce a state of fiscal emergency and to begin to curtail its expenditures, including these programs. Since 1983, several major reforms were carried out, which I regard as the first-round adjustments in these programs. In the first half of this paper, I will follow the developments that led to them and describe their outlines. Mainly as a result of these reforms, the expansion of government expenditure was brought under control, and the renewed strength of economic growth during the last few years is finally restoring the balance in the national budget for now.

Nevertheless, it is not clear how much these reforms have accomplished in the long run. While some reforms were fundamental reforms that reduced the costs of the plans themselves, others simply shifted the national government's burden to the private sector. Moreover, the long-run outlook for the costs of these transfer programs is still an open question. According to the latest government estimates, the cost of public annuity benefits will go up to 7.5 percent of national income in 1986 and to 15.5 percent of national income in 2010. In the same period, the cost of public medical insurance benefits will go up from 7.5 percent of national income to between 9 and 11.5 percent.

In the past, however, the government's cost projection had a very pronounced downward bias, and one must worry whether these figures are biased as well. I will provide some insight into the problem by focusing on changes in the costs of these programs as a result of the changes in the demographic composition over time. The idea is very similar to Laspeyres quantity index, with 1986 costs as fixed weights, or the notion of a "current service" budget under constraint prices.

The design of the rest of the paper is as follows. In the first section, I present the basic structure of the Japanese public health insurance system and follow what took place during the fiscal crisis. In the second section, I repeat the same process for the public annuity insurance system. In the third section, I explain my population allocation model, which I used to generate demographic variables. In the fourth section, I present the results of the simulation.

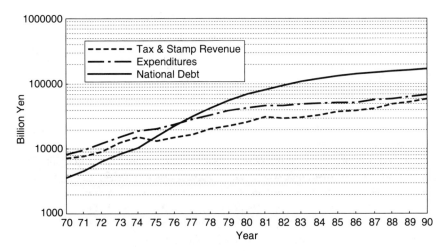

Fig. 6.1   Budget of national government and national debt

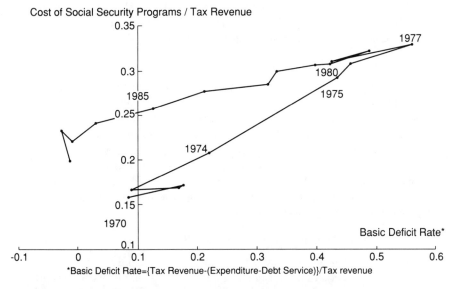

Fig. 6.2   Budget deficit and the cost of Social Security programs for the Japanese national government

6.1   The Public Health Insurance System

Every Japanese must carry a public insurance plan. When an individual gets ill, a doctor will provide medical care as an agent of the insurance plan, following the standard treatment procedure. The procedure is common to all public insurance plans and gives detailed instructions on the range of permissible treatments for each ailment and their costs. A patient must pay a part of the costs at the doctor's office and the pharmacy. The proportion varies from one plan to another in a range from 0 to 30 percent, but the total cost of insurance copayments to a household can be no more than ¥60,000 (¥33,600 for poor households) during any given month (in 1991). The rest of the cost will be billed to the insurance plan once a month, together with the other patients' bills. To maintain the public health insurance system, the national government reimburses administrative expenses and gives subsidies to weaker plans through many channels.

In this section, I outline the coverage of four major public health insurance plans: (1) Health Insurance Managed by Associations (HIMA), (2) Health Insurance Managed by Government (HIMG), (3) Mutual Aid Association Insurance (MAAI), and (4) National Health Insurance (NHI). While these terms are rather awkward, they are nevertheless used in the *Statistical Yearbook of Japan*, and for this reason I use them also. I should point out that, except for HIMG, these are decentralized systems where authorized insurers individually set and collect insurance taxes and pay out insurance benefits under the supervision of the Ministry of Health and Welfare. Naturally, uniform rules govern this process, but they do permit plans to provide extra benefits when they can afford them, including smaller insurance copayment ratios.

6.1.1   Employee's Health Insurance Plans

A majority of employed workers and their family members are covered by plans belonging to HIMA, HIMG, and MAAI; for them, the present coverage has probably begun with their employment and will end with their retirement. Collectively, all such plans are referred to as *employee's health insurance* plans. At most, their insurance copayment ratio is 10 percent for the workers, but, for their dependents, it is 20 percent for inpatient care and 30 percent for outpatient care. Roughly speaking, insurance taxes are collected as fixed proportions of employees' wages and salaries, and the employer must pay at least half the tax, but may choose to contribute more.[1]

Health Insurance Managed by Associations (HIMA)

An employee's health insurance plan can be independently managed by an insurance association of a corporation. Under such a plan, membership is limited to the corporation's employees, and insurance coverage is usually limited to the members and their dependents. Legally, it is a (public) entity independent from the corporation, but in reality its day-to-day operation relies heavily on corporate resources, even though the national government reimburses administrative expenses. For a corporation to qualify for this plan, called a Kumiai-Kenko-Hoken, it must have at least 700 employees. As of March 1991, there were 1,777 such associations, covering more than 14.7 million member-

---

1. The health insurance tax base is referred to as the *standard monthly wage,* and each worker is classified into one of thirty-nine classes, ranging from ¥68,000 to ¥710,000 per month (in 1987).

workers as well as their 17 million dependents. More than 60 percent of these workers belong to associations with more than 20,000 members.

Each association can set its own tax rate within the range between 30/1,000 and 95/1,000, of which the employer is required to contribute at least half. In 1988, the average tax rate of all the plans in HIMA was 8.248 percent, 57 percent of which was contributed by employers. Since the members of these associations are the employees of large corporations, they tend to be healthier and receive higher pay than the average worker of the same age and sex. As a result, these associations usually offer better benefits at lower tax rates. In many large corporations, for example, surplus funds are used to establish facilities in resort areas that accommodate employees and their dependents for a small cost. Most regard these facilities as effective means for recruiting and keeping good workers.

Health Insurance Managed by the Government (HIMG)

Smaller corporations, or most businesses employing more than five workers, must join Seifu-Kansho-Kenko-Hoken, Health Insurance Managed by the Government. As of March 1991, this huge insurance plan covered close to 1 million businesses, with almost 18 million workers and their 19 million dependents.

The tax rate is currently set at 8.2 percent, which is shared equally between employer and employee. The average HIMG tax base is more than 20 percent smaller than HIMA's. Since it is such a gigantic plan, a change in its tax rate used to become a hot political issue when the cost of benefits exceeded the tax revenue. Several times in the past, the government had to reach into its own pocket to solve HIMG's financial crises, which explains why it contributes 16.4 percent of the cost of insurance benefit payments to HIMG, or ¥879 billion in 1990.

Mutual Aid Association Insurance (MAAI)

Most public-sector employees are covered by the health insurance plan managed by the Kyosai-Kumiai, or Mutual Aid Association (MAA), of the particular agencies for which they work. There are 118 MAAs for national and local government agencies, covering 11.2 million individuals, including dependents. Reflecting a wide variance in the employees' age structure, tax rates also vary widely among MAAs—that for the national government is from 6.4 to 11.46 percent, and that for local governments is 8.868 percent. These costs are split equally between employees and the employer.

6.1.2   National Health Insurance System (NHI)

Since 1961, the rest of the population has been covered by plans under Kokumin-Kenko-Hoken, or the National Health Insurance System. Altogether the NHI system covers 43 million individuals, but it is divided into 3,424 separate plans managed independently by municipal governments. More than half of them are relatively small plans that cover no more than 5,000 individuals each. In addition, there are 166 professional association plans.

Currently, among the covered households of the NHI system, about 30 percent are self-employed workers, while another 30 percent are those employed either in very small businesses or only on a part-time basis. About 25 percent are households headed by the unemployed or the retired. In the past, the government has regarded NHI as an insurance system for the poor and has reserved for it the highest subsidy rates among public health plans.

Since 1968, the standard copayment rate for all care has been set at 30 percent for all members. The government contributes 40 percent of the cost of the benefit payments to each NHI plan, and an extra 10 percent of it is committed to grants to weaker plans. Each municipal government sets its tax schedule, but usually it consists of proportional taxes on (*a*) a household's taxable income, (*b*) its real assetholdings, and (*c*) the number of individuals in it, in addition to (*d*) a flat household charge. In 1990, an average household in the NHI system had 1.7 members and paid ¥150,000 for the coverage. Out of this amount, 71.5 percent represented taxes on the household's income, 6.6 percent taxes on real assetholdings, 15.4 percent the tax on the number of individuals, and 6.6 percent the flat household charge.[2]

6.1.3   Aging and the NHI Problem

Japan's public health insurance plans are "risk blind"; a person's insurance tax is based only on his ability to pay. A seventy-year-old person may consume several times as much medical care as a thirty-year-old person but does not pay higher taxes because of it. If each insurance plan must pay for itself, the others in the plan must subsidize the elderly person by paying higher taxes. But if the old and/or the poor are concentrated in a particular plan, that plan may never be able to collect enough tax revenue to cover the standard insurance benefits.

Such was the case for the NHI plans. From the very start, since it was a system without many younger and healthier people who were in employees' plans, it was a relatively "old" system. It lost more young people during the high economic growth period to employee plans as agriculture shrank. Had NHI been left alone, it would have been bound for serious financial problems as the NHI population kept on aging. The last straw, however, came from the influx of a large number of retired workers from employee insurance plans. When an employed worker retires, he and his family usually must withdraw from an employee health insurance plan and join an NHI plan. The influx of retired employees from HIMA and HIMG is estimated to have doubled between 1970 and 1980, from 150,000 to 300,000 persons annually. (Currently, it is close to 1 million a year.)

2. Until the reform of 1984, the national government had been contributing 45 percent of the total medical costs of the NHI participants. After the reform of 1984, the rate has been set at 50 percent of the insurance payments, which is said to be equivalent to 38.5 percent of the total medical cost.

This also meant that the national government had to start paying 45 percent of these retirees' medical bills, the rate it used to subsidize NHI plans. This was the long-run cause for the increased costs of the NHI subsidy, but, in 1973, the government helped the costs skyrocket by eliminating insurance copayments for anyone over 70 years old. Zero coinsurance did not simply mean that the national and other governments now had to pay the extra 30 percent of the medical bills of these people. It also meant that their bills would become much more expensive.

While there has been no firm quantitative analysis yet on the effects of the zero copayment policy, apparently this induced the aged to seek medical care more often (see Ogura and Futagami 1992), and, more significantly, it induced doctors to give them more expensive care, including longer hospitalization. As a result, in ten years, the share of national medical expenditures for patients over 70 years old has almost doubled, from 11 percent in 1973 to 20 percent in 1982. Considering the 50 percent increase in their number, from 4.2 to 6.5 million, their medical costs have increased 50 percent faster than those for the rest of the population during this period. The national government had to increase its subsidy to the NHI from ¥489 billion in 1972 to ¥2,203 billion in 1982, in addition to paying ¥517 billion for its share of the insurance copayment scheme in 1982.[3]

6.1.4   The Fiscal Crisis and 1983 and 1984 Reforms

In 1973, the Japanese economy was shaken by the first oil shock, and, for more than a decade following the shock, economic growth remained sluggish. While tax revenues stagnated in real terms from the slowdown, government expenditures kept on growing. The national debt continued to increase, and soon interest payments became the single largest item in the national budget. During the unprecedented fiscal crisis of the early 1980s, there was a national consensus that substantial cuts had to be made in social welfare expenditures.

It was clear that neither the NHI system nor the national government was any longer able to cope with the influx of retired workers from the employee plans. In order to offset the fiscal burdens that accompanied the influx, the government introduced Rojin-Hoken, or the Health Maintenance System for the Aged (HMSA), in 1983, and Taishokusha-Iryou-Seido, or the Retired Workers' Medical System (RWMS), in 1984.

The Health Maintenance System for the Aged (HMSA)

This system introduced new user fees for the medical care of those over 70 years old, but so far they are mostly symbolic; the current rates are ¥900 per month for outpatient care and ¥600 per day for inpatient care. With the intro-

---

3. Actually, after the Ministry of Finance rejected the measure proposed by the Ministry of Health and Welfare in 1969, paying the copayments for the aged became very common among municipal and prefectural governments by the early 1970s. In 1973, finally, the national government decided to take over two-thirds of these costs (i.e., 20 percent of the medical bill), leaving the municipal and prefectural governments paying one-sixth each (i.e., 5 percent).

duction of HMSA, municipal governments must provide medical care for any resident who is 70 years old or older, regardless of membership in an NHI plan. The national government contributes 20 percent of this cost, and prefectural and municipal governments are each expected to contribute 5 percent, as under the old insurance copayment scheme.

The remaining 70 percent of the cost is reimbursed by a special fund set up to collect the money from every public health insurance plan. Instead of billing each plan for the actual costs incurred for caring for its member patients, from 1990 on the fund will raise the necessary amount by charging each plan in proportion to the total number of individuals in the plan (as well as the average medical cost of its aged patients).

Since the NHI system has a population share of 37 percent, it will have to pay only 37 percent of this amount, even though 67 percent of those over 70 belong to NHI plans. Currently, HMSA costs about ¥6 trillion per year, and NHI will pay about ¥1.4 trillion, instead of the ¥3 trillion that it paid prior to HMSA. The government subsidy to NHI will be ¥0.7 trillion (= 0.5 × 1.4) instead of ¥1.8 trillion (= 0.45 × 0.67 × 6).

The Retired Workers' Medical System (RWMS)

In this system, the NHI offers reduced copayment rates (20 percent for the insured person and for his family's inpatient care) to an "old boy" retired from an employee plan who is too young to qualify for HMSA. Retired workers are defined as those who receive Welfare Annuity Plan (WAP) benefits or MAA retirement benefits.

Benefit claims will be paid out of pooled premiums, and the resulting shortage will be charged to all employee insurance plans in proportion to payroll size. For 1990, HIMA paid ¥234 billion and HIMG ¥232 billion to RWMS. Equivalent amounts were saved by NHI plans, half of which was saved by the national government.

These reforms together shifted ¥2 trillion from government budgets to employee health insurance taxes in 1990. The amount will easily double in later years.

6.2   Japanese Public Annuity Insurance Plans

Prior to the 1986 reform, by and large, the coverage of public annuity insurance plans overlapped with those of public health insurance systems. Kosei-Nenkin, or Welfare Annuity Insurance, was the public annuity insurance plan for the workers covered by HIMA and HIMG. Kyosai-Kumiai, or mutual aid associations, offered their own annuity insurance plans in addition to health insurance plans. Kokumin-Nenkin, or the National Pension Plan (NPP), was the public annuity insurance plan for self-employed workers and their spouses. In contrast to the public health insurance plans, however, public annuity plans are centralized and managed by the national government (with MAAs as curious exceptions). All benefits are indexed against any inflation greater than 5 percent annually.

6.2.1   Public Annuity Insurance Plans under the 1973 Regime

The Welfare Annuity Plan (WAP)

The Welfare Annuity Plan was created in 1942 as the Worker's Annuity Insurace to provide annuity insurance for employed workers and families against the loss of their earning capacity due to old age, disability, or death. It was the public annuity insurance plan for the households of 27 million workers covered by HIMA and HIMG until the 1986 reform (fig. 6.3). In 1990, WAP paid ¥11.4 trillion in benefits to 10.8 million individuals. Retirement benefits accounted for ¥8.4 trillion, or 73 percent of the total cost of WAP benefits. Less important are survivor's benefits, which accounted for 15 percent, partial credit benefits, which accounted for 8 percent, and disability annuities, which accounted for 3 percent (fig. 6.4).

Roughly speaking, a worker's WAP contribution is determined as a fixed percentage, currently set at 14.5 percent for male workers, of his or her monthly paycheck, half of which should be paid by the employer (table 6.1). Participation is mandatory at any site of business with more than five employees.[4]

Retirement benefits started at age 60 for males and age 56 for female workers, with the condition that the worker be in the system for twenty years or more, or for fifteen years or more after the age of 40/35 for males/females.

The basic formula for computing the WAP benefit (in yen) was given by

$$y = a \times n + b \times z \times n,$$

where a and b are constants, n is the number of months the individual had paid the WAP tax, and z is the individual's revaluated average monthly pay. The last value of a was 2,050 (before the 1986 reform took effect), and the value of b had been 0.01. The first term ($a \times n$) was referred to as the *flat benefit,* and the second term ($b \times z \times n$) was referred to as the *proportional benefit.* The survivor's benefit was three-quarters of the original benefit. The average full retirement WAP benefit for those under the old system was ¥1,680,000 in 1990.

The National Pension Plan (NPP)

This plan was created in 1961 to provide annuity insurance for self-employed workers and their spouses against old age, disability, or death. Self-employed workers and their spouses between the ages of 20 and 60 were re-

---

4. WAP's tax base is also referred to as the *standard monthly wage,* and a worker is classified into one of thirty classes ranging from ¥80,000 to ¥570,000 (in 1989). Unlike the public health insurance tax, there is no exemption in the WAP tax, since anyone earning less than ¥80,000 is classified as earning ¥80,000.

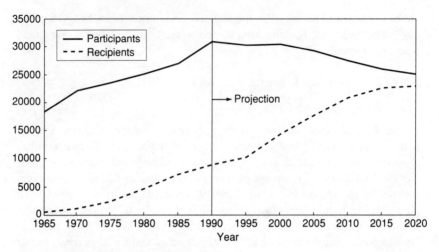

Fig. 6.3   JCER projection of participants and recipients of Japanese Welfare Annuity Pension plan (1,000 persons)

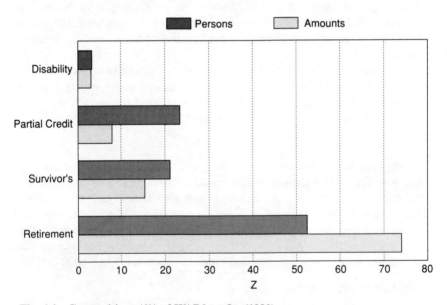

Fig. 6.4   Compositions (%) of WAP benefits (1990)

quired to join the plan, but the dependent spouses of employed workers (who are covered by WAP) were encouraged to join the plan voluntarily (fig. 6.5). In 1990, NPP paid ¥5 trillion in benefits to 10 million individuals. Eighty percent of the amount was for the old-age pension, while the partial credit pension accounted for 10 percent and the disability pension for 7 percent (fig. 6.6).

Table 6.1   **WAP Tax Rate**

Date	Male (%)	Female (%)	Date	Male (%)	Female (%)
1942, June	6.4	6.4	1971, Nov.	6.4	4.8
1944, Oct.	11	11	1963, Nov.	7.6	5.8
1947, Sep.	9.4	6.8	1966, Aug.	9.1	7.3
1948, Aug.	3	3	1980, Oct.	10.6	8.9
1960, May	3.5	3	1985, Oct.	12.4	11.3
1965, May	5.5	3.9	1990, Jan.	14.3	13.8
1969, Nov.	6.2	4.6	1991, Jan.	14.5	14.3

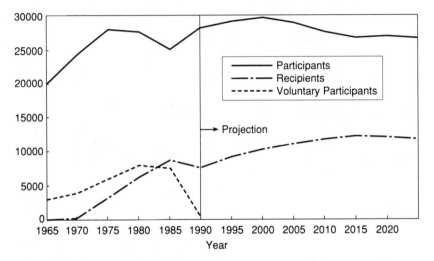

Fig. 6.5   JCER projection of participants and recipients of Japanese National Pension Plan (1,000 persons)

Survivor's benefits are limited to those with dependent children and hence accounted for less than 2 percent.[5]

Unlike the WAP tax, the NPP tax is a fixed-sum, monthly tax, and both husband and wife must join NPP, even if only one member of the household is working (table 6.2). The NPP retirement benefits started at age 65, compared with WAP's age 60, and to qualify for NPP benefits one must pay the NPP monthly tax for at least twenty-five years, compared with WAP's twenty years.

The formula for computing NPP's old-age benefits (in yen) was given by

$$y = c \times n,$$

where c is a constant (whose last value was 800 before the 1986 reform), and

5. At the end of 1985, altogether, there were 25.1 million individuals in NPP, out of which 17.6 million were mandatory and 7.5 million voluntary participants. Since the number of dependent spouses of WAP workers is given at 10.9 million, three out of four housewives of WAP workers were participating in NPP on their own.

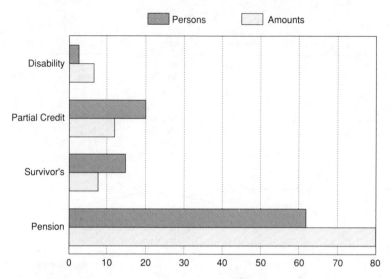

Fig. 6.6   Compositions (%) of NPP benefits (1990)

n is the number of months the individual had paid the NPP tax. In 1985, the average size of the existing NPP full old-age pension was ¥336,000.[6]

Retirement Benefits after the 1973 Welfare Reform

All these plans started as fully funded plans, for they were never intended to be tools for transferring income between generations until 1973, when a revolutionary change was brought into WAP in computing the benefits. Prior to the change, a worker's retirement benefit had been based on the mathematical average of his actual monthly payments during the insured period.

Since 1973, however, a worker's past wages are reevaluated once every five years by a set of multipliers that reflect the increases in the market wage that have occurred since the last evaluation. The government adopted this change to let a "model WAP retirement benefit" pay 60 percent of a worker's current monthly earnings. For NPP, in 1973, the government increased the constant c from ¥320 to ¥800 to provide a pension income of ¥50,000 per month for a couple who had been in the plan for twenty-five years.

Since the changes were retroactive, they affected all the existing claims as well as future ones. In just two years, the cost of WAP benefit payments tripled, while that of NPP quintupled. Later, because of all its revolutionary measures, 1973 came to be known as the first year of the welfare era. These were measures that would require higher rates of subsidization, but the government never followed through with sufficient quantities of new funds. It is possible that the

6. For those who were already 50 years old or older in 1961 and could not join NPP, the national government provides an old-age welfare pension (which should not be confused with the Welfare Annuity Plan below) when they reach 70. The sum is about ¥329,000 per year, and there are 2 million recipients.

Table 6.2   **NPP Tax (in yen)**

Date	Aged 20–34	Date	Uniform
1961, Apr.	100	1979, Apr.	3,300
1967, Jan.	200	1980, Apr.	3,770
1969, Jan.	250	1981, Apr.	4,500
	————	1982, Apr.	5,220
	Aged 35–49	1983, Apr.	5,830
1961, Apr.	150	1984, Apr.	6,220
1967, Jan.	250	1985, Apr.	6,740
1969, Jan.	300	1986, Apr.	7,100
	————	1987, Apr.	7,400
	Uniform	1988, Apr.	7,700
	————	1989, Apr.	8,000
1970, July	450	1990, Apr.	8,400
1972, July	550	1991, Apr.	9,000
1974, Jan.	900	1992, Apr.	9,700
1975, Jan.	1,100		
1976, Apr.	1,400		
1977, Apr.	2,200		
1978, Apr.	2,730		

fiscal crunch after the first oil shock prevented the government from doing so. But it is more likely that the government never had a clear idea of what it was getting into. The ideas were politically very popular, and the ruling party had to grab them to stay in power.

6.2.2 The NPP Crisis and the National Fiscal Crisis

The first program to feel the pinch was the NPP, which had two to three times as many recipients for each taxpayer as WAP did (fig. 6.7). Unlike WAP, NPP did not have much time to accumulate substantial financial assets, and, as a result, NPP taxes had to be raised ten times between 1975 and 1983, to more than tenfold the original level, or from ¥450 to ¥5,220 per month (table 6.2). The government subsidy had also grown from ¥213 billion in 1975 to ¥790 billion in 1982, but it was still too little. Moreover, in 1983, in view of its own fiscal crisis, the government declared that it must postpone its NPP subsidy payments for the following six years.[7]

It was also clear that rapid increases in insurance fees were eroding the NPP's revenue base very fast and that, before too long, the government would have to start contributing substantially more to keep the plan solvent. But, at that time, it did not even have enough money to pay for the current commitment.

7. One can see how things were getting out of hand in the following episode: in 1976, in an attempt to increase NPP's cash flow, the government changed the subsidy scheme from half the NPP tax revenue to one-third of the cost of NPP benefit payments. In this year, the cost of NPP benefits increased by more than 50 percent, owing to inflation.

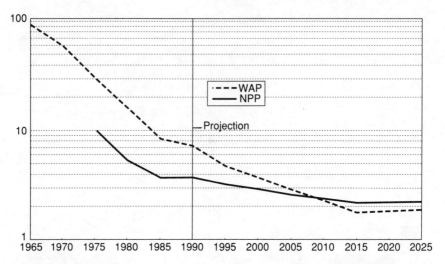

Fig. 6.7   JCER projections of the numbers of participants per full-benefit recipient

Compared with the situation at NPP, things were not nearly as critical at WAP, but just as serious. At the present moment, WAP does not have a cash-flow problem, and, in fact, it will be accumulating considerable surplus cash for at least another ten years. Yet, by the early 1980s, the government began to admit openly that the measures adopted in 1973 left a monstrous structure that may require a 40 percent payroll tax rate in the third decade of the twenty-first century. The government, which had to contribute 20 percent of the cost of WAP benefits, saw its subsidy payment jump from ¥38 billion in 1972 to ¥124 billion in 1974 and then to ¥595 billion in 1983. In 1986, it would have been ¥1.2 trillion had the government not postponed paying a quarter of it because of the fiscal crisis.

6.2.3   The 1986 Pension Reforms

NPP Reforms

The government solved the short-run problem in the NPP by infusing sur-plus funds from WAP. It replaced what used to be called WAP's *flat benefit* by NPP benefits. Formally, NPP's coverage was extended to those who had been covered by WAP (or MAA's annuity plans). In addition, housewives of em-ployed workers are awarded automatic independent insurance coverage by NPP. With these changes, a new name was given to the NPP benefit, and it is now called the *basic old-age pension benefit*.

In exchange for this extended coverage, the WAP (and MAAs) is now asked to bear a part of the cost of the basic old-age pension benefits net of govern-ment subsidies equal to WAP's share of the number of all (employed and self-employed) workers and their dependent spouses, under the new NPP scheme. Currently, this share is about 70 percent. The resulting net annual infusion of WAP funds into NPP is currently more than ¥1 trillion, about the size of total NPP tax revenues, or over 10 percent of WAP tax revenues. This will stabilize NPP taxes for the next decade or so, at the cost of depleting WAP's funds.

To curb the expansion of future basic old-age pension benefits taxes for the full 480 months, the annual benefit would be ¥626,500 instead of ¥950,000, as before. This change will be phased in gradually over the fifteen-year period beginning in 1992.[8]

WAP Reform

One of the most important ingredients of the 1986 reform was the cut in the "proportional part" of the WAP benefit. Namely, the value of the constant *b* in the benefit equation will decrease from 10/1,000 to 7.5/1,000 over twenty years, by approximately 0.125/1,000 for every birth year between 1927 and 1946.

On the other hand, the reform that transferred WAP's flat benefit to the NPP seemed to be neutral with respect to the value of the retirement benefit received by a married WAP worker. The reform converted one WAP flat benefit into two NPP pensions, that is, one for the WAP worker himself and the other for his dependent wife. Even in monetary terms, this seemed to be true; the flat part in the old WAP added ¥2,472 for every extra month, while the new basic pension will (in fifteen years) add only ¥1,298 for every extra month.

In many respects, however, this change implied very substantial cuts in the value of WAP benefits. Most affected are unmarried workers or female workers without dependent spouses, who will lose almost 50 percent of the original WAP flat benefit. For married workers, WAP's dependent allowances, which used to add ¥180,000 for a dependent wife, will be phased out after the wife reaches 65. Moreover, dependent wives of WAP workers who participated in the NPP voluntarily will not receive an extra benefit as they had expected, other than their own basic old-age pension, while those housewives who had not participated in the NPP voluntarily will not be given credit for their husbands' WAP coverage prior to 1986.

Reduction in Government Subsidies

After this reform, the government discontinued its subsidy to WAP of 20 percent of WAP benefits. Instead, it now contributes a third of the cost of the basic old-age pension benefits, as it did for NPP. This change in the subsidy

8. More precisely, the new NPP benefit formula after the 1986 reform is given by

$$y = 626,500 \times n/v,$$

where n is the number of months one had paid NPP taxes, and v is the policy parameter standing for the maximum number of covered months. For those born in 1926, v is set at 300; for every year after that 12 will be added, until it reaches 480 for those born in 1941 and after.

scheme will save the government a considerable amount of money since an average WAP benefit claim (¥1,436,000) was 4.5 times as large as an NPP claim (¥336,000). By converting one WAP subsidy into two NPP subsidies (namely, for a husband and wife), the government can save a quarter of an NPP claim, or about ¥80,000, since

$$0.2 \times 4.5 - 0.333 \times 2 \times 1 = 0.23.$$

The change also saves the government money because the new subsidy starts at age 65, which is five years later than the start of WAP benefits. In the 1986 reform, however, the government could not postpone the start of the WAP benefit itself from age 60 to age 65. For the moment, a retiree between the ages 60 and 65 is receiving essentially the same amount as a person receiving a basic pension benefit with dependent allowances and a WAP retirement benefit as a special WAP benefit entirely at the expense of WAP. The government wanted to phase this benefit out by the year 2022, but the WAP reform bill submitted to the Diet in 1989 met strong political opposition and was passed without this part.

6.3   What Our (Children's) Future Will Look Like

In general, it is difficult to predict what it will be like even ten years from now. Consider the case of medical costs as a good example. First of all, medical technology can change. So much medical research is carried out all over the world, and researchers may very well change the fundamental medical technologies and the cost structure of health care in the near future. Second, institutions can change. The medical industry is far from perfectly competitive. It has a very strong professional union and an equally determined government. Almost all its demand is derived from public health insurance plans. Its supply is rigidly regulated by government at all levels. Any substantial change in these institutional factors is bound to have its effect on future medical costs.

Rather than trying to make an uneducated guess regarding how these factors change over time, I assume that these factors remain constant. After all, what we want to find out is not so much the absolute size of the medical cost for the elderly in years to come as its size relative to what the working generation will be earning then.

6.3.1   The Population Allocation Model

As a first approximation to our future, I project it directly on the economic and sociological structure of our present society. Consider a world where, for example, a future 40-year-old man earns exactly the same amount of money as today's 40-year-old man. In that world, he marries at the same age and has just as many children. His family gets ill just as often, his doctor is just as expensive, and his wife even goes back to work just as often. When his children finish school, they will start working too, just as today's youngsters do. His mortality rate at each age is exactly the same as that of his present counterparts.

Demographic Disaggregation

Since our concern here is aging and its social costs, it is natural to disaggregate our population by biological ages. In many aspects, however, there seem to be substantial differences between the two sexes, and we have to differentiate our population by sex, too. Ideally, we would like to disaggregate our population both by age and by sex. I express this disaggregation by *sex/age*.

Unfortunately, most vital and social statistics are available only for age groups rather than for each age. For these variables, I use almost exclusively the following demographic groupings for each sex: 0–4, 5–9, 10–14, 15–19, 20–24, 25–29, 30–34, 35–39, 40–44, 45–49, 50–54, 55–59, 60–64, 65–69, 70–74, 75–79, 80–84, 85–89, 90+. To save space, I use *sex/age-group* to express this disaggregation.

The Demographic Structure

I start from the sex/age profile of the 1986 population. Each year, I take account of how many babies of each sex are born and how many men and women die at each age and then construct a new age profile for the next year.

The number of new births is obtained by multiplying the female population in each of the following reproductive age groups by its rate of reproduction, taken from the *1989 Vital Statistics.* According to it, an adult female gives birth to 1.52 children in her life at the rate of 0.047 per year between the ages of 20 and 24, 0.146 between 25 and 29, 0.091 between 30 and 34, and 0.019 between 35 and 39.

The number of deaths in each sex/age group is obtained by multiplying each sex/age-group population by its mortality rate, taken from the *1986 Vital Statistics* (fig. 6.8).

The Employment Structure

Every year, the Ministry of Welfare publishes the *State of Affairs of Workers Covered by Health Insurance,* which reports a number of sample statistics on the workers covered by HIMA and HIMG. Contained in this report are the number of workers and their average monthly pay in each sex/age group. From the 1988 sample figures for each system, I obtained estimates of the number of workers of each sex/age group in each system.

As for the workers in the public sector who are covered by MAAs, there is no consolidated report. I had to rely on the *Labor Force Survey* compiled by the Management and Coordination Agency for the 1986 sex/age-group decomposition of these workers.

Inflow. I compute the number of workers coming into the system each year for two entry-level age groups, namely, ages 15–19 and 20–24. I assume that the numbers of people entering the system are fixed proportions of the general population of these two sex/age groups given in table 6.3. As for the new workers in the public sector, I assume that the absolute numbers are fixed for each sex/age group rather than their shares of the population.

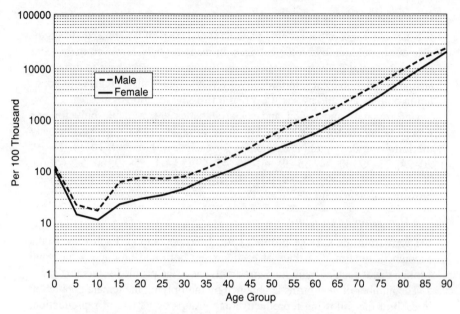

Fig. 6.8   Mortality rates for Japanese population (1989)

Table 6.3   Fraction of the Population Working in HIMA and HIMG and the
                   Number of Workers in MAA

Age Group and Sex	HIMA (%)	HIMG (%)	MAA (No.)
15–19:			
Male	4	5	59,000
Female	5	5	3,000
20–24:			
Male	23	22	317,000
Female	26	25	180,000

Outflow. I then subtract the number of workers leaving the system by multiplying the "net dropout rate" of each sex/age group by the stock of workers in that group. This rate can be loosely interpreted as the probability of a worker of a given sex/age dropping out of the system during the next year. To obtain these rates, first I observe the proportional rate of change in the number of workers moving up from one age group to the next older one in five years, adjusted for the change in the system's overall employment level during the period.

I have computed two such sets over two consecutive five-year periods, one from 1975 to 1980, and another from 1980 to 1985, and averaged them. Such important behaviors as changing jobs, temporarily retiring for family reasons, or permanently retiring due to old age are presumably reflected in these figures. I reproduce the rates that I used for HIMA in figure 6.9.

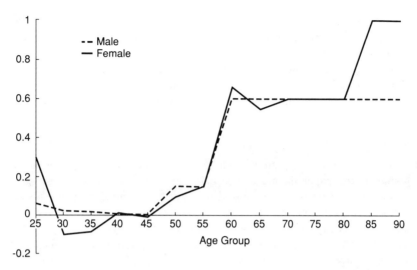

Fig. 6.9   Net dropout rates (HIMA)

Dependents in Each System

The Ministry of Welfare reports cited above also contain the sex/age-group relations between workers and their dependents, which can be transformed into the following matrix: the (i, j)th element of this matrix shows what percentage of dependents in the jth age group are supported by 1 percent of the workers in the ith age group who are in a particular program. Multiplying the ith row by the share of this program in the number of workers in the ith age group of any year and summing over the rows will give the age-group profile of the dependents supported by the workers of the system.

Since there is a matrix for each of the four possible combinations of workers' and dependents' sexes (i.e., male/female supported by male/female), this procedure must be repeated four times each year. I then add male dependents supported by male workers to those supported by female workers and obtain the age-group profile of male dependents. Likewise, by adding female dependents supported by male workers to those supported by female workers, I obtain the age-group profile of female dependents.

For public-sector employees, I adjusted the matrices of HIMA by a common factor to obtain the same total number of dependents for 1986. The same procedure as above is then followed for each year.

6.3.2   Medical Costs

Medical Costs of Each Sex/Age Group

Since our population allocation model differentiates male/female and worker/dependent for each age group, ideally one would like to have medical information on these four different groups, as is the case for HIMA. For the rest, however, I had to do with the available cost figures; for example, for

HIMG cost computations, I use a common set of costs for male and female workers in the same age group and another set for male and female dependents in the same age group.

Since no consolidated benefit report is published for MAAI, I averaged HIMA and HIMG rates for each sex/age group and adjusted them by a common factor until I obtained the total medical expenditure on MAAI individuals for 1989.

Medical Cost Allocation Models

According to the structure of each health insurance plan outlined at the beginning of this paper, the medical cost allocation model divides the (estimated future) medical costs of the covered individuals of a given system into four parts: the part that patients pay, the part that governments pay, the part that other systems pay, and the part that the system itself pays. Each system then adds all the costs charged to it and subtracts the government subsidies to it. The difference between the two will have to be raised by insurance taxes. The model also computes the payroll of the covered workers, and the tax rate will be determined. For the NHI system, the per capita premium is computed.

6.3.3   The Cost of Public Retirement Benefits

The Welfare Annuity Plan (WAP) Model

Existing benefits. The Social Insurance Agency's 1989 *Annual Report* provides a sex/age breakdown of the retired workers who are receiving WAP benefits as well as the distribution of the number of covered years among old-age annuity recipients of each sex. From these two sets of statistics, I estimated the average size of existing old-age annuities for each sex/age group.

The number of recipients is then reduced each year by the expected number of deaths in each sex/age group. Each deceased male recipient is replaced by five-sevenths of a female spouse, who then receives three-quarters of the original annuity as a survivor's benefit until her death. I ignored the possibility of a male spouse claiming a survivor's benefit. The *Annual Report* cited above, however, does not allow one to construct an age-group profile of survivor's benefit recipients, and I simply depreciate the total cost of the existing survivor's benefit at the rate of 14.3 percent per year.

New benefits. One-fifth of the HIMA/HIMG workers who were in the 55–59 and 60–64 age groups during the previous period and who drop out of HIMA/ HIMG employment in the current period are counted as recipients of the WAP special benefit during that period. In the next period, they will move to regular WAP benefits with basic old-age pensions. Older workers who drop out of employment during the period are added directly to the group receiving regular WAP benefits with basic old-age pensions.

To estimate the future WAP benefits for the new recipients, it is necessary to estimate their average number of years covered by WAP and their lifetime average wages. As to the number of covered years, I projected that it will increase from 32.5 years in 1989 to 34.9 years in 2019 for new male recipients and from 26.5 years in 1989 to 30.3 years in 2019 for new female recipients. After 2019, the length of coverage will increase only very slightly for both sexes. At this moment, however, this projection is based on an ad hoc computation carried outside the simulation model, using the cross-distribution tables of number of covered months and age/sex of WAP workers (contained in Department of Public Pensions [1986]) and their assumed differential entry/quit probabilities. The lifetime wage profile is approximated by starting from the average wage for 55–59 age group and going down the age structure until a sufficient number of years are obtained to match the number of covered years.

The NPP Model

NPP participants' sex/age-group structure. The relationship between NPP and NHI is far weaker than the relation between WAP and HIMA/HIMG because monthly NPP tax payments are handled by individual passbooks independently whereas WAP and HIMA/HIMG taxes are automatically withheld from workers' paychecks at the same time. Nevertheless, information about the NPP participants' sex/age structure is very scarce, and I have to rely on the NHI sex/age-group data.

According to my estimation of each sex, there are approximately 11 million individuals between the ages 20 and 59 who should be participating in NHI *and* NPP. Out of these individuals, from each sex, about 10 million participate in NHI and 9 million in NPP. Since the coverage of NPP is essentially identical to that of NHI, and in the absence of direct information, in order to estimate the NPP sex/age-group structure one must rely on NHI sex/age-group data. But the NHI data contain workers who are "old boys" or "old girls" of HIMA/HIMG or their dependents who are in the RWMS. Since these people are unlikely to join NPP, I subtracted them from the NHI participants and multiplied the NHI data by the factor 0.9 to obtain the NPP sex/age structure for 1989.

NPP benefits: Existing NPP benefits. The 1989 *Annual Report* cited above gives the sex/age-group profile of NPP recipients and the size distribution of NPP benefits separately. I assume that all NPP benefits are identical regardless of age group in each sex and that the male recipient's benefit is fixed at ¥385,700 and the female recipient's benefit at ¥368,300. In each sex/age group, I then depreciate the total of these benefits each year by the mortality rate. The average size of current benefits suggests that the current NPP recipients had paid NPP taxes for only 55 percent of the months that they had been presumably covered, or for about twenty-two years of a forty-year base, which is not yet long enough to qualify for the pension without special provisions.

NPP benefits: Future NPP benefits. The surviving participants of the 1989 NPP sex/age-group structure who enter the 65–69 age group are counted as new recipients of the old-age benefit in this period. According to my projection, the fraction of the months that the new retirees will have paid the taxes will increase steadily over the next thirty years, but only to around 0.7, or to twenty-eight years, which will barely exceed the minimum twenty-five years required.

Compared with private annuity contracts, the NPP no longer looks attractive. Its annual costs now exceed ¥100,000, and, for each "paid" year, its annuity will increase by less than ¥16,000. Younger people can do far better in the private capital market. In fact, for the last two years, registered NPP participants have paid only a little more than 80 percent of the taxes due. In addition, as a result of repeated increases in NPP taxes, now there is a significant number of "poor" individuals who are exempt from NPP taxes. Their share of the population is about 15 percent.[9]

6.4   Simulation Results

6.4.1   Demographic Changes

In order to give an idea of the speed and the degree of aging in the Japanese economy, three sets of figures are produced. One set of figures (fig. 6.10) shows the 1986 distribution of population across sex/age groups and insurance systems. Another set (fig. 6.11) shows the situation early in the next century, just before the baby boomers begin to retire. The third set (fig. 6.12) shows the population in 2019 at its most aged state, when there will be almost as many women older than 60 as younger than 20. The distribution of the population over more aggregated groups is given in table 6.4 for these three years.

6.4.2   Medical Costs

Absorption of Medical Care

No less dramatic is the change in the absorption of medical care. Figure 6.13 shows the shares of the medical care resources absorbed by each age group (both sexes combined) in 1989, regardless of who paid the costs. The top of the hill appears to be around the 60–64 age group, but it is a low hill. The baby boom generation is in the 40–44 age group and causes no alarm at this stage. Things look a little serious in 2004, but still manageable (fig. 6.14). The baby boomers are in the 55–59 age group, and their costs are just starting to show. Things look extremely serious in 2024 (fig. 6.15), when the baby boomers

---

9. I assumed that the ratio of n to v in t years will be given by

$$p = 0.55 \times (30 - t)/30 + 0.7 \times t/30,$$

which I multiply by 625,000 by p to obtain the average NPP value.

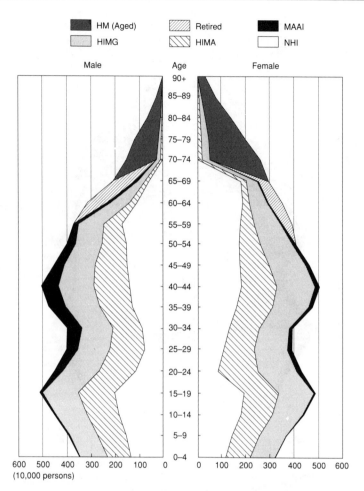

Fig. 6.10   Population pyramid and its distribution to health insurance programs (1989)

appear as a steep mountain in the 70–74 age group. In 2024, in fact, the retired collectively consume more medical care than the working generation and their children, compared to 43 percent in 1986.

Table 6.5 gives the medical costs for each super age group in these three years (age groupings here are more aggregated than the standard one.) Needless to say, they are expressed in 1989 prices. According to this table, in 2004, the national medical expenditure will be about 30 percent higher than in 1989, and, in 2024, it will be about 1.5 times the 1989 size.

Allocation of Medical Costs

Given the bulging medical costs of the aged in coming years, how are they going to be paid if we maintain the present system of public medical insur-

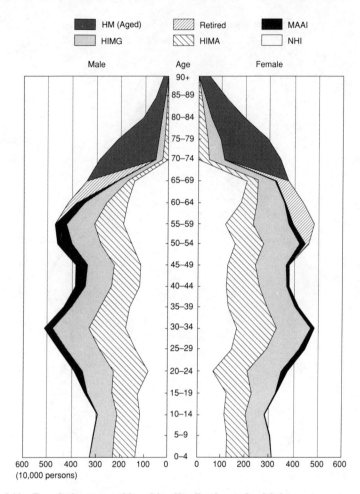

Fig. 6.11   Population pyramid and its distribution to health insurance programs (2004)

ance? I distinguish three different sources of payment: (i) government subsidies, (ii) patients' direct payments, and (iii) insurance taxes. Figure 6.16 shows the allocation of the national medical costs to these three sources under the present system. In 1989, about 25 percent of all medical costs are paid by governments from general tax revenue funds, and the share will increase by about 5 percentage points by 2024.

Insurance taxes paid slightly less than 60 percent in 1989, and the share will decrease by about 5 percentage points by 2024. Nevertheless, because the increase in the national medical expenditure will be accompanied by a decline in employment, employee insurance tax rates will have to be about 1.5 times the current levels by 2024. Close to 50 percent of the taxes imposed on the

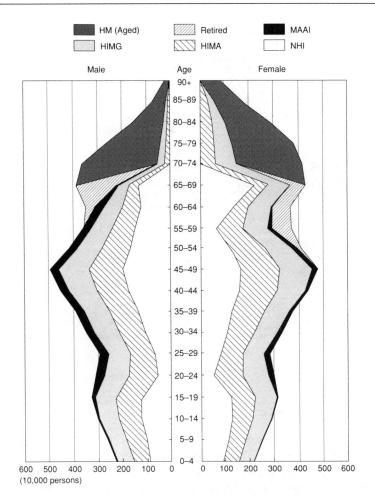

Fig. 6.12   Population pyramid and its distribution to health insurance programs (2019)

working generation will go to support HMSA and RWMS as a part of financing the medical costs of the aged.

The Effects of the 1983–84 Reforms

The effects of HMSA (and RWMS to a lesser degree) can be clearly seen by comparing figure 6.16 with figure 6.17, which represents the cost allocation under the old system. Without the reform, in 1986, government subsidies would have paid about ¥2.5 trillion more, or almost 15 percentage points more in terms of relative share. In 2024, the amount of money charged to the government would have been 60 percent more than under the present system, or close to 50 percent of all medical costs of that year. The cost charged to insurance

Table 6.4   **JCER Population Projection, 1991 (in thousands of persons)**

Year	Age 0–19	20–39	40–59	60–79	80+	Total
Male:						
1989	16,964	17,326	17,341	7,891	966	60,488
	(0.138)	(0.141)	(0.141)	(0.064)	(0.008)	(0.491)
2004	13,621	17,902	17,184	12,378	1,502	62,587
	(0.107)	(0.141)	(0.135)	(0.097)	(0.012)	(0.491)
2019	12,399	13,772	17,358	13,701	2,552	59,782
	(0.102)	(0.113)	(0.142)	(0.112)	(0.021)	(0.49)

Year	Age 0–19	20–39	40–59	60–79	80+	Total
Female:						
1989	16,130	16,914	17,601	10,207	1,764	62,616
	(0.131)	(0.137)	(0.143)	(0.083)	(0.014)	(0.509)
2004	12,904	17,165	17,254	14,337	3,127	64,787
	(0.101)	(0.135)	(0.135)	(0.113)	(0.025)	(0.509)
2019	11,742	13,159	17,021	15,787	4,456	62,165
	(0.096)	(0.108)	(0.14)	(0.129)	(0.037)	(0.51)

Note: Numbers in parentheses are the proportion of each age group/sex in total national population.

taxes, on the other hand, would have been relatively stable under the old system.

6.4.3 Public Pension Costs

Using simulation models as described in Ogura (1993), I have computed the costs of NPP benefits and WAP benefits as well as MAA retirement benefits. NPP participants are computed as a fixed proportion of NHI participants, while participants in HIMA and HIMG are collectively regarded as WAP participants, even though some may not qualify for the pension benefits in both programs owing to the extraordinarily long vesting period of twenty-five years. MAAs provide both health insurance and retirement benefits for all public-sector employees and hence are treated as identical in terms of participants.

Cost of NPP

In 1989, the total cost of NPP benefits was ¥3.1 trillion, of which the old-age pension benefits accounted for ¥2.5 trillion. According to the simulation results, the total cost of NPP benefits will go up to ¥5.7 trillion in 2019 and will come down slowly thereafter. During the same period, the number of NPP pension benefit recipients will increase from 7.6 to 11.4 million. These numbers do not include the WAP workers and their dependent spouses, to whom the 1986 reform extended mandatory coverage. The voluntary participants prior to 1989 are assumed to receive their basic old-age pension benefits from WAP.

Cost (10 Billion Yen)

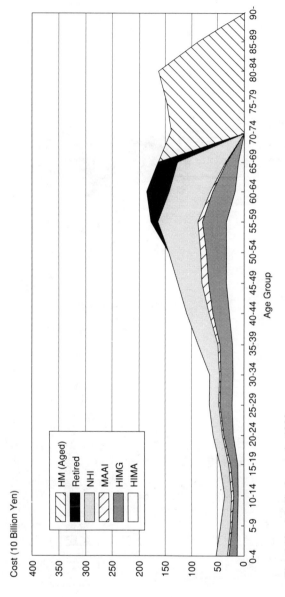

Fig. 6.13   Medical costs in 1989

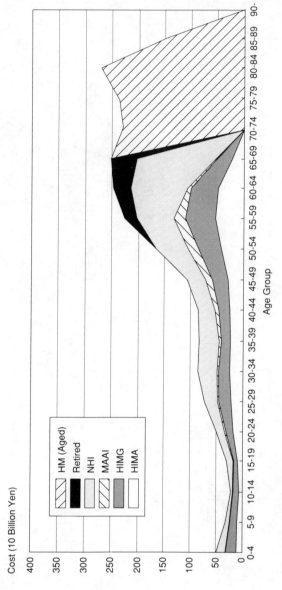

Cost (10 Billion Yen)

400

350

300

250

200

150

100

50

0

HM (Aged)
Retired
NHI
MAAI
HIMG
HIMA

0-4 5-9 10-14 15-19 20-24 25-29 30-34 35-39 40-44 45-49 50-54 55-59 60-64 65-69 70-74 75-79 80-84 85-89 90-

Age Group

Fig. 6.14 Medical costs in 2004

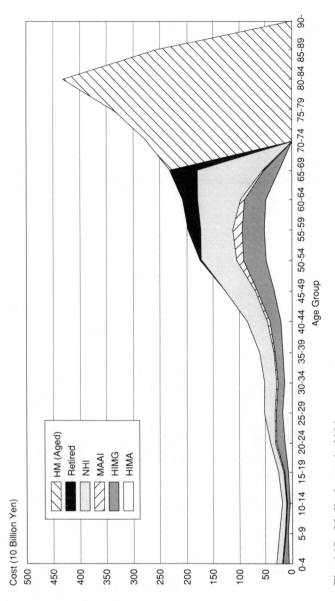

Fig. 6.15　Medical costs in 2024

Table 6.5   **Annual Medical Cost Projection (in 1989 billion yen)**

Year	Age					
	0–19	20–39	40–59	60–79	80+	Total
1989	145	234	489	623	257	1,749
	(0.08)	(0.13)	(0.28)	(0.36)	(0.15)	(1.00)
2004	111	252	508	956	450	2,277
	(0.05)	(0.11)	(0.22)	(0.42)	(0.20)	(1.00)
2024	83	175	506	1,051	726	2,541
	(0.03)	(0.07)	(0.20)	(0.41)	(0.29)	(1.00)

Note: Numbers in parentheses are the proportion of each age group in national health care costs.

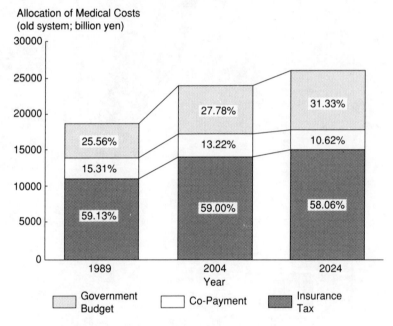

Fig. 6.16   Allocation of medical costs

Costs of the WAP and MAA

In 1989, the total cost of WAP benefits was ¥10 trillion, including the basic old-age annuity. It should go up to ¥21 trillion, or more than twice the present cost, in the second decade of the twenty-first century. Of this amount, about a third (¥7 trillion) will be for the basic old-age annuity. The increase in cost will be primarily due to the increase in the number of full benefit recipients from 7 million to over 14 million individuals during this period.

In 1989, MAA paid almost ¥7 trillion in retirement benefits. The cost will increase to ¥9 trillion at the end of this century, but it will start declining there-

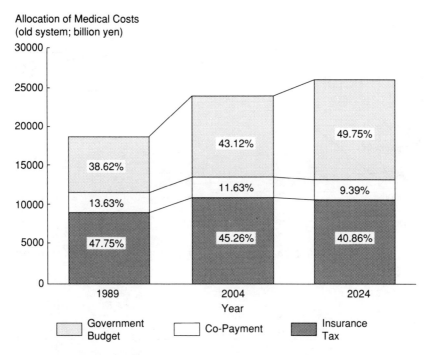

Allocation of Medical Costs
(old system; billion yen)

Fig. 6.17   Allocation of medical costs (old system)

after to less than half the present level in the middle of the next century, if the current low level of hiring persists in the public sector. Currently, MAA is in the worst shape of all the public pension programs for employed workers. The present level of benefits is already more than 40 percent of the total payroll of the workers in the public sector.

Effects of the 1986 Reforms

I also computed how much the benefits would cost in 2021 had we kept the system prior to the 1986 reform. The combined costs of WAP and MAA benefits would reach ¥38 trillion instead of ¥31 trillion in 2034 (fig. 18*a*), and the cost of NPP benefits would reach ¥8.2 trillion instead of ¥5.7 trillion in 2019 (fig. 6.18*b*). Therefore, without the 1986 reform, in 2019, the total cost of NPP, WAP, and MAA would be ¥46 trillion instead of ¥36.7 trillion.

Thus, the 1986 reform will reduce the combined costs by more than 30 percent. As was pointed out earlier, the savings in NPP costs come from both the cut in the unit NPP benefit and the de facto cancellation of 7 million voluntary participants' claims that will be "paid" by WAP. The savings in the WAP cost come from the one-quarter cut in the "proportional" benefit and the implicit cuts in the "flat" benefits.

A

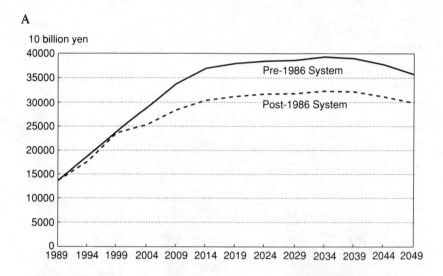

B

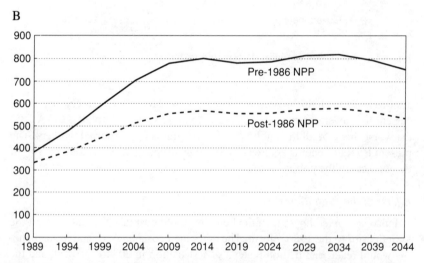

Fig. 6.18   (A) Comparison of pre-1986 and post-1986 systems: WAP and MAA integrated costs. (B) Comparison of pre-1986 and post-1986 systems: NPP costs

6.5 Concluding Remarks

6.5.1 Magnitude of the Costs

In fiscal year 1986, the Japanese national medical expenditure was estimated at ¥17 trillion, or 6.4 percent of the national income that year. Of this amount, only ¥2 trillion was paid directly out of patients' pockets, and the rest paid out of government budgets and by public medical insurance plans. In the same year, ¥16.6 trillion, or 6.3 percent of national income, was paid out as benefits of public annuity insurances, of which WAP and NPP together accounted for two-thirds.

Population aging will increase these costs over the next several decades. The peak will come around the year 2021, when the national medical expenditure will be close to 50 percent higher, at around ¥25 trillion. At the same time, the costs of the benefits of all public annuity plans may well exceed ¥35 trillion if we maintain the current system of starting the retirement benefits at age 60 for employees. Figure 6.19 shows estimates of future combined costs of all public pension costs and national medical costs, as well as the costs of all public pension costs alone, in the first half of the next century. According to this figure, the combined costs will increase from ¥40 trillion in 1994 to ¥60 trillion in the second decade of the next century (both figures are given in 1989 yen). While these costs increase, the size of our labor force will shrink, along with the tax base of our social insurance in real terms, as can be seen clearly from the estimates of the employees' payroll in the same figure. Thus, medical costs and retirement benefit costs will either absorb or transfer about one-quarter of national income, or twice their current share.

6.5.2 Reforms in the 1980s

If this simulation model is correct, the 1986 pension reform has reduced NPP's long-run cost by ¥2.5 trillion and WAP's long-run cost by ¥7 trillion. This amounts to a cut of 30 percent. It also reduced the government's subsidy to WAP. On the other hand, the 1984–85 medical insurance reforms simply redistributed the medical costs of the old from the government budgets to employee insurance plans.

These reforms have left us a fiscal structure that depends too heavily on social insurance taxes. In 1986, the revenue from social insurance taxes reached ¥28.7 trillion, compared with ¥42.1 trillion of national general tax revenue. The share of the social insurance taxes will keep on ballooning as the expanding costs of public annuity plans are scheduled to be financed mainly by annuity insurance taxes, and the combined social insurance tax rates of future working generations will easily be in excess of 50 percent. In figure 6.20, I computed the necessary payroll tax rate to maintain health insurance programs and keep all public pension programs on a pay-as-you-go basis for all employees including those in the public sector. By 2019, the combined tax

10 billion yen

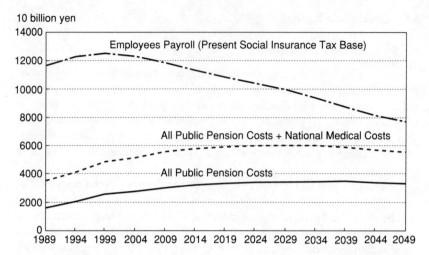

Fig. 6.19   Effects of aging on Japanese public pension costs and medical costs (JCER projection)

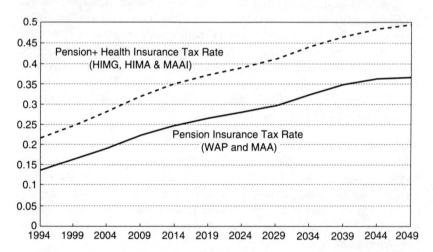

Fig. 6.20   JCER projection of combined health and pension insurance tax rates

rate will be close to 40 percent, or double the current rate, and still increasing for another twenty years.

6.5.3   Future Reforms

There are two problems that need to be resolved in these programs. One is the size of the burden of these programs itself. It still is too much for future working generations. In order to provide economic incentives for the supply of labor and capital, it would be wise to trim the costs of these programs further.

In fact, these programs still contain substantial fat. When being old was synonymous with being poor, providing free medical care and generous public annuity benefits might have been a desirable policy for achieving distributional justice. But now there are rich old people and poor old people. One can say that the present benefit structure of these programs does not try to direct benefits toward relatively needy old people. One may even say that the present public annuity provides very regressive benefits; rich old people receive more benefits because of longer coverage and better pay. An attempt must be made to relax the very stringent vesting period and make the benefit schedule a more progressive one, as is the case in the United States.

In the working generation, there are rich people and poor people, and, as a tax borne by them, a social insurance tax is far from ideal. Typically, it is a linear tax on labor income between the lower and the upper limits. Compared with the personal income tax, it is far less progressive, and its tax base is much narrower, as the projected future tax rate shows. For low-income households, it provides little or no exemption but imposes a fixed-sum tax. For high-income households, it becomes another fixed-sum tax. In these regions, it is regressive. Income transfer between generations has become an essential part of any of these social insurance programs. Financing them primarily by such imperfect taxes is a very questionable proposition.

References

Department of Public Pensions. Ministry of Health and Welfare. 1986. *Official projection of public pension programs of 1986* (in Japanese). Tokyo.

Ogura, S., 1993. Projection of Japanese public pension costs in the first half of the 21st century and the effects of three possible reforms. Paper presented at the JCER-NBER Joint Conference on Aging at Hakone, Japan, 14–16 September 1993.

Ogura, S., and R. Futagami. 1992. On the decline of the mortality rate from cerebrovascular diseases since 1965. Mimeo.

Social Security Administration. 1980–90. *Annual report* (in Japanese). Tokyo.

7

Financing Health Care for Elderly Americans in the 1990s

Alan M. Garber

Although elderly Americans are better able to pay for medical care than ever before, there is a widespread perception that financing the health care of the elderly will pose a tremendous challenge to policymakers in the United States during the coming decades. The elderly have more comprehensive protection against the financial burden of paying for hospital and physicians' services than other segments of the population; more than 13 percent of all Americans lack health insurance, but only six-tenths of 1 percent of Americans 65 and older are uninsured (U.S. Bureau of the Census 1989, 96). The great majority participate in at least one of the two government programs that finance health care for the elderly, Medicare and the need-based Medicaid program. About two-thirds of the elderly purchase supplemental private insurance as well. Even as the elderly enjoy more comprehensive medical insurance than younger Americans, their well-being has improved absolutely and in relation to other demographic groups. For example, between 1970 and 1984, median incomes for families headed by 25–64-year-olds barely changed, rising from $29,113 to $29,292 (in 1984 dollars). During the same period, median incomes for families headed by persons 65 years of age or older rose from $13,522 to $18,236 (U.S. Senate Special Committee on Aging 1986, 57). Why, then, speak of a crisis in financing the health care of the elderly?

The challenge lies in the observation that government expenditures for the

Alan M. Garber is health services research and development senior research associate, Department of Veterans Affairs; associate professor of medicine, Division of General Internal Medicine, Stanford University Medical School; and a research associate of the National Bureau of Economic Research. He was a Henry J. Kaiser Family Foundation Faculty Scholar in General Internal Medicine when this was written.

This work was supported in part by grant AG07651 from the National Institute on Aging and grant 12761 from the Robert Wood Johnson Foundation. Hiroo Urushi made helpful comments. Opinions expressed here should be attributed to the author alone.

health care of the elderly are rising rapidly, yet the elderly continue to risk catastrophic health expenses. The growth in Medicare expenditures, which pay for hospital and physicians' services, has outstripped general inflation and cannot be attributed to demographic change alone. In 1967, its first full year of operation, total Medicare expenditures were $4.6 billion. By 1984, Medicare expenditures had increased to $62.9 billion (Division of National Cost Estimates 1987). The annual compound real rate of growth was 9.1 percent, far in excess of the growth in the number of Medicare enrollees. Only a small part of this growth rate could be explained by the increasing average age of Medicare enrollees. Rapid expenditure growth has continued despite well-publicized and controversial cost-containment programs.

Advocates of a greater role for public insurance emphasize that out-of-pocket expenditures for health care among Americans age 65 and older have not decreased in real terms since the Medicare program began. There are several explanations for the persistence of substantial out-of-pocket expenditures. One is the growth and diffusion of cost-increasing medical technology, which may have improved the care delivered to Medicare recipients and certainly has increased its cost (Schwartz 1987; Division of National Cost Estimates 1987). Because of relatively complete insurance coverage, however, hospital and physician services are rarely responsible for catastrophic out-of-pocket expenditures. Nursing home care and related services, however, can lead to large out-of-pocket costs. Largely because its eligibility rules are so restrictive, the Medicare program pays for relatively little long-term care, which consists of nursing home care, home health care, and other services for chronic illnesses and disabilities. Only a small fraction of total nursing home care expenditures in the United States are reimbursed by the Medicare program. Medicaid spends much more for long-term care, paying for about 44 percent of all nursing home expenditures in 1987 (Letsch, Levit, and Waldo 1988). However, because it is a need-based program, Medicaid is unavailable to middle-class Americans until they have become impoverished by health expenditures.

Discussions of long-term care financing usually emphasize institutional care because it accounts for the preponderance of long-term care expenditures. In 1982, for example, when total expenditures for nursing home care in the United States were $27 billion, Medicare and Medicaid together spent less than $1.6 billion for home health care. Private expenditures for home health care in 1981 were estimated to be $2.3 billion (Doty, Liu, and Wiener 1985).

While many recognize the need for improved financing of long-term care, opinions about the best solutions diverge. Some groups emphasize the need for a greater government role either in the provision of long-term care or in its financing. Others, noting the unexpectedly rapid rise in Medicare expenditures, argue that it would be preferable to develop private initiatives for long-term care.

In this paper, I briefly describe demographic trends that influence the utilization of health care, examine some of the financial issues surrounding hospital and physicians' services for the elderly, and discuss obstacles to more comprehensive financing and delivery of long-term care. Cost containment is the central theme of current discussions about financing hospital and physicians' services, while the issues in long-term care concern expanding coverage and reducing the risk of catastrophic costs for the elderly who are subject to the risk of institutionalization.

7.1   Demographic Change and Financing Health Care

Even if prices and the mix of health services do not change, the "graying" of the U.S. population will promote health expenditure growth. Demographic changes account for only part of the recent inflation in health costs, but they will have a greater effect in the future. The 12 percent of the U.S. population age 65 and older are responsible for more than a third of all health expenditures. The number of Americans in this age group is expected to double by the time all the postwar "baby boom" generation reaches old age. Furthermore, among the elderly, health care utilization rises dramatically with age, so projections that the number of very old—age 85 and older—will quadruple in the next fifty years (U.S. Bureau of the Census 1984) suggest that health expenditures will soar.

Long-term care is even more closely tied to aging. A negligible fraction of the under-65 population reside in nursing homes. Among all individuals age 65 and older, between 4 and 5 percent will be in a nursing home at any time (table 7.1). The likelihood of being in a nursing home rises with age, reaching as high as 25 percent for a person who is age 85 or older. Over the past decade or so, the age-specific risk of being institutionalized appears to have declined slightly, but, even if this trend continues, if all else is equal, the shift in the age distribution of the American population will expand the number of nursing home residents. The effect on utilization of long-term care services, which are delivered primarily to the elderly, may even exceed the change in demand for physician or hospital care.

As health service utilization increases, the range of feasible options for financing care may become more limited. When the baby boom generation reaches older ages, the population that uses health care services and long-term care most heavily will grow as the working-age population shrinks. The ratio of elderly Medicare enrollees to currently employed adults may rise to 40 percent—that is, two retirees for every five workers (U.S. Senate Special Committee on Aging 1986, 21). Thus, even though today's Medicare budget deficit might be funded out of general revenues, that option will become less viable when the number of employed persons as a fraction of retirees shrinks. Political, economic, and demographic trends make it likely that the generation receiving the care will pay for it, either during their working years or after they have reached advanced age.

Table 7.1   **Nursing Home and Personal Care Home Residents 65 Years of Age and Over and Rate per 1,000 Population: United States, 1963, 1973–74, 1977, and 1985**

	1963	1973–74	1977	1985
All ages	25.4	44.7	47.1	46.2
65–74 years	7.9	12.3	14.4	12.5
75–84 years	39.6	57.7	64.0	57.7
85 years and older	148.4	257.3	225.9	220.3

Source: National Center for Health Statistics (1989, 123).

7.2   Current Financing of Health Care for the Elderly

The vast majority of America's elderly participate in Medicare. The hospital insurance component of Medicare, Part A, formerly paid for up to ninety days of hospital care per year. The Supplemental Medical Insurance (SMI) component, or Medicare Part B, covers physicians' fees and fees for other professional services and supplies. More than 95 percent of elderly Americans participate in Part A, and a similar number pay a small monthly premium to participate in Part B (Health Care Financing Administration 1989).

At least until recently, about two-thirds of all elderly Americans purchased private health insurance to extend or complement their Medicare coverage. Much of this private insurance, usually called *medigap* insurance, paid for some or all of the deductibles and copayments under Medicare. Many of the policies also extended the number of days of coverage for hospital care, nursing home care, or both. Relatively few services that were excluded from Medicare benefits, such as prescription drugs and eyeglasses, were covered by medigap policies. The role of medigap policies is in flux because of the series of revisions of the Medicare program that began in 1988 with the passage of the Medicare Catastrophic Coverage Act.

The Catastrophic Coverage Act contained many of the features of medigap insurance policies. The new benefit structure, which was to be implemented in a series of steps, would have limited out-of-pocket expenditures for several covered services and expanded the services covered by Medicare. The Catastrophic Coverage Act mandated that, as of 1990, Medicare would pay for all Part B services in excess of $1,370. After payment of a $560 deductible, Medicare recipients would have unlimited coverage for inpatient hospital care. Prior to the passage of this bill, coverage was limited to ninety days of hospitalization, and patients bore a significant coinsurance burden. The catastrophic illness benefit was also designed to reduce out-of-pocket expenditures for outpatient prescription drugs, which Medicare had not covered previously. As of 1991, there was to be a $600 deductible for prescription drugs and 50 percent copayments. In subsequent years, the copayment rate was to diminish, while a flexible deductible was planned, its size depending on the number of Medicare beneficiaries who used the drug benefit. The deductible was to be indexed so that approximately 16.8 percent of all Medicare beneficiaries would qualify for the drug benefit at any time. Consequently, the deductible would have increased if pharmaceutical use or prices rose.

The Catastrophic Coverage Act added little to Medicare's limited coverage of long-term care. Only individuals confined to their homes ("homebound") were to be reimbursed for home health care. Coverage for several routine home health care services, such as occupational therapy and part-time services of home health aides, would have been extended only to persons who needed part-time skilled nursing care and met all other eligibility conditions. Homemaker services, drug administration, and blood transfusions were not covered.

Although the Catastrophic Coverage Act liberalized some of the rules for nursing home coverage under Medicare, the scope of coverage was not expanded dramatically. Prior to passage of the Catastrophic Coverage Act, Medicare paid for up to 100 days of nursing home care. The hospital insurance component of Medicare paid for all the covered services during the first twenty days in a nursing home, leaving a copayment for the twenty-first through the 100th day of hospital care. Several conditions had to be met, however, before a beneficiary could be reimbursed for any nursing home care. Nursing home coverage was limited to care in skilled nursing facilities, institutions that provide full-time or nearly full-time skilled nursing care. The patient had to be transferred to the skilled nursing facility in order to receive care for a condition that was treated in a hospital. The hospital admission preceding entry to the nursing home had to be at least three days long and had to occur in the thirty days prior to the nursing home admission. Admission to the nursing home required the approval of both a doctor and a utilization review committee. The Catastrophic Coverage Act eliminated the prior hospitalization requirement and raised the limit on nursing home care from 100 to 150 days per year. No deductible for skilled nursing care was proposed.

The Catastrophic Coverage Act was repealed before it was fully implemented. Controversy over its provisions erupted soon after it was passed. The funding mechanism—a surtax on the income tax of elderly Medicare enrollees—divided older Americans. Many of them faced added tax payments far exceeding the premiums they formerly paid for private supplemental insurance and far in excess of the actuarial value of the added benefits. A Congressional Budget Office report estimated that the program's benefits in 1989 were worth $62.00 per enrollee while premiums *averaged* $145 and were substantially more for high-income Medicare enrollees. For persons subject to the maximum surtax (incomes over $35,000), the cost was fourteen times the value of the benefits (Tolchin 1989). Although the pressure for repeal came from people who objected to the surtax, others attacked the Catastrophic Coverage Act because it failed to extend long-term care coverage.

In recent years, because it limited eligibility for nursing home reimbursements and covered only 100 days of nursing home care each year, Medicare has accounted for a small percentage of the overall payments for nursing home care. Of the $40.6 billion spent for nursing home care, Medicare paid for 1.4 percent in 1987. Private long-term care insurance paid for less than 1 percent. The elderly and their families paid for about half of nursing home care. Medicaid paid for just under 44 percent, while other government and private sources paid the remainder (see table 7.2).

Although Medicaid, which is administered jointly by the states and the federal government, was designed to provide health insurance to low-income persons, its "spend-down" provisions have enabled many other Americans who have substantial medical or long-term care expenditures to draw on its benefits. The rules for Medicaid eligibility vary from state to state, but most state Medicaid programs have an eligibility category called *medically needy.* In the thirty-five states with medically needy programs, persons whose income net of health expenditures falls below 133 percent of the welfare level income are said to "spend down" and are eligible to receive Medicaid benefits. In 1984, the "allowed resources" or value of assets allowed for two-person households under state medically needy programs ranged from $2,250 (in several states) to $9,500 (in North Dakota). The allowed income after health expenditures for a two-person household ranged from $135 (Tennessee) to $583 (Wisconsin). Long stays in nursing homes are expensive—in 1986, it was estimated that nursing home care cost an average of $22,000 annually in the United States (Bowen 1986). Because the long-term care expenditures of many middle-class institutionalized elderly approach or exceed total income, many are able to participate in Medicaid.

Largely because of its spend-down provision, Medicaid pays nearly half of all U.S. nursing home expenditures. The Medicaid benefit has been the source of discontent among many groups with disparate interests and opinions. Spending down is viewed by the elderly as a disruptive and often humiliating experience, discomfiting a group that is already disabled by chronic disease and forced to leave home for an institution. In some states, spouses' assets are not protected if an individual enters a nursing home and spends down. Anec-

Table 7.2   **U.S. Aggregate Nursing Home Care Expenditures by Source of Funds: Selected Calendar Years, 1980–87 (billions of dollars)**

Year	Total	Direct Patient Payments	All Third Parties	Private Health Insurance	Medicare	Medicaid
1980	20.4	8.9	11.5	.2	.4	9.8
1983	29.4	14.1	15.3	.3	.5	13.0
1984	31.6	15.5	16.1	.3	.5	13.8
1985	34.7	17.2	17.4	.3	.5	15.0
1986	37.4	18.8	18.6	.3	.6	16.0
1987	40.6	20.0	20.6	.4	.6	17.8

Source: Letsch, Levit, and Waldo (1988).

dotes are told about elderly couples divorcing in order to preserve the assets of the independently living spouse. Yet Medicaid often bears the cost of nursing home care for a group of people who were never intended beneficiaries of the program. Furthermore, some people transfer assets prior to the spend-down period in order to escape loss of assets and income. The federal Office of the Inspector General claims that millions of dollars are lost to the Medicaid program each year because of lax efforts to recover assets for decedents who received Medicaid benefits. If all states recovered money "owed" to Medicaid by the estates of Medicaid beneficiaries as effectively as Oregon, the state with the most effective estate recovery program, $589 million would be collected annually, according to the inspector general (Kidwell 1988).

Private insurance plays a smaller role in financing the health care of the elderly. Although the role of medigap policies will change in response to government actions, they are unlikely to begin to provide extensive coverage for long-term care. Nevertheless, private insurance has an important potential role in long-term care. Long-term care represents a frontier for private health insurers: although policies have been available for several years, private insurance currently pays less than 1 percent of all nursing home expenditures. To know why the role of private insurers has been so limited, it is necessary to review the characteristics of long-term care and the people who use it.

7.3   Long-Term Care Utilization and Determinants

Because the number of disabled elderly is expected to grow over the coming years, and because the market for insurance against the financial risks generated by nursing home admission is poorly developed, there is substantial interest in promoting private long-term care insurance and innovative approaches to long-term care. Why has private insurance made few inroads into long-term care, and why has there been so little innovation in long-term care delivery? Many of the elements of demand for insurance are present: to the extent that elderly people who have prolonged admissions to nursing homes deplete their assets and income, they face financial catastrophe. The risk of institutionalization is small but not negligible. However, efforts to change long-term care financing and delivery have been stymied by our inadequate knowledge of the forces leading to nursing home admission, of the characteristics that distinguish individuals who spend long periods in nursing homes from those whose nursing home admissions are brief, of the interactions between nursing home utilization and hospital utilization, and of the distinctions between those health factors associated with high mortality and those that lead to nursing home admission.

Without this kind of information, both insurers and the elderly themselves have found it difficult to anticipate the risk of nursing home admission. There is even less information about the extent of adverse selection that would be faced by a private insurer. Regulatory barriers, uncertainty about future government programs directed toward long-term care, and concerns about moral hazard aggravate these problems. For quite some time, economists have proposed that, by raising the demand for health care, health insurance is responsible for much of the growth in U.S. medical expenditures in recent decades (Feldstein 1973).

In view of the relative underdevelopment of insurance for long-term care, it is noteworthy that long-term care expenditures have grown much more slowly than expenditures for hospital and physicians' services. The experience of Medicare is instructive. Medicare expenditures rose from $4.5 billion in 1967 to $76 billion in 1986 (table 7.3). There is substantial disagreement about its causes, but the rapid rise in Medicare expenditures cannot be attributed to the rate of inflation in input prices, such as labor, nor can it be attributed to simple expansion of the number of Medicare recipients. Several experts believe that much of the growth in expenditures can be attributed to the development and dissemination of new health care "technology." Many new operations and diagnostic procedures had been developed during that period, and operations that were once performed only on middle-aged adults or younger people were performed increasingly often on the elderly. For example, in the 1970s, it was unusual for elderly Americans to undergo coronary artery bypass surgery. In 1972, Americans age 65–74 accounted for 8 percent of all coronary bypass operations. By 1981, they accounted for 28 percent of the procedures. The number of such operations performed in this age group rose from 2,500 in 1972 to 46,000 in 1981. The volume of other major operations performed on the elderly also grew during the same period (Valvona and Sloan 1985).

The circumstance that most favorably affected the development of such technology was the widened availability of health insurance, which lowered the price to the patient of having an operation or an expensive diagnostic procedure to the amount of the copayment. No such phenomenon has characterized

Table 7.3   **Medicare Enrollees and Expenditures and Percentage Distribution, According to Type of Service: United States, Selected Years, 1967–86**

Type of Service	1967	1970	1975	1980	1983	1984	1985	1986
Enrollees[a]	19.5	20.5	25.0	28.5	30.0	30.5	31.1	31.7
All expenditures[b]	4.5	7.1	15.6	35.7	57.4	62.9	70.5	76.0
All services[c]	100.0	100.0	100.0	100.0	100.0	100.0	100.0	100.0
Hospital care[c]	69.1	71.5	73.8	72.6	70.5	70.1	69.3	68.0
Physician services[c]	24.7	22.8	21.6	22.1	23.4	23.3	24.0	25.0
Nursing home care[c]	4.6	3.7	1.9	1.1	.9	.9	.8	.8
Other health services[c]	1.6	1.9	2.8	4.1	5.3	5.7	5.9	6.2

Source: National Center for Health Statistics (1989, 174).
[a]Millions.
[b]Billions of dollars.
[c]Percentage distribution of expenditures.

long-term care. Direct payments by the elderly and their families or fixed, low payments by Medicaid account for virtually all expenditures for nursing home care. Anecdotal evidence that Medicaid patients face very long waits for admission supports the claim that Medicaid reimburses nursing homes less than private payers do. Because most full payments are out-of-pocket expenditures, and because Medicaid, which pays less, is responsible for most third-party expenditures, nursing homes and other providers have had little incentive to develop possibly cost-increasing but more attractive long-term care.

Successful methods to limit utilization of long-term care would allay much of the concern that insurers have about long-term care insurance. They would still need to know, however, the likelihood that insurance subscribers will use long-term care, and they will need accurate predictions of long-term care expenditures for enrollees. Consequently, analyses of the utilization of nursing home care, particularly in relation to observable characteristics of the individuals, have become very important. In fact, if observable characteristics could explain a great deal of the variation in nursing home utilization, adverse selection might not be a severe problem for insurers. Of course, if insurers possess detailed risk information, many elderly men and women would be unable to purchase private long-term care insurance at an affordable premium.

Few studies have provided comprehensive estimates or forecasts of long-term care utilization. Many studies have been designed simply to estimate the risk that an individual will enter a nursing home during that person's remaining life or during a fixed time interval. Many other studies have examined the distribution of length of stay in a nursing home without reference to the probability of admission. Relatively few of them have examined the expected future utilization of nursing home care by an individual who currently lives in the community. This is the measure of utilization that is most important for estimating expenditures on behalf of a potential purchaser of long-term care insurance.

A full characterization of the demand for and supply of long-term care would be the best basis for anticipating the effect of insurance coverage. However, attempts to estimate supply and demand curves for long-term care services have been nearly absent from the literature. Furthermore, nearly all studies of long-term care utilization have concentrated on nursing homes, although several studies have examined substitution between home health services and nursing home utilization. These studies did not, however, attempt to estimate price elasticities. The most prominent exception is a paper by Chiswick (1976), which combined state- and metropolitan-level cross-sectional and time-series data to analyze nursing home supply and demand. Data and methodological limitations cast doubt on the validity of its findings, yet many of the results are plausible. The price elasticity of demand for nursing home care was negative, and aggregate demand for nursing home care was higher in areas with an older, more disabled, and wealthier population. Because the author did not have data on such characteristics as the percentage of elderly persons living alone, only limited conclusions can be drawn about the effect of these correlates of area-wide utilization. Particularly because other authors did not even attempt to control for some of the exogenous characteristics that influence the supply of nursing home care, such as average wage levels, this study represents a noteworthy attempt to characterize the market for nursing home services.

A number of problems make it difficult to estimate the supply and demand for long-term care services. Nursing homes are not homogeneous, so price variation may reflect differences in the services offered. More important, the price faced by the elderly person who enters a nursing home may not be observable; the price paid for six months of nursing home care by an elderly person facing spend down is much lower if his or her assets have already been depleted. Typically, a middle-class woman who spends down is first a "private pay" patient and enters a relatively desirable nursing home with little difficulty. She can stay in the nursing home after becoming a Medicaid beneficiary, but, if she is transferred to a hospital for a long admission (perhaps two weeks or longer), she may lose her nursing home bed. She must then apply for readmission, but, now that she is a Medicaid patient, she is more likely than a private pay patient to be rejected. Uncertainty about current and expected assets and the subjective probability distribution of the duration of institutionalization make it particularly difficult to infer the price faced by an individual.

Given these difficulties, it is not surprising that other studies of long-term care utilization have had narrower goals: predicting the number of people entering nursing homes, examining the determinants of nursing home utilization, or studying the interactions between nursing home and home health care. Many studies only attempted to predict the probability that a person will enter a nursing home during some fixed time interval or during that person's lifetime. Others examined only the duration of nursing home admissions. Finally, some studies used comprehensive measures of utilization, estimating the distribution of expected nursing home utilization for various groups of older people living in the community. Within this group are several studies that also attempt to examine interactions between home health care and nursing home utilization as well as the interactions between hospital and nursing home care.

Several studies (Shapiro and Webster 1984; Shapiro and Tate 1988; Cohen, Tell, and Wallack 1988; Greenburg and Ginn 1979; Branch and Jette 1982; and Lane et al. 1985) have examined the risk of admission to a nursing home in a fixed period. Others estimated the number of people who will be admitted to a nursing home at any time in their life (Palmore 1976; Vicente, Wiley, and Carrington 1979; McConnel 1984; and Cohen, Tell, and Wallack 1986b). These studies are a heterogeneous group, examining different populations, applying different statistical methods, predicting different aspects of utilization, and controlling for different underlying sources of variation in utilization. Consequently, estimates of the likelihood of admission to a nursing home vary greatly. However, the best estimate of the probability that a 65-year-old will later enter a nursing home is approximately 25 percent.

Several characteristics have been found to be consistently associated with the risk of institutionalization. Chief among these are advanced age, female gender, the presence of certain health conditions, severe functional impairments, and living alone. Those who receive Medicaid are more likely to enter nursing homes, while some studies, but not all, find that more wealthy people are less likely to enter nursing homes (Garber and MaCurdy 1989).

Few studies have attempted to forecast overall nursing home utilization. The studies of overall utilization that were not conducted as part of a trial of a health intervention include those by Manheim and Hughes (1986) and Cohen, Tell, and Wallack (1986a). There have been several investigations of the effects of community care interventions on nursing home utilization, but many did not have an appropriate control group, nor did they control for relevant characteristics of the participants. Others studied populations that may not be representative of the general U.S. population of elderly (Weissert 1985). Community care demonstrations directed toward preventing nursing home admission have been reviewed by Kemper, Applebaum, and Harrigan (1987). For the most part, these demonstrations have tested whether enriched sets of home health services and other community services could obviate admission to nursing homes. One national randomized controlled trial, the National Long-Term Care ("Channeling") Demonstration, has tested whether enhanced home health services can prevent nursing home admission and decrease long-term care expenditures. This study, which was sponsored by the Department of Health and Human Services, selected a group of very disabled elderly people who were predominantly poor, relatively old, and lacking in social supports (Kemper 1988). More than half of the Channeling participants were incontinent, and 84 percent were disabled in at least one activity of daily living. The intervention was case management, or the assignment of an individual, usually a social worker, to coordinate and help obtain care for Channeling participants (Phillips, Kemper, and Applebaum 1988). Although the enrollees who received the intervention obtained more home health services, their outcomes were not improved by the intervention. Furthermore, overall costs in the intervention group were somewhat higher than in the control group (Thornton, Dunstan, and Kemper 1988). During the first year of the randomized trial, participants who received the intervention spent an average of twenty-five days in nursing homes, while control group utilization averaged twenty-nine days. Increased use of home services offset the slightly lower expenditures for nursing home care. The use of hospitals and physicians' services was unaffected by case management (Wooldridge and Schore 1988). Nursing home utilization was no higher than expected for other persons of the same age, but mortality rates in both the treatment and the control groups were very high (nearly a third of the participants died within a year of enrollment), and it is possible that nursing home utilization would have been greater in a disabled but less sickly group of elderly (Garber and MaCurdy 1989).

The findings of research on the determinants of long-term care utilization suggest that social factors play an important part. These factors, which are not as easily quantified as a laboratory test or a physical characteristic, pose problems for third-party payers who reimburse long-term care. In view of the challenges posed by long-term care, we next turn to the solutions that are currently being evaluated or marketed.

7.4   New Approaches to Private Financing of Long-Term Care

The slow development and adoption of long-term care insurance reflects the unique characteristics of long-term care. There can be little doubt that insurers were slow to develop and market insurance for long-term care because they feared that adverse selection, moral hazard, and demographic uncertainty would be serious obstacles. In many respects, the informational asymmetries and inefficiencies that have characterized health care insurance are likely to be magnified in the case of long-term care. As a result, thin coverage and rigorous exclusions have characterized most of the policies offered.

Perhaps the most important barrier to the development of either private long-term care insurance or capitated health care plans is adverse selection. Poverty, lack of social supports, and functional disability are important risk factors for institutionalization. While insurance companies may partially observe these characteristics, the purchaser knows a great deal more about the beneficiary's health status and level of function. Any party that indemnifies, reimburses services, or directly provides care faces these same problems. If the insurer or provider had sufficient information about the functional status and social supports of elderly people, reluctance to provide insurance might diminish.

Protection against adverse selection takes many forms. For example, the premiums for private long-term care insurance rise rapidly with the age at enrollment. Presumably a woman at age 40 or 50 has little information about her future risk of nursing home admission, relative to others at the same age. At age 70, she is much more likely than the insurer to know whether she is particularly likely (or unlikely) to enter a nursing home. Other methods to deter adverse selection are the imposition of waiting periods before benefits can be collected and the exclusion of preexisting conditions or particular conditions that are very common among nursing home residents, such as dementia. Of course, while narrow coverage and multiple exclusions may deter adverse selection, they diminish insurance coverage for all enrollees and compromise the desirability of the long-term care insurance package. Thus, it is not surprising that few policies with highly restrictive benefits have been sold.

Moral hazard may have a greater effect on long-term care utilization than on hospital or physicians' services. In health care, the presence of moral hazard means simply that there is a price effect—that insurance that pays a substantial fraction of the cost of medical care will increase the quantity demanded. It is no longer tenable to hold that the demand for hospital and physicians' services is inelastic in the long run and that only "needed" services will be provided to patients. There is no obvious standard for either the quantity or the quality of care "needed." Even if the demand for care were inelastic in the short run, long-run expenditures for treating specific conditions can rise because of the adoption and diffusion of more costly new medical technology or the wider application of existing technology. Thus, as the price to the consumer (the co-payment) falls, the quantity demanded rises, and the long-run effects are likely to be magnified by technological change.

Demand for long-term care is likely, in the long run, to be highly sensitive to price because there are substitutes for the housing and many of the service components of nursing home care. Food, homemaking, and other personal services are potentially desirable to any elderly person, whether disabled or not. The likelihood that these services will be "overused" is great. Even large co-payments and deductibles are unlikely to eliminate what is perceived as inappropriate use of these services. Thus, insurers and care providers often allocate these services by using a rationing mechanism based on screening examinations, which determine "need" for long-term care, rather than price. The ability to evaluate the need for long-term care services is at a primitive stage and relies heavily on subjective reports by the family and the enrollee, who have an obvious incentive to obscure disabilities when seeking to buy insurance and to emphasize impairments when they seek reimbursement. For many acute medical services, laboratory tests and other measures that are less subject to direct manipulation by the enrollee are available. Thus, moral hazard is likely to remain a significant challenge to any form of prepayment or insurance for long-term care.

Uncertainty about the length of life and trends in the disability of elderly persons further complicate long-term care financing. There is little information about changes in average morbidity over time among elderly Americans and the resulting changes in expected utilization of long-term care services. Usually, long-term care insurance plans allow individuals to pay fixed premiums that vary with the age of initial enrollment. If the elderly live longer but age-specific levels of disability do not diminish, insurers who charge a fixed premium will face unexpected liabilities. Furthermore, if spouses and children provide less care for disabled elderly in the future, the demand for paid long-term care services will grow. However, the demographic uncertainty is likely to become less important as information about the determinants and magnitude of long-term care utilization improves.

Uncertainty regarding government action is another potential deterrent. Will new government policies obviate the need for private long-term care insurance or other private financing mechanisms? If this is an important reason for the reluctance of elderly Americans to purchase long-term care insurance, it is one that some insurers have already addressed. Some plans have arrangements to refund premiums if government policy creates insurance with similar coverage for all elderly Americans.

Long-term care insurance plans and other private plans for delivering or financing long-term care have addressed these problems in several ways. Reducing the insurer's risk means, however, increasing the risk faced by the insured or denying coverage to many potential enrollees. There is every reason to believe that insurers and providers will refine their ability to assess enrollee risk as they gain more experience with long-term care insurance and as new findings emerge from research on predictors of institutionalization.

Despite the remaining challenges, private long-term care insurance is becoming an important component of long-term care financing. The Health Insurance Association of America reported that, in 1988, the number of companies selling long-term care insurance was six times the number in 1984. By December 1988, an estimated 1.1 million policies had been sold. It seems clear that broader coverage promoted expansion in the market for long-term care insurance. Plans introduced in 1988 and later tended to eliminate prior hospitalization requirements for nursing home admission and to provide benefits for a longer period. Furthermore, exclusions for such conditions as Alzheimer's disease and for preexisting conditions became less common. A greater proportion of policies guaranteed renewability (Van Gelder and Johnson 1989). It seems likely that private long-term care insurance, which was unattractive to purchasers because it formerly paid benefits only under a restrictive set of circumstances, will become an increasingly important means of financing nursing home care in the next decade.

Nevertheless, private insurance may not finance all or most long-term care in the coming years. Long-term care insurance is likely to be affordable if purchased during working years, so private insurance could have an expanded role by the time baby boomers have aged. According to simulation estimates from the Brookings-ICF long-term care financing model, about 58 percent of all elderly early in the next century will be covered by private long-term care insurance purchased during working years. Insurance purchased after retirement will cover fewer people (Rubin, Wiener, and Meiners 1989). Private insurance, unless subsidized, is also unlikely to finance care for low-income, high-risk men and women, like many Medicaid enrollees.

Attention to private long-term care insurance is complemented by interest in social health maintenance organizations and continuing-care retirement communities or life-care communities. Social HMOs extend the concept of a prepaid capitated health care plan to provision of long-term care services. Like conventional HMOs, social HMOs typically rely on fixed annual payments to give providers an incentive to limit the quantity of services delivered. Preliminary results from a nationwide demonstration of social HMOs indicate that this form of care, which seeks to diminish costs by placing the health care provider at risk for any costs arising from care of the subscribers, may not be profitable. Although the reasons for the lack of success of the demonstration social HMOs is unclear, unexpectedly low enrollment is a major contributing factor.

Life-care communities, which usually combine housing with social and health services, are also becoming popular. Their characteristics vary greatly from one state to another because they are subject to state regulation. These communities, which often provide long-term care services to their members, frequently self-insure. Nursing homes are sometimes on the campus of these communities, although nursing home care is often provided off premise under contractual arrangements. The fees for joining these communities vary greatly. Typically, there is a large initial payment for the purchase of a condominium in the life-care community, with additional monthly fees. For life-care communities that insure or provide long-term care services, the incentives and risks are the same as for social HMOs: because they bear the financial risk for any nursing home care or other costly long-term care required by its members, they have an incentive to underprovide such care.

Federal agencies and Congress have discussed several other options for government financing of long-term care. One of the options is expansion of Medicare benefits so that reimbursement for long-term care would parallel coverage under Medicaid but would be extended to all elderly Americans (Blumenthal et al. 1986). Financing such a program would likely prove contentious. It might be much more costly than the Medicare Catastrophic Coverage Act coverage; younger Americans would resist paying more for health care for the elderly, and older Americans who would bear the cost of a surtax would object even more strongly. As an alternative, the Reagan administration had discussed the feasibility of utilizing tax-deferred saving vehicles to induce individuals to save money for possible catastrophic health care or long-term care costs. The tax-saving vehicle, called an individual medical account (IMA), has not progressed far in legislative debates or within the Department of Health and Human Services. The drawbacks, according to several critics, are that participation would be lower than for IRAs, that participation in the IRA program was limited, and that such a program would favor the wealthy. Thus, the IMAs are viewed as a potential tool to help a small minority of elderly Americans at risk of long-term care pay for their future long-term care services.

Other saving devices might diminish the need for long-term care insurance if the elderly had enough liquid assets at the time they needed long-term care. One alternative would enable the elderly to convert their main asset, the homes that many of them own, into liquid wealth. Reverse annuity mortgages are one means of converting housing wealth into cash, without selling or leaving one's residence, but thus far few elderly persons have participated in the programs. It remains to be seen whether these or other mechanisms to convert assets will contribute substantially to long-term care financing; however, according to a report from the Brookings Institution based on a simulation model, because many of the elderly have substantial home equity, equity conversions could be a valuable source of funds to pay for long-term care insurance (Rivlin and Wiener 1988).

Moral hazard is likely to remain a significant challenge for long-term care insurance, whether privately or publicly funded. There are several mechanisms for limiting utilization of free or heavily subsidized long-term care services, and while (acute) health care services have long been a testing ground for plans to limit moral hazard, there is far less experience in long-term care. Functional status testing, as noted above, can be used to determine eligibility for benefits. Large copayments and deductibles can limit service use by providing less than full indemnification for costs of long-term care. Of course, such mechanisms are likely to be less than fully effective, and they limit the extent of insurance. Insurers may explore other mechanisms for limiting their costs, such as contracting with nursing homes directly. They have taken a similar approach to hospital and physicians' services, and, while there is little evidence that contracting (with "preferred providers") limits utilization, it may limit expenditures inasmuch as it lowers the price that insurers pay. However, none of these solutions has eliminated the effect of moral hazard in the market for physicians' and hospital services. Partly because HMOs have been more successful than conventional fee-for-service plans in this regard, the conventional wisdom is that provider incentives are a key component of successful efforts to control moral hazard.

Another way to limit utilization, and to ensure appropriate utilization, is case management. Case management, such as the intervention in the Channeling demonstration, means that a professional is designated to coordinate the delivery of long-term care services to an elderly disabled individual. The motivation for such an approach is the hope that, with adequate provision of home health care and related services, people who are otherwise likely to enter nursing homes will not do so. Furthermore, case management might deter inappropriate utilization of long-term care services generally. Unfortunately, the evidence that such an intervention would lower nursing home utilization or costs of long-term care is at best mixed, as noted above. Consequently, while case management appears to be a sensible approach to improving long-term care delivery, and while it could be applied with either public or private insurance, there is little evidence that it will help insurers or capitated health plans reduce their risk.

7.5   Concluding Comments

Because demographic factors will increase demand for both long-term care and conventional medical services, financing the health care of the elderly is sure to remain an important issue in the United States throughout the coming decades. Like other forms of insurance, long-term care insurance should protect subscribers from the risk of catastrophic expenditures, but moral hazard and adverse selection may render comprehensive coverage unprofitable. Will these considerations lead to greater federal involvement in long-term care financing? Are private financing mechanisms likely to overcome these obstacles and play a larger role in the future?

After experiencing years of escalating health expenditures, legislators and voters are understandably reluctant to add long-term care to federal expenditures for health care. Efforts to contain Medicare expenditures have had mixed success; in the 1980s, when prospective payment dampened the growth in Medicare's hospital expenditures, physicians' payments rose sharply. The consequences of expanded government financing of long-term care are unknown, but there are many reasons to be cautious. Because expenditures for long-term care costs may be more difficult to control than expenditures for hospital and physicians' services, legislators may be reluctant to augment benefits for nursing homes and home health care. Medicaid does pay for a substantial fraction of long-term care, but it is not an attractive model for future financing. Private approaches to financing and delivering long-term care seem to be a more viable first step.

Many of the elderly will be unable to purchase private long-term care insurance because they have manifest disabilities. In the longer run, marketing long-term care insurance to younger persons should help prevent adverse selection. That is one reason why private long-term care insurance is expected to play a larger role in the future and a larger fraction of the elderly will be protected from the costs of long-term care. However, moral hazard will remain an obstacle to the efficient functioning of a long-term care insurance market. In order to make sure that costs do not rise as rapidly as the costs of conventional health insurance, payers will need to adopt a more deliberate approach to evaluating new forms of long-term care. Medical treatments have been adopted and widely disseminated before their benefits were tested. In many cases, they were later found to be ineffective. Because pharmaceutical companies, equipment manufacturers, and care providers had an incentive to provide innovative care and patients bore little of the cost themselves, new technology has become synonymous with increased costs. At least in the near term, insurance is not likely to induce major technological innovations in long-term care. But the major components of long-term care include housing and food services. As large numbers of people purchase long-term care insurance, nursing homes are likely to change their character, many of them providing higher-quality housing and related services. Many individuals who would not consider entering a nursing home today would be willing to do so if quality improved in this sense. Unless insurers learn to allocate long-term care services by criteria that are judged as fair and acceptable to enrollees, the costs of long-term care insurance could grow as rapidly as the costs of conventional health insurance.

An alternative approach would emphasize the prevention of the disabilities that lead persons to seek long-term care. Some (e.g., Somers 1984) have argued that well-placed efforts to prevent chronic disability might be effective. If the disabilities due to the chronic syndromes and diseases that lead to the heavy use of long-term care services—such as dementia, heart disease, musculoskeletal disease, stroke, and urinary and fecal incontinence—can be reduced, the demand for long-term care might well diminish.

Unfortunately, there is little evidence that available treatments can significantly diminish the morbidity of these conditions. The specific cause of Alzheimer's disease, the most common form of dementia in the elderly, is unknown, and it cannot be prevented or effectively treated. One can be more sanguine about other illnesses. Medications that prevent heart attacks and stroke by lowering cholesterol and by lowering elevated blood pressure are available. The overall mortality rates from cardiovascular disease in the United States have fallen in recent years. However, the reduction in coronary heart disease that results from either cholesterol reduction or the lowering of a mildly elevated blood pressure (the most common form of high blood pressure) is modest. While there are treatments that effectively relieve some of the symptoms of arthritis and other forms of musculoskeletal disease, most forms can be neither prevented nor cured. In fact, there are few data available to determine whether age-adjusted disability levels among the elderly in the United States have fallen in recent years. While there is some evidence that there may have been a modest reduction in age-adjusted disability (Fries 1980; Palmore 1986; Poterba and Summers 1987), it is unlikely that future reductions in disability will offset the growing number of elderly who are at risk for developing disability (Verbrugge 1984). Thus, it is doubtful that either prevention or new developments in the treatment of disabling conditions will substantially diminish the need for long-term care within the next two decades.

Because Americans will continue to be subject to the risk of developing the health impairments that make long-term care necessary, long-term care financing will remain an important policy issue. No simple change in long-term care financing will satisfy the desire for complete coverage without leading to "overutilization," particularly because moral hazard will remain an important obstacle for both public and private insurance. Insurers have entered the market for long-term care insurance cautiously, well aware of these problems and of the cost inflation that has plagued health insurance during the past thirty years. Along with the private insurers, the government will play a large role in financing long-term care, as a regulator and as a payer. Although the mix will change, a combination of public and private sources will almost surely continue to finance long-term care. Recent experience suggests, however, that any program that increases net governmental outlays will meet with resistance and that private financing mechanisms will pay for a growing fraction of long-term care. Furthermore, because transfers across generations will not pay for long-term care indefinitely, funding for both publicly and privately financed long-term care will ultimately come from savings: enforced savings (taxation or mandatory program participation), tax-favored voluntary savings, and insurance premium payments that have a large savings component.

Perhaps a technological breakthrough will someday obviate the need for long-term care by preventing the chronic diseases associated with institutionalization. Until such a solution becomes available, the mode of financing long-term care will have a profound effect on the well-being of elderly Americans.

References

Blumenthal, David, Mark Schlesinger, Pamela Drumheller, et al. 1986. The future of Medicare. *New England Journal of Medicine* 314:722–28.

Bowen, Otis A. 1986. *Catastrophic illness expenses.* Department of Health and Human Services, Report to the president. Washington, D.C.: U.S. Government Printing Office.

Branch, L. G., and A. M. Jette. 1982. A prospective study of long-term care institutionalization among the aged. *American Journal of Public Health* 72:1373–79.

Chiswick, Barry R. 1976. The demand for nursing home care: An analysis of the substitution between institutional and noninstitutional care. *Journal of Human Resources* 11:295–316.

Cohen, M. A., E. J. Tell, and S. S. Wallack. 1986a. Client-related risk factors of nursing home entry among elderly adults. *Journal of Gerontology* 41:785–92.

———. 1986b. The lifetime risks and costs of nursing home use among the elderly. *Medical Care* 24:1161–72.

———. 1988. The risk factors of nursing home entry among residents of six continuing care retirement communities. *Journal of Gerontology* 43:S15–S21.

Division of National Cost Estimates. Office of the Actuary. Health Care Financing Administration. 1987. National health expenditures, 1986–2000. *Health Care Financing Review* 8:1–36.

Doty, Pamela, Korbin Liu, and Joshua Wiener. 1985. An overview of long-term care. *Health Care Financing Review* 6:69–78.

Feldstein, Martin S. 1973. The welfare loss of excess health insurance. *Journal of Political Economy* 81:251–80.

Fries, James F. 1980. Aging, natural death, and the compression of morbidity. *New England Journal of Medicine* 303 (17 July): 130–35.

Garber, Alan M., and Thomas MaCurdy. 1989. Predicting nursing home utilization among the high-risk elderly. NBER Working Paper no. 2843. Cambridge, Mass.: National Bureau of Economic Research.

Greenberg, J. N., and A. Ginn. 1979. A multivariate analysis of the predictors of long-term care placement. *Home Health Care Services Quarterly* 1:75–99.

Health Care Financing Administration. 1989. Medicare and Medicaid data book, 1988. U.S. Department of Health and Human Services, HCFA Publication no. 03270. Washington, D.C.: U.S. Government Printing Office.

Kemper, Peter. 1988. The evaluation of the National Long-Term Care Demonstration: 10. Overview of the findings. *Health Services Research* 23:161–74.

Kemper, Peter, Robert Applebaum, and Margaret Harrigan. 1987. Community care demonstrations: What have we learned? *Health Care Financing Review* 8:87–100.

Kidwell, K. D. 1988. Medicaid estate recoveries: National program inspection. Office of Inspector General, Office of Analysis and Inspections, Department of Health and Human Services (OAI-09–86–00078). Washington, D.C.: U.S. Government Printing Office.

Lane, D., D. Uyeno, A. Stark, E. Kliewer, and G. Gutman. 1985. Forecasting demand for long-term care services. *Health Services Research* 20:435–60.

Letsch, S. W., K. R. Levit, and D. R. Waldo. 1988. National health expenditures, 1987. *Health Care Financing Review* 10:119.

McConnel, C. E. 1984. A note on the lifetime risk of nursing home residency. *Gerontologist* 24:193–98.

Manheim, L. M., and S. L. Hughes. 1986. Use of nursing homes by a high-risk long-term care population. *Health Services Research* 21:161–76.

National Center for Health Statistics. 1989. *Health, United States, 1988.* DHHS Publication no. (PHS) 89–1232. Washington, D.C.: U.S. Government Printing Office.

Palmore, Erdman B. 1976. Total change of institutionalization among the aged. *Gerontologist* 16:504–7.

———. 1986. Trends in the health of the aged. *Gerontologist* 26:298–302.

Phillips, Barbara R., Peter Kemper, and Robert A. Applebaum. 1988. The evaluation of the National Long-Term Care Demonstration: 4. Case management under channeling. *Health Services Research* 23:67–82.

Poterba, James M., and Lawrence H. Summers. 1987. Public policy implications of declining old-age mortality. In *Work, health, and income among the elderly,* ed. Gary Burtless. Washington, D.C.: Brookings Institution.

Rivlin, Alice M., and Joshua M. Wiener. 1988. *Caring for the disabled elderly: Who will pay?* Washington, D.C.: Brookings Institution.

Rubin, Rose M., Joshua M. Wiener, and Mark R. Meiners. 1989. Private long-term care insurance: Simulations of a potential market. *Medical Care* 27:182–93.

Schwartz, William B. 1987. The inevitable failure of current cost-containment strategies: Why they can provide only temporary relief. *Journal of the American Medical Association* 257:220–24.

Shapiro, Evelyn, and Robert Tate. 1988. Who is really at risk of institutionalization? *Gerontologist* 28:237–45.

Shapiro, Evelyn, and L. M. Webster. 1984. Nursing home utilization patterns for all Manitoba admissions, 1974–1981. *Gerontologist* 24:610–15.

Somers, Anne R. 1984. Why not try preventing illness as a way of controlling medicare costs? *New England Journal of Medicine* 311:853–56.

Thornton, Craig, Shari Miller Dunstan, and Peter Kemper. 1988. The evaluation of the National Long-Term Care Demonstration: 8. The effect of channeling on health and long-term care costs. *Health Services Research* 23:129–42.

Tolchin, M. 1989. Expansion of Medicare is painful for Congress. *New York Times,* 27 August 1989, E4.

U.S. Bureau of the Census. 1984. Projections of the population of the U.S. by age, sex, and race: 1983 to 2080. *Current Population Reports,* ser. P-25, no. 952. Washington, D.C.: U.S. Government Printing Office.

———. 1989. *Statistical Abstract, 1989.* Washington, D.C.: U.S. Government Printing Office.

U.S. Senate Special Committee on Aging. 1986. *Aging America: Trends and projections* (1985–86 ed.). Washington, D.C.: U.S. Government Printing Office.

Valvona, J., and Frank Sloan. 1985. Rising rates of surgery among the elderly. *Health Affairs* 4:108–19.

Van Gelder, S., and Diane Johnson. 1989. Long-term care insurance: Market trends. Washington, D.C.: Health Insurance Association of America.

Verbrugge, Lois M. 1984. Longer life but worsening health? Trends in health and mortality of middle-aged and older persons. *Milbank Memorial Fund Quarterly/Health and Society* 62:475–519.

Vicente, L., J. A. Wiley, and R. A. Carrington. 1979. The risk of institutionalization before death. *Gerontologist* 19:361–67.

Weissert, W. G. 1985. Seven reasons why it is so difficult to make community-based long-term care cost-effective. *Health Services Research* 20:423–33.

Wooldridge, Judith, and Jennifer Schore. 1988. The evaluation of the National Long Term Care Demonstration: 7. The effect of channeling on the use of nursing homes, hospitals, and other medical services. *Health Services Research* 23:119–28.

Contributors

Alan M. Garber
National Bureau of Economic Research
204 Junipero Serra Boulevard
Stanford, CA 94305

Michael D. Hurd
Department of Economics
SUNY, Stony Brook
Stony Brook, NY 11794

Robin L. Lumsdaine
Department of Economics
Princeton University
Princeton, NJ 08544

Daniel L. McFadden
Department of Economics
655 Evans Hall
University of California, Berkeley
Berkeley, CA 94707

Yukio Noguchi
Department of Economics
Hitotsubashi University
2–1 Naka, Kunitachi-shi
Tokyo, 186
JAPAN

Seiritsu Ogura
Department of Economics
Hosei University
4342 Aihora-cho
Machida City, Tokyo 194–0
JAPAN

Atsushi Seike
Faculty of Business and Commerce
Keio University
2–15–45, Mita, Minato-ku
Tokyo, 108
JAPAN

Haruo Shimada
Faculty of Economics
Keio University
2–15–45, Mita, Minato-ku
Tokyo, 108
JAPAN

Noriyuki Takayama
Institute of Economic Research
Hitotsubashi University
2–1 Naka, Kunitachi-shi
Tokyo, 186
JAPAN

David A. Wise
National Bureau of Economic Research
1050 Massachusetts Avenue
Cambridge, MA 02138

195

Author Index

Ai, C., 113
Allen, Steven G., 22n11, 71
Applebaum, Robert, 185
Arita, F., 105
Atkinson, A. B., 94n9

Barton, M., 51n9
Berkovec, James, 33–34n20
Blinder, Alan, 22
Blumenthal, David, 189
Börsch-Supan, A., 129n8
Boskin, Michael, 22, 50n8, 69, 70
Bowen, Otis A., 180
Branch, L. G., 184
Bridges, Benjamin, 70n2
Bulow, Jeremy, 23
Burkhauser, Richard V., 22, 77, 78, 81n10
Burtless, Gary, 22, 33

Carrington, R. A., 184
Carroll, Chris, 20
Chiswick, Barry, 183
Clark, Robert L., 22n11, 23, 70n2, 71, 79n6, 81n10
Cohen, M. A., 184, 185

Danziger, Sheldon, 76t
Doty, Pamela, 176
Dunstan, Shari Miller, 185

Feaster, Daniel, 78, 81n10
Feinstein, J., 126
Feldstein, Martin S., 182

Fields, Gary S., 22n12, 23
Frant, Howard L., 23
Fries, James F., 192
Futagami, R., 145

Garber, Alan M., 185
Ginn, A., 184
Gordon, Roger, 22
Greenburg, J. N., 184
Gustman, Alan, 22

Harrigan, Margaret, 185
Harrison, A. J., 94n9
Hausman, Jerry A., 22, 33nn18,19, 51n9
Health Care Financing Administration, Division of National Cost Estimates, 176, 178
Heckman, J. J., 48, 49
Hogarth, Jeanne, 22n12
Holden, Karen, 77, 78, 81n10
Hughes, S. L., 185
Hurd, Michael D., 18–19, 22, 69, 70, 74n4, 78t, 79t, 80, 81t

Ito, T., 129

Japan Institute of Population Problems, 129n6
Japan Statistical Bureau, 129nn7,8, 133n12, 134n13
Jette, A. M., 184
Johnson, Diane, 188
Judge, G. G., 54n12

Kemper, Peter, 185

Subject Index

Annuity insurance plans, Japan, 146–54
Assets, Japan: of elderly people, 106; holding changes, 99–104; household and distribution of household, 88–97; net worth distribution by asset component and age, 97–100
Assets, U.S.: homeownership, 123–26; income of elderly from, 68, 73, 75; measurement of, composition of, and income from, 116–23

Case management, 190
Consumption: behavior in elderly and nonelderly households, 72–75; effect for very old people, 65, 77; postretirement in United States, 8, 13; U.S.-Japanese comparison of elderly, 134–35

Data sources: analysis of housing and economic status of elderly, 112; analysis of Japanese household asset- and wealth-holdings, 86; relation of Social Security to labor supply of elderly in Japan, 52

Early retirement decision, U.S., 35–36
Earnings. *See also* Market wage, Japan; Reservation wage, Japan
Earnings of older employees, U.S., 17, 20–21
Earnings test, Japan: effect on earnings distribution of eligible Social Security recipients, 51, 56–57; implications for public policy, 58–60

Elderly people. *See* Elderly people, Japan; Elderly people, U.S.; Living arrangements, elderly
Elderly people, Japan: comparison of housing with U.S., 129–35; health maintenance system, 145–46; as homeowners, 104–5, 131–32; living arrangements, 105–7; mobility, 131–32; public policy related to working elderly, 45; retired workers' medical system, 146
Elderly people, U.S.: characteristics of population, 112–15; comparison of housing with Japanese, 129–35; current health care financing, 178–81; economic and housing status, 112–13; health care programs, 175; as homeowners, 123–26, 131–32; incomes, 18–19, 65–67; issues related to housing of, 109–12; mobility, 131–32; proposals related to insurance-underwritten long-term care, 181–86; proposed long-term care options, 188–90; as recipients of insurance-underwritten benefits, 178–81
Employment policy, Japan: implications of pension benefits for employed elderly, 58–60; related to regulation of elderly in work force, 45

Health care insurance, U.S.: coverage and costs, 175–76; effect of demographic changes in cost, 177–78; interest in promoting long-term care, 181–86; Medicaid